MASS COMMUNICATION & SOCIETY

Volume 3, Number 1, 2000 • Winter

SPECIAL ISSUE:
Communication Theory in the 21st Century

EDITOR'S NOTE

David Demers
   Communication Theory in the 21st Century:
   Differentiation and Convergence   1

ARTICLES

Thomas E. Ruggiero
   Uses and Gratifications Theory in the 21st Century   3

K. Viswanath and Pamela Arora
   Ethnic Media in the United States: An Essay on Their Role
   in Integration, Assimilation, and Social Control   39

Bryant Paul, Michael B. Salwen, and Michel Dupagne
   The Third-Person Effect: A Meta-Analysis of the Perceptual Hypothesis   57

Karin Wahl-Jorgensen
   Rebellion and Ritual in Disciplinary Histories of U.S. Mass
   Communication Study: Looking for "The Reflexive Turn"   87

SCHOLARLY MILESTONES ESSAY

Everett M. Rogers
   The Extensions of Men: The Correspondence of Marshall McLuhan
   and Edward T. Hall   117

BOOK REVIEWS

Matthew C. Ehrlich
   Reviews John Corner's *Critical Ideas in Television Studies*   137

Sharon R. Mazzarella
   Reviews Norma Odom Pecora's *The Business of Children's Entertainment*   141

Kevin M. Carragee
   Reviews Barry Dornfeld's *Producing Public Television,*
   Producing Public Culture   145

Mead Loop
   Reviews Richard H. Reeb, Jr.'s *Taking Journalism Seriously:*
   Objectivity As a Partisan Cause   149

ANNOUNCEMENTS   153

MASS COMMUNICATION & SOCIETY DIVISION INFORMATION

Division Head
 Carol J. Pardun, *University of North Carolina*
Division Vice Head
 Daniel A. Panici, *University of Southern Maine*
Secretary and Newsletter Editor
 Paul S. Voakes, *Indiana University*
Program Chair
 Daniel A. Panici, *University of Southern Maine*
 Carol J. Pardun, *University of North Carolina*
Professional Freedom and Responsibility Committee
 John Beatty, *University of North Carolina at Pembroke*
Research Committee Chair/Paper Competition Chair
 Kathy Brittain McKee, *Berry College*
Teaching Standards Committee Chair
 Jennifer Greer, *University of Nevada at Reno*
Graduate Student Liaison
 Lois A. Boynton, *University of North Carolina at Chapel Hill*
Membership
 Donica Mensing, *University of Nevada at Reno*
Webmaster
 Thomas Gould, *Kansas State University*

Mass Communication & Society is published four times a year by Lawrence Erlbaum Associates, Inc., 10 Industrial Avenue, Mahwah, NJ 07430–2262. Subscriptions are available only on a calendar-year basis.

Printed subscriptions for Volume 3, 2000 are US $35 for individuals and $185 for institutions within the United States and Canada; US $65 for individuals and $215 for institutions outside the United States and Canada. Faculty members of the Mass Communication & Society Division of the Association for Education in Journalism and Mass Communication pay $21 (individuals only); student members of the Mass Communication & Society Division of the Association for Education in Journalism and Mass Communication pay $12 (individuals only). Address changes: AEJMC Division members send changes to AEJMC; all others to the Journal Subscription Department, Lawrence Erlbaum Associates, Inc., 10 Industrial Avenue, Mahwah, NJ 07430–2262. Address changes should include the mailing label or a facsimile. Claims for missing issues cannot be honored beyond 4 months after mailing date. Duplicate copies cannot be sent to replace issues not delivered due to failure to notify publisher of change of address.

The **electronic** version of this journal is available through OCLC (Online Computer Library Center) at no additional cost (excluding OCLC's access charges) to all 2000 institutional subscribers. The 2000 electronic-only subscription rate is $166.50. To set up electronic access to this journal or to obtain more information, please contact OCLC at 1–800–848–5878 (ext. 6462). E-mail: brownchr@oclc.org or visit http://www.oclc.org/oclc/eco/main.htm

This journal is abstracted and/or indexed in *Sociological Abstracts*.

Microform copies of this journal are available through Bell & Howell Information and Learning, P.O. Box 1346, Ann Arbor, MI 48106–1346.

Copyright © 2000, Association for Education in Journalism and Mass Communication. No part of this publication may be used, in any form or by any means, without permission from AEJMC or the publisher. Printed in the United States of America. ISSN 1520-5436.

Special requests for permissions should be addressed to the Permissions Department, Lawrence Erlbaum Associates, Inc., 10 Industrial Avenue, Mahwah, NJ 07430–2262.

Visit LEA's website at http://www.erlbaum.com and *Mass Communication & Society*'s website at www.wsu.edu/~mcs

Communication Theory in the 21st Century: Differentiation and Convergence

David Demers
Editor

During one of my job interviews several years ago, a faculty interviewer mentioned in passing that he was a "logical positivist." Later, I asked a member of the search committee whether there were any other logical positivists on his faculty.

"Why, all of them are logical positivists," the search committee member said. My jaw almost hit the floor. Luckily, the search committee member was not looking directly at me, but it probably did not matter, because I did not get the job.

You see, most of my master's and Ph.D. work was in sociology, and sociologists all but abandoned logical positivism many decades ago. In fact, the growth of functional and critical and cultural models after the 1930s came partly in response to the Vienna Circle's overly deterministic, inductive, atheoretical approach.

Although small pockets of logical positivism survive, it is safe to say that as the 20th century comes to a close, logical positivism—or *naive empiricism,* as some scholars call it—is having a near-death experience in most of the social sciences. There are two major reasons for this: (a) the unfulfilled promise of being able to explain large amounts of variance, and (b) the philosophical problem of theory-neutral observation. You can credit (or blame) philosophers of science for the latter problem. All empirical observations are embedded with ontological and epistemological assumptions about the natural and social worlds. Data are not self-explanatory. They need a logical system to be interpreted. In short, today there is a much greater appreciation for theory in the social sciences.

Yet, despite increased emphasis on theory, as we move into the 21st century, there is little or no evidence to suggest that any particular theory or perspective will dominate the social sciences in general or the field of communication in particular. Critical and cultural studies has grown in stature, to be sure. However, instead of greater theoretical homogeneity, this has brought even more theoretical diversity. And, ironically, the biggest critics of cultural works today are not the hard-core positivists, but the cultural theorists themselves.

Theoretical pluralism is not a bad thing, mind you. It provides a much more realistic portrait of our complex social world. However, increasing theoretical pluralism does mean that those social scientists who wish for greater unity in our field will be disappointed.

From a deductive sociological framework, the growth (or should I say explosion) of theoretical models and perspectives is not surprising. As I outline in much greater depth in my recent book, *Global Media: Menace or Messiah?* (Demers, 1999), three key factors are responsible for this growth. The first is simply that there are a lot more scholars, professional groups, universities, and scholarly journals around today than there were at the beginning of the 20th century. Second, as social systems grow and become more structurally complex, they tend to place a high value on a diversity of ideas itself—that is, pluralistic systems are much more tolerant of new and unorthodox ideas. The third factor enhancing the development of theories and ideas is simply the ability to record them in writing or electronic form—in fact, technology is speeding up the process through which ideas are generated and disseminated.

In short, as we move into the 21st century, the number and variety of theories in the social sciences will grow exponentially. Pluralism is in. In fact, the four articles and the Scholarly Milestones essay in this special issue are a testament to that diversity. The perspectives include cognitive (the third-person effect; Bryant, Salwen, & Dupagne), structural (ethnic media; Viswanath & Arora), cultural (rebellion and ritual in disciplinary histories; Wahl-Jorgensen), and social psychological (uses and gratifications; Ruggiero).

Although it is highly unlikely that any single theoretical perspective will ever again dominate our field as functionalism once dominated sociology, theoretical pluralism does not mean that everything "is in." Logical positivism is not likely to grow as quickly as some cultural perspectives. Many of the old dogmas are out. For example, many critical and cultural theorists have abandoned the dominant ideology (full-incorporation) thesis. Mass media are agents of social control, to be sure. However, there is increasing appreciation for ideological pluralism and the role that mass media play in promoting social change that can benefit disadvantaged groups.

Similarly, theoretical perspectives that have advocated a strong role for human agency (e.g., free-will models, active audience models) or, conversely, a strong role for social structure (e.g., deterministic models, passive audience models) are giving way to perspectives that appreciate the fact that social forms and action are products of both agency and structure. Social actors, in other words, make choices between social structured alternatives.

In sum, I believe the 21st century will bring, in terms of theory, both increasing differentiation and convergence to the social sciences and to the field of communication. It is an exciting time to be a scholar.

REFERENCE

Demers, D. (1999). *Global media: Menace or messiah?* Cresskill, NJ: Hampton.

Uses and Gratifications Theory in the 21st Century

Thomas E. Ruggiero
Communications Department
University of Texas at El Paso

Some mass communications scholars have contended that uses and gratifications is not a rigorous social science theory. In this article, I argue just the opposite, and any attempt to speculate on the future direction of mass communication theory must seriously include the uses and gratifications approach. In this article, I assert that the emergence of computer-mediated communication has revived the significance of uses and gratifications. In fact, uses and gratifications has always provided a cutting-edge theoretical approach in the initial stages of each new mass communications medium: newspapers, radio and television, and now the Internet. Although scientists are likely to continue using traditional tools and typologies to answer questions about media use, we must also be prepared to expand our current theoretical models of uses and gratifications. Contemporary and future models must include concepts such as interactivity, demassification, hypertextuality, and asynchroneity. Researchers must also be willing to explore interpersonal and qualitative aspects of mediated communication in a more holistic methodology.

What mass communication scholars today refer to as the *uses and gratifications* (U&G) *approach* is generally recognized to be a subtradition of media effects research (McQuail, 1994). Early in the history of communications research, an approach was developed to study the gratifications that attract and hold audiences to the kinds of media and the types of content that satisfy their social and psychological needs (Cantril, 1942). Much early effects research adopted the experimental or quasi-experimental approach, in which communication conditions were manipulated in search of general lessons about how better to communicate, or about the unintended consequences of messages (Klapper, 1960).

Requests for reprints should be sent to Tom Ruggiero, Print Journalism, 102–B Cotton Memorial Communication Department, University of Texas, El Paso, TX 79968. E-mail: truggier@miners.utep.edu

Other media effects research sought to discover motives and selection patterns of audiences for the new mass media. Examples include Cantril and Allport (1935) on the radio audience; Waples, Berelson, and Bradshaw (1940) on reading; Herzog (1940, 1944) on quiz programs and the gratifications from radio daytime serials; Suchman (1942) on the motives for listening to serious music; Wolfe and Fiske (1949) on children's interest in comics; Berelson (1949) on the functions of newspaper reading; and Lazarsfeld and Stanton (1942, 1944, 1949) on different media genres. Each of these studies formulated a list of functions served either by some specific content or by the medium itself:

> To match one's wits against others, to get information and advice for daily living, to provide a framework for one's day, to prepare oneself culturally for the demands of upward mobility, or to be reassured about the dignity and usefulness of one's role. (Katz, Blumler, & Gurevitch, 1974, p. 20)

This latter focus of research, conducted in a social-psychological mode, and audience based, crystallized into the U&G approach (McQuail, 1994).

Some mass communication scholars cited "moral panic" and the Payne Fund Studies as the progenitor of U&G theory. Undertaken by the U.S. Motion Picture Research Council, the Payne Fund Studies were carried out in the late 1920s. Leading sociologists and psychologists including Herbert Blumer, Philip Hauser, and L. L. Thurstone sought to understand how movie viewing was affecting the youth of America (Lowery & DeFleur, 1983). Rosengren, Johnsson-Smaragdi, and Sonesson (1994), however, argued that the Payne Fund Studies were primarily effects-oriented propaganda studies, as opposed to the U&G tradition, which focuses on research of individual use of the media. Likewise, Cantril's (1940) study of Orson Welles's "War of the Worlds" radio broadcast was more narrowly interested in sociological and psychological factors associated with panic behavior than in developing a theory about the effects of mass communication (Lowery & DeFleur, 1983).

Wimmer and Dominick (1994) proposed that U&G began in the 1940s when researchers became interested in why audiences engaged in various forms of media behavior, such as listening to the radio or reading the newspaper. Still others credit the U&G perspective with Schramm's (1949) immediate reward and delayed reward model of media gratifications (Dozier & Rice, 1984).

Regardless, early U&G studies were primarily descriptive, seeking to classify the responses of audience members into meaningful categories (Berelson, Lazarsfeld, & McPhee, 1954; Katz & Lazarsfeld, 1955; Lazarsfeld, Berelson, & Gaudet, 1948; Merton, 1949).

Most scholars agree that early research had little theoretical coherence and was primarily behaviorist and individualist in its methodological tendencies (McQuail, 1994). The researchers shared a qualitative approach by attempting to group gratification statements into labeled categories, largely ignoring their frequency distribution in the population. The earliest researchers for the most part did not attempt to explore the links between the gratifications detected and the psychological or sociological origins of the needs satisfied. They often failed to search for the interrelations among the various media functions, either quantitatively or conceptually, in a manner that might have led to the detection of the latent structure of media gratifications.

Criticisms of early U&G research focus on the fact that it (a) relied heavily on self-reports, (b) was unsophisticated about the social origin of the needs that audiences bring to the media, (c) was too uncritical of the possible dysfunction both for self and society of certain kinds of audience satisfaction, and (d) was too captivated by the inventive diversity of audiences used to pay attention to the constraints of the text (Katz, 1987). Despite severe limitations, early researchers, especially those at the Bureau of Applied Social Research of Columbia University, persevered, particularly in examining the effects of the mass media on political behavior. They studied voters in Erie County, Ohio, during the 1940 election between Roosevelt and Wilkie (Lazarsfeld et al., 1948) and voters in Elmira, New York, during the 1948 Truman–Dewey election (Berelson et al., 1954). Both studies suggested that the mass media played a weak role in election decisions compared with personal influence and influence of other people. As a result, Berelson et al. began amplifying the two-step flow theory, moving away from the concept of an "atomized" audience and toward the impact of personal influence (Katz, 1960).

1950S AND 1960S RESEARCH

Despite disagreement by communication scholars as to the precise roots of the approach, in the next phase of U&G research, during the 1950s and 1960s, researchers identified and operationalized many social and psychological variables that were presumed to be the precursors of different patterns of consumption of gratifications (Wimmer & Dominick, 1994). Accordingly, Schramm, Lyle, and Parker (1961) concluded that children's use of television was influenced by individual mental ability and relationships with parents and peers. Katz and Foulkes (1962) conceptualized mass media use as escape. Klapper (1963) stressed the importance of analyzing the consequences of use rather than simply labeling the use as earlier researchers had done. Mendelsohn (1964) identified several generalized functions of radio listening: companionship, bracketing the day, changing mood, counteracting loneliness or boredom, providing useful news and information, allowing vicarious participation in events, and aiding social interaction. Gerson (1966) introduced the variable of race and suggested that race was important in predicting how adolescents used the media. Greenberg and Dominick (1969) concluded that race and social class predicted how teenagers used television as an informal source of learning.

These studies and others conducted during this period reflected a shift from the traditional effects model of mass media research to a more functionalist perspective. Klapper (1963) called for a more functional analysis of U&G studies that would restore the audience member to "his rightful place in the dynamic, rather than leaving him in the passive, almost inert, role to which many older studies relegated him" (p. 527). Markedly, Geiger and Newhagen (1993) credited Klapper with ushering in the "cognitive revolution" in the communication field. From the 1950s forward, cross-disciplinary work between U&G researchers and psychologists has produced abundant research on the ways human beings interact with the media.

1970S RESEARCH

Until the 1970s, U&G research concentrated on gratifications sought, excluding outcomes, or gratifications obtained (Rayburn, 1996). During the 1970s, U&G researchers intently examined audience motivations and developed additional typologies of the uses people made of the media to gratify social and psychological needs. This may partially have been in response to a strong tide of criticism from other mass communication scholars. Critics such as Elliott (1974), Swanson (1977), and Lometti, Reeves, and Bybee (1977) stressed that U&G continued to be challenged by four serious conceptual problems: (a) a vague conceptual framework, (b) a lack of precision in major concepts, (c) a confused explanatory apparatus, and (d) a failure to consider audiences' perceptions of media content.

U&G researchers produced multiple responses. Katz, Gurevitch, and Haas (1973) assembled a comprehensive list of social and psychological needs said to be satisfied by exposure to mass media. Rosengren (1974), attempting to theoretically refine U&G, suggested that certain basic needs interact with personal characteristics and the social environment of the individual to produce perceived problems and perceived solutions. Those problems and solutions constitute different motives for gratification behavior that can come from using the media or other activities. Together media use or other behaviors produce gratification (or nongratification) that has an impact on the individual or society, thereby starting the process anew. Seeking to more closely define the relation between psychological motives and communication gratifications, Palmgreen and Rayburn (1979) studied viewers' exposure to public television and concluded that the U&G approach served well as a complement to other determinant factors such as media availability, work schedules, and social constraints. Palmgreen and Rayburn argued that the primary task facing media researchers was to "integrate the roles played by gratifications and other factors into a general theory of media consumption" (p. 177). Essentially, Palmgreen and Rayburn were responding to earlier researchers' (Greenberg, 1974; Lometti et al., 1977) call to investigate gratification sought and gratifications received. Blumler (1979) identified three primary social origins of media gratifications: normative influences, socially distributed life changes, and the subjective reaction of the individual to the social situation. Also, in response, McLeod, Bybee, and Durall (1982) theoretically clarified audience satisfaction by concluding that gratifications sought and gratifications received were two different conceptual entities that deserved independent treatment in any future U&G research.

Another related theoretical development was the recognition that different cognitive or affective states facilitate the use of media for various reasons, as predicted by the U&G approach. Blumler (1979) proposed that cognitive motivation facilitated information gain and that diversion or escape motivation facilitated audience perceptions of the accuracy of social portrayals in entertainment programming. In related research, McLeod and Becker (1981) found that individuals given advanced notice that they would be tested made greater use of public affairs magazines than did a control group. Bryant and Zillmann (1984) discovered that stressed individuals watched more tranquil programs and bored participants opted for more exciting fare.

1980S AND 1990S RESEARCH

Rubin (1983) noted that gratifications researchers were beginning to generate a valid response to critics. He concluded that his colleagues were making a systematic attempt to (a) conduct modified replications or extensions of studies, (b) refine methodology, (c) comparatively analyze the findings of separate investigations, and (d) treat mass media use as an integrated communication and social phenomenon. Examples include Eastman's (1979) analysis of the multivariate interactions among television viewing functions and lifestyle attributes, Ostman and Jeffers's (1980) examination of the associations among television viewing motivations and potential for lifestyle traits and television attitudes to predict viewing motivations, Bantz's (1982) exploration of the differences between general medium and specific program television viewing motivations and the comparability of research findings, Rubin's (1981) consideration of viewing motivations scale validity and the comparability of research results in U&G research, and Palmgreen and Rayburn's (1985) empirical comparison of alternative gratification models.

Likewise, Windahl (1981) also sought to advance U&G theoretically. In his "Uses and Gratifications at the Crossroads," he argued that the primary difference between the traditional effects approach and the U&G approach is that a media effects researcher usually examines mass communication from the perspective of the communicator, whereas the U&G researcher uses the audience as a point of departure. Believing it was more beneficial to emphasize similarities than differences, Windahl coined the term *conseffects* and argued for a synthesis of the two approaches. Thus, he suggested, observations that are partly results of content use in itself and partly results of content mediated by use would serve as a more useful perspective. Windahl's approach served to link an earlier U&G approach to more recent research.

Aspiring to heighten the theoretical validity of structural determinants, Webster and Wakshlag (1983) integrated the dissimilar perspectives of U&G and "models of choice," attempting to locate the interchange between programming structures, content preferences, and viewing conditions in the program choice process. Likewise, Dobos (1992), using U&G models applied to media satisfaction and choice in organizations, predicted television channel choice and satisfaction within specific communication technologies.

ACTIVE AUDIENCE

Also, in the 1980s, researchers reevaluated the long-held notion of an active audience. During this time, some researchers reiterated that although both uses and effects sought to explain the outcomes or consequences of mass communication, they did so by recognizing the potential for audience initiative and activity (Rubin, 1994b). Levy and Windahl (1984) attempted to articulate a theoretically more complete notion of audience activity and to test a model of audience orientations that linked activity to U&G, and Rubin (1984) suggested that audience activity is not an absolute concept, but a variable one. Notably, Windahl (1981) argued that "the notion of activeness leads a picture of the audience as superrational and very selective, a tendency which invites criticism" (p. 176). Instead, he argued audience activity covers a range of possible orientations to the communication process, a range that "varies across phases of the communication sequence" (Levy & Windahl, 1984, p. 73). More succinctly, different individuals tend to display different types and amounts of activity in different communication settings and at different times in the communication process.

In support of this, theoretical active audience models have increasingly emerged that range from high audience activity to low levels of involvement. For example, both dependency and deprivation theories suggest that some individuals under certain conditions such as confinement to home, low income, and some forms of stress form high levels of attachment to media. These include television (Grant, Guthrie, & Ball-Rokeach, 1991), newspapers (Loges & Ball-Rokeach, 1993), and communication technologies such as remote control devices (Ferguson & Perse, 1994).

DEPENDENCY THEORY

Media dependency theory itself posits that media influence is determined by the interrelations between the media, its audience, and society (DeFleur & Ball-Rokeach, 1982). The individual's desire for information from the media is the primary variable in explaining why media messages have cognitive, affective, or variable effects. Media dependency is high when an individual's goal satisfaction relies on information from the media system (Ball-Rokeach, 1985). Rubin and Windahl (1986) augmented the dependency model to include the gratifications sought by the audience as an interactive component with media dependency. For Rubin and Windahl, the combination of gratifications sought and socially determined dependency produced media effects. They argued that dependency on a medium or a message results when individuals either intentionally seek out information or ritualistically use specific communication media channels or messages. For example, McIlwraith (1998) found that self-labeled "TV addicts" often used television to distract themselves from unpleasant thoughts, to regulate moods, and to fill time. This link between dependency and functional alternatives illustrates how U&G is a theory "capable of interfacing personal and mediated communication" (Rubin, 1994b, p. 428).

DEPRIVATION THEORY

Deprivation theory has an even longer history in U&G research than dependency theory. Berelson (1949) studied the effects of the 1945 strike of eight major New York City daily newspapers on audience behavior. Since that time, additional studies of media strikes have emerged: Kimball (1959) replicated Berelson's study during the 1958 New York City newspaper strike; de Bock (1980) studied the effects of newspaper and television strikes in the Netherlands in 1977; Cohen (1981) examined a general media strike; and Walker (1990) analyzed viewers' reactions to the 1987 National Football League players' strike.

Related, Windahl, Hojerback, and Hedinsson (1986) suggested that the consequences of a media strike for adolescents were connected to the total degree of perceived deprivation of television as well as the specific content such as entertainment, information, and fiction. These deprivations are related both to media variables like exposure, involvement, and motives, and nonmedia variables such as socioconcept orientation and activities with friends and parents. Windahl et al. found that individuals in more socially oriented environments tended to feel more deprived than those in conceptually oriented settings.

THEORIES OF LOW-LEVEL AND VARIABLE AUDIENCE ACTIVITY

Conversely, other factors such as (a) different time relations (advance expectations, activity during the experience, postexposure), (b) variability of involvement (as background noise, companionship), and (c) ritualistic or habitual use (as mild stimulation) suggest a much less active audience than traditionally believed. Specifically, time relations theory argues that individuals are differentially selective and goal directed at different times: before, during, and after exposure to media (Levy & Windahl, 1984). For example, Lemish (1985) discovered that college students arranged their busy schedules to view a specific soap opera, formed program-centered groups, paid attention to the program, and discussed the content with others.

Variability of involvement suggests that the motivation to use any mass medium is also affected by how much an individual relies on it (Galloway & Meek, 1981), and how well it satisfies her or his need (Lichtenstein & Rosenfeld, 1983). Thus, many U&G researchers have included some aspect of expectancy in their models and have turned to established theories of expectancy to explain media consumption (Rayburn, 1996). Rayburn cited Fishbein and Ajzen's (1975) expectancy value theory as illustrative. Fishbein and Ajzen's model poses three beliefs: (a) Descriptive beliefs result from direct observation of an object, (b) informational beliefs are formed by accepting information from an outside source that links certain objects and attributes, and (c) inferential beliefs are about the characteristics of objects not yet directly observed, or that are not directly observable. Palmgreen and Rayburn (1982) developed an expectancy model that successfully predicted gratifications sought from television news. Rayburn and Palmgreen combined U&G with expectancy value theory to generate an expectancy value model of gratifications sought (GS) and gratifications obtained (GO).

For example, a study about talk radio by Armstrong and Rubin (1989) concluded that individuals who called in found face-to-face communication less rewarding, were less mobile, believed talk radio was more important to them, and listened for more hours a day than listeners who did not call in.

In terms of ritualistic and habitual media use, audience activity involves the concept of utility, an individual's reasons and motivations for communicating, but little intentionality or selectivity (Blumler, 1979; Hawkins & Pingree, 1981). Rubin (1984) suggested that ritualized viewing involved more habitual use of television for diversionary reasons and a greater attachment with the medium itself. Instrumental viewing, on the other hand, reflected a more goal-oriented use of television content to gratify information needs or motives. Notably, however, Rubin (1984) cautioned that ritualized and instrumental media use are not neatly dichotomous but are more likely interrelated. Just as audience activity is variable, individuals may use media ritualistically or instrumentally depending on background, time, and situational demands. Thus, Perse and Rubin (1988) suggested a multidimensional view of audience activity, reinforcing an emphasis on media use instead of media exposure. Additionally, Rubin (1994a) argued that U&G research needed to "continue its progression from simple exposure explanations of effects and typologies of media motivation to conceptual models that explain the complexity of the media effects process" (p. 103).

ATTEMPTS TO REFINE U&G

Paradoxically, U&G scholars may have been their own toughest critics. Throughout the decades, U&G researchers challenged their own model and argued for a more comprehensive theoretical grounding (Klapper, 1963; Rubin, 1994a; Schramm et al., 1961). Rubin (1986) called for a clearer picture of the relation between media and personal channels of communication and sources of potential influence. Swanson (1987) urged that research focus on three areas: the role of gratification seeking in exposure to mass media, the relation between gratification and the interpretive frames through which audiences understand media content, and the link between gratifications and media content. Windahl (1981) argued that a synthesis of several viewpoints would be most productive: (a) that media perceptions and expectations guide people's behavior; (b) that besides needs, motivation is derived from interests and externally imposed constraints; (c) that there are functional alternatives to media consumptions; and (d) that media content plays an important role in media effects. Rubin (1994b) agreed that a fruitful direction was a synthesis between U&G and media effects research as proposed by Windahl.

CONTINUED CRITICISMS OF U&G

Thus, during the last several decades, U&G researchers have continued to conceptually refine their perspective. Nevertheless, critics such as Stanford (1983) have assailed perceived deficiencies such as the confusing of operational definitions and the analytical model, a lack of internal consistency, and a lack of theoretical justification for the model offered. Stanford complained, "the discussion ranges far from the results, which do not support their theoretical underpinnings" (p. 247). Likewise, media hegemony advocates have contended that the U&G theory overextends its reach in asserting that people are free to choose the media fare and interpretations they want (White, 1994). J. A. Anderson (1996) conceded that U&G is an "intelligent splice of psychological motivations and sociological functions, [but nonetheless noted that] materialism, reductionism, and determinism, as well as foundational empiricism, are all firmly in place" (p. 212).

Thus, much contemporary criticism of U&G challenges assumptions that include (a) media selection initiated by the individual; (b) expectations for media use that are produced from individual predispositions, social interaction, and environmental factors; and (c) active audiences with goal-directed media behavior (Wimmer & Dominick, 1994).

Outside of the United States, particularly in non-Western countries, even a diffused notion of an active audience has limited acceptability and U&G scholars differ in their methodological approach. For example, Cooper (1997) noted that Japan's communication researchers view media's individual-level impact as a limited effects perspective, in that media serve only to reinforce preexisting attitudes and behaviors.

CONTINUED FLAWS IN U&G THEORY

Thus, despite attempts to produce a more rigorous and comprehensive theory, several flaws continue to plague the perspective, and U&G researchers have acknowledged this. First, by focusing on audience consumption, U&G is often too individualistic (Elliott, 1974). It makes it difficult to explain or predict beyond the people studied or to consider societal implications of media use. Second, some studies are too compartmentalized, producing separate typologies of motives. This hinders conceptual development because separate research findings are not synthesized. Third, there still exists a lack of clarity among central concepts such as social and psychological backgrounds, needs, motives, behavior, and consequences. Fourth, U&G researchers attach different meanings to concepts such as motives, uses, gratifications, and functional alternatives, contributing to fuzzy thinking and inquiry. Fifth, the cornerstones of U&G theory, the notion of an active audience and the validity of self-report data to determine motives, are assumed by researchers, and that assumption may be "a little simplistic or naive" (Severin & Tankard, 1997, p. 335). Thus, some critics continue to argue that traditional U&G methodologies, particularly those dependent on self-reported typologies and relying on interpretation of lifestyle and attitude variables rather than observable audience behavior, are suspect (Rosenstein & Grant, 1997). Self-reports may not be measuring the individual's actual behavior so much as his or her awareness and interpretation of the individual's behavior. This dilemma is further complicated by evidence that suggests that individuals may have little direct introspective access to the higher order cognitive processes that mediate their behavior (Nisbett & Wilson, 1977), and therefore may base their self-reports on "a priori, casual theories influenced by whatever stimuli happen to be salient" (Rosenstein & Grant, 1997, p. 4).

U&G THEORY BUILDING

Despite these perceived theoretical and methodological imperfections, I would argue that reproach of U&G must be tempered with encouragement. A typology of uses, although not providing what some scholars would consider a refined theoretical perspective, furnishes a benchmark base of data for other studies to further examine media use. Furthermore, Finn (1997) suggested that due to a contemporary preference for more parsimonious models of human personality, the design of U&G studies committed to a "broad range of personality traits has become a more tractable endeavor" (p. 1). For example, current scholars favor a typology of five (K. J. Anderson & Revelle, 1995; Costa & McCrae, 1988), and in some cases as few as three fundamental personality traits (Eysenck, 1991). Contrast this to the earlier system of 16 primary personality factors as advanced by Cattell, Edger, and Tatsuoka (1970) and McGuire (1974).

Second, there has been a trend toward enlarging and refining theories concerning affective motivations toward media use (Finn, 1997). For instance, Finn noted that the rigid dichotomy between instrumental and ritualistic behaviors that formerly esteemed information-seeking over entertainment-seeking behaviors has been infused with new motivational theories. These take into consideration the individuals' need to manage affective states (D. R. Anderson, Collins, Schmitt, & Jacobvitz, 1996; Kubey & Csikszentmihalyi, 1990) or achieve optimum levels of arousal (Donohew, Finn, & Christ, 1988; Zillmann & Bryant, 1994).

Third, fully focusing on the social and cultural impacts of new communication technologies may be premature until we grasp more fully how and why people are making use of these media channels (Perse & Dunn, 1998). It stands to reason that in the information age, media users will seek information. Equally reasonably, World Wide Web (Web) survey respondents are most attracted to information formats that speak to them in a more personalized voice and in a broader entertaining context (Eighmey & McCord, 1995).

Thus, the media uses and effects process is an increasingly complex one that requires careful attention to antecedent, mediating, and consequent conditions (Rubin, 1994b). A continued emphasis on theory building must proceed, particularly by scholars who will attempt to develop theories that explain and predict media consumption of the public based on sociological, psychological, and structural variables. Some current research illustrates the plausibility of changing the scope of U&G research from an "exaggerated emphasis on using mass media to meet social deficits, to the function it fulfills," as Blumler (1985, p. 41) previously suggested to aiding people in promoting social identities (Finn, 1997). A serious potential problem facing U&G researchers, however, may be the practical impossibility of probability sampling on the Internet. At this point, studies may only be able to tentatively generalize to a very specific population. Also, Web-administered surveys may pose problems with tracking precise and reliable response rates. Additionally, a current lack of standardization among browsers, servers, and operating systems may create a serious challenge to methodically sound quantitative research. However, as we invent more sophisticated methods of tracking users and become more familiar with their demographics, generalizability to well-studied segments of the overall population should become less problematic (Smith, 1997).

TELECOMMUNICATIONS TECHNOLOGY AND THE REVIVAL OF U&G

U&G fell out of favor with some mass communication scholars for several decades, but the advent of telecommunications technology may well have revived it from dormancy. The deregulation of the communications industry and the convergence of mass media and digital technology have altered the exposure patterns of many media consumers (Finn, 1997). Improved compression algorithms now allow for the compression of video data for online transmission down telephone copper wire, coaxial, fiber optic cable, and by broadcast satellite, cellular, and wireless technologies (Chamberlain, 1994, p. 279). As new technologies present people with more and more media choices, motivation and satisfaction become even more crucial components of audience analysis. Not surprisingly, researchers have been busy applying U&G theory to a wide range of newly popularized video media technologies. For example, Donohew, Palmgreen, and Rayburn (1987) explored how the need for activation interacts with social and psychological factors to affect media U&G sought by cable television audiences. They identified four lifestyle types whose members differed significantly on a wide range of variables, including newspaper and newsmagazine readership and gratifications sought from cable television. They found that individuals with a high need for activation had lifestyles involving greater exposure to media sources of public affairs information than individuals with a lower need for activation and less cosmopolitan lifestyles. LaRose and Atkin (1991) also examined cable subscribership in U.S. households, including the factors that lead to initial subscription and to subscription retention. Walker and Bellamy (1991) related television remote control devices to audience member interest in types of program content. Lin (1993) conducted a study to determine if VCR satisfaction, VCR use, and interpersonal communication about VCRs were related to three functions: home entertainment, displacement, and social utility. James, Wotring, and Forrest (1995) investigated adoption and social impact issues possessed by the characteristic bulletin board user and how board use affected other communication media. Jacobs (1995) examined the relation between sociodemographics and satisfaction by studying the determinants of cable television viewing satisfaction. Jacobs identified antecedents in the study that included performance attributes, complaint call frequencies, and cable system characteristics. Funk and Buchman (1996) explored the effects of computer and video games on adolescents' self-perceptions. Perse and Dunn (1998) examined home computer use, and how CD–ROM ownership and Internet capability were linked to computer utility. Each of these scholars questioned whether new telecommunications media are used to satisfy the same needs they had been theorized to satisfy with traditional communication media (Williams, Phillips, & Lum, 1985). For example, the parasocial aspects of television soap opera viewing may soon pale in comparison to the interactive relation possibilities offered by electronic chat rooms and multiuser domains. Researchers are now being challenged to "decode the uses and gratifications of such communication experiences" (Lin, 1996, p. 578).

This increasing interest by communication scholars in online audiences may be particularly intense because of the makeup of these newer media forms: interactive media obscure the line between the sender and receiver of mediated messages (Singer, 1998). Furthermore, new media like the Internet possess at least three attributes of data not commonly associated with traditional media: interactivity, demassification, and asynchroneity.

INTERACTIVITY

Interactivity significantly strengthens the core U&G notion of active user because it has been defined as "the degree to which participants in the communication process have control over, and can exchange roles in their mutual discourse" (Williams, Rice, & Rogers, 1988, p. 10). Communication literature reflects six user-oriented dimensions of interactivity that should be useful for the U&G approach: threats (Markus, 1994), benefits (S. Ang & Cummings, 1994), sociability (Fulk, Flanagin, Kalman, Monge, & Ryan, 1996), isolation (Dorsher, 1996), involvement (Trevino & Webster, 1992), and inconvenience (Stolz, 1995; Thomas, 1995). Additionally, Ha and James (1998) cited five dimensions of interactivity: playfulness, choice, connectedness, information collection, and reciprocal communication. Ha and James suggested that for "self-indulgers" and "Web surfers," the playfulness and choice dimensions of interactivity fulfill self-communication and entertainment needs. For task-oriented users, the connectedness dimension fulfills information needs. For expressive users, the information collection and reciprocal communication dimensions allow them to initiate communication with others of common online interests. Ha and James assessed dimensions such as information collection and reciprocal communication as higher levels of interactivity. Playfulness, choice, and connectedness were viewed as lower levels of interactivity.

Heeter (1989) also defined interactivity as a multidimensional concept: amount of choice provided to users, amount of effort a user must exert to access information, how actively responsive a medium is to users, potential to monitor system use, degree to which users can add information to the system that a mass undifferentiated audience can access, and degree to which a media system facilitates interpersonal communication between specific users.

Thus, the real advantage to interactivity for individual users is not simply multimedia videos, online shopping, or obtaining information on demand. Just as the Lotus 1-2-3 spreadsheet allowed users to create their own business plans and models, interactivity may offer users the means to develop new means of communication (Dyson, 1993) and greatly increase user activity. After all, interactivity is not only the ability to select from a wide array of Internet merchandise or "surf" 500 or more television channels. Technologists such as Nelson (1990) argued that human–computer activities represent the human impulse to create interactive representation. Dutton, Rogers, and Jun (1987) suggested that interactivity displays "the degree to which the new communication systems are capable of responding to user commands" (p. 234). However, interactivity, at least on the Internet with current technology, does pose some serious practical limitations for users. The ability to access information is limited to three means: entering the address of a location the user already knows, scrolling through a single document, and following a hypertext link (Jackson, 1997). A further serious downside to interactivity continues to exist. More and more often, a Web search using a keyword or a hypertext link results in an extensive list and the user must choose from hundreds or even thousands of destinations, often with few or no contextual clues (Bergeron & Bailin, 1997).

DEMASSIFICATION

Williams et al. (1988) defined *demassification* as the control of the individual over the medium, "which likens the new media to face-to-face interpersonal communication" (p. 12). Demassification is the ability of the media user to select from a wide menu. Chamberlain (1994) argued that we have entered an era of demassification in which the individual media user is able, through newer technologies, to pick from a large selection of media, previously shared only with other individuals as mass media. Unlike traditional mass media, new media like the Internet provide selectivity characteristics that allow individuals to tailor messages to their needs. Kuehn (1994) cited *The New York Times* as an example. Those who wish to receive the paper version of *The New York Times* must pay for the whole paper, whereas those receiving the electronic version may select only those articles of interest to them. Mass messages will be able to be viewed as second-class by recipients and "individual, one-on-one dialogue will be the preferred mode of communication" (Chamberlain, 1994, p. 274).

ASYNCHRONEITY

Asynchroneity refers to the concept that messages may be staggered in time. Senders and receivers of electronic messages can read mail at different times and still interact at their convenience (Williams et al., 1988). It also means the ability of an individual to send, receive, save, or retrieve messages at her or his convenience (Chamberlain, 1994). In the case of television, asynchroneity meant the ability of VCR users to record a program for later viewing. With electronic mail (e-mail) and the Internet, an individual has the potential to store, duplicate, or print graphics and text, or transfer them to an online Web page or the e-mail of another individual. Once messages are digitized, manipulation of media becomes infinite, allowing the individual much more control than traditional means.

For U&G researchers, each of these accelerated media aspects—interactivity, demassification, and asynchroneity—offer a vast continuum of communication behaviors to examine.

TRADITIONAL MODELS OF U&G

Rogers (1986) concluded that these novel attributes make it nearly impossible to investigate the effects of a new communication system using earlier research. Rogers argued that "conventional research methodologies and the traditional models of human communication are inadequate. That's why the new communication technologies represent a new ball game for communication research" (p. 7).

Other mass media scholars, however, suggested that traditional models of U&G may still provide a useful framework from which to begin to study Internet and new media communication (December, 1996; Kuehn, 1994; Morris & Ogan, 1996). All four of these scholars contend that a U&G model provides a productive method of examining Internet use at this time. Much of the current activity on the Web involves exploratory behavior, offering an environment in which users can contact thousands of sources, find information presented in a wide range of formats, and interact with many of the sources they contact (Eighmey, 1997). Kuehn (1994) emphasized this interactive capacity of computer-mediated communication and suggested a group of U&G statements be used as rating scales to evaluate computer-aided instructional programs. His typology included convenience, diversion, relationship development, and intellectual appeal.

For December (1996), more traditional typologies of mass media consumption translate appropriately to the Internet. U&G researchers can continue to use categories such as surveillance, entertainment and diversion, interpersonal utility, and parasocial interaction to test people's attitudes toward media consumption through such variables as GO and GS. Also in line with previous U&G scholars, Morris and Ogan (1996) argued that the concept of active audience, whether instrumental or ritualized, should continue to be included in current and future Internet research.

Perse and Dunn (1998) also suggested that U&G offers a convincing theoretical explanation for changes in media use patterns following the adoption of new communication technologies such as personal computers. Because they are increasingly filling similar needs, personal computers may be displacing the use of traditional media like newspapers and television. When television was adopted, for instance, it tended to replace other entertainment activities such as radio, movies, and comics. A more recent study concluded that displacement of other media and forms of television occurred with an individual's acquisition of a VCR (Anonymous, 1989). Significantly, some predict that television, the Internet, and the telephone may soon merge into one instrument, displacing other media choices.

TWO THEORETICAL DICHOTOMIES

In general, although the media industry is based on the strategy that audiences are at least somewhat active, two dichotomies concerning media and U&G research have long prevailed (Zillman & Bryant, 1985). In the first group are those scholars who view the mass audience as predominantly passive and those who hold that audience members are active and discriminating. In the second group are those studies that underscore the explanatory power of individual characteristics and those that attribute power to structural factors (Cooper, 1996).

Those scholars that supported a passive audience conception often cite the escapist model of media use, particularly in television viewing (Stone & Stone, 1990). The escapist model presumes that television viewing consists largely of a leisurely way to pass the time (Barwise, Ehrenberg, & Goodhardt, 1982; Kubey, 1986) and that television programming is primarily homogeneous in gratifying a time-filling behavior (McQuail, Blumler, & Brown, 1972). Goodhardt, Ehrenberg, and Collins's (1987) study of British television audience behavior is frequently cited as corroboration that audience availability, not selectivity, is paramount in shaping patterns of viewing. In their study, the researchers examined three variables: repeat viewing, audience duplication, and audience appreciation. They discovered that (a) 55% of the viewers of one episode of a television program also watched the following episode; (b) for any two programs, the level of audience viewing duplication depends on the programs' ratings and not their content; and (c) a viewer's average appreciation score does not depend on the program's rating or its incidence of repeat viewing. Goodhardt et al. concluded that television viewing behavior and audience appreciation appeared to follow "a few very general and simple patterns" (p. 116) rather than involving great differentiation between distinct groups of viewers and between the audiences of different programs. Horna (1988) found specific relations between leisure and an individual's U&G of mass media. Specifically, the majority of media audiences are seeking entertainment, relaxation, or escape, and for most people, leisure and mass media are nearly synonymous.

Conversely, a chief tenet of U&G theory of audience behavior is that media use is selective and motivated by rational self-awareness of the individual's own needs and an expectation that those needs will be satisfied by particular types of media and content (Katz et al., 1974). Rubin (1983) argued that "viewing motivations are not isolated static traits, but rather, comprise a set of interactive needs and expectations" (p. 39). Studies by scholars such as Garramone (1984, 1985) suggested that motivation leads to higher knowledge regardless of attention to a specific medium. Other studies that support the active audience assumption include work by Fry and McCain (1983), who found that a person's expectations, evaluations, and motivations determined the usefulness of a medium; and work by Gandy, Matabane, and Omachonu (1987), who discovered that the strongest factors predicting knowledge from a medium were an individual's gender and personal interest in the issues. Furthermore, Grunig (1979) suggested that people sometimes seek media content that has a functional relation to situations in which they are involved. Perse and Courtright (1993) concluded that individuals are aware of communication alternatives and select channels based on the normative images those channels are perceived to have.

STRUCTURAL MODELS OF U&G

On the other hand, those scholars who attribute media use behavior to structural factors, particularly in television viewing, have used complex statistical procedures to show that channel loyalty, inheritance effects, repeat viewing, and availability are stronger predictors of program choice than any measure of program typology (Goodhardt et al., 1987; Webster & Wakshlag, 1983). Supporting this perspective, in Heeter's (1989) study of program choice and channel selection, 23% of all respondents were unable to identify what channels they commonly viewed. Structural scholars interpret this to mean that most audience members pay little attention to content or channel but use television in a relatively undiscriminating fashion. A viewer's primary relation may be with the medium itself rather than with any specific channel or program (Rosenstein & Grant, 1997). This has serious ramifications, particularly for critical scholars, who argue that "new media technologies will be funded almost exclusively by private enterprise" (Chamberlain, 1994, p. 280). This will restrict the use of the latest technology to those who can afford it, widening the gap between the haves and have nots, perpetuating information-rich and information-poor individuals, groups, and societies.

Despite their usefulness, however, most structural models should be viewed as "a set of complex, surrogate variables that can have great predictive power" (Cooper, 1996, p. 10) but lack ability to explain the underlying processes. Research has yet to fully explicate how the structure of television program offerings, for example, influence the actual choices made by individual viewers. Thus, U&G continues to be exceedingly useful in explaining audience activity when individuals are most active in consciously making use of media for intended purposes. For example, Lind's (1995) study concluded that television viewers did not want their news fare limited by the government, the industry, or even concerned viewers.

NEWER COMMUNICATION MEDIA

Additionally, the active audience concept is gaining credibility with newer media researchers. As emerging technologies provide users with a wider range of source selection and channels of information, individuals are selecting a media repertoire in those areas of most interest. Heeter and Greenburg (1985) suggested that given the many entertainment options on cable television, most viewers choose a subset of channels, or a repertoire, that they prefer. Ferguson (1992) discovered that the main component of television channel repertoire was whether the viewer subscribed to cable television. Atkin (1993) identified the phenomenon of repertoire when studying the interrelations between cable and noncable television, and subscriptions to them by owners of VCRs, camcorders, personal computers, walkman radios, and cellular telephones. Reagan (1996) argued that each individual is now able to rely on easy-to-use media for low-interest topics and more complex repertoires for higher interest topics. He suggested that researchers should move away from labeling media users as television oriented or newspaper oriented, and consider them more as users of "cross-channel clusters of information sources" (p. 5).

Similarly, some communications scholars are viewing the Internet as the ultimate in individualism, "a medium with the capability to empower the individual in terms of both the information he or she seeks and the information he or she creates" (Singer, 1998, p. 10). Inversely, others see the Web as the ultimate in community building and enrichment, through which users can create relationships online in ways that have never been possible through traditional media. Despite this optimistic portrait, Rafaeli (1986) speculated that computer-mediated communication by individuals may lead to loneliness and isolation. Moreover, Young (1996) raised concern that excessive use of new media such as the personal computer may leave users vulnerable to technological dependencies like "Internet addiction."

Whatever the approach, most U&G scholars agree that concepts such as *active* and *audience* will have to be revised when applied to Internet communication. Reasons for using the Internet differ from person to person. Some individuals are goal directed and may want to complete a task through visiting specific Web sites. Others may only be curious and surf the Web for fun. Additionally, in electronic discussion groups, for example, some users are quiet observers and "lurkers" who never participate, whereas others frequently participate in the discussion (Ha, 1995). Fredin and David (1998) argued that audience activity, as it applies to hypermedia use, has three interrelated components that place elevated demands on individual user interaction. First, hypermedia obligate frequent audience responses because, unlike radio or television, hypermedia freeze or halt if responses are not made. Second, the audience is presented with a seemingly unending variety of options from which they must choose. Third, an individual's choices are often highly contingent on a series of earlier responses. Moreover, differences in quality and quantity of activity exist among individual online users. Sundar (1998) contended that experienced Internet users make different choices than do novices, particularly in matters such as attentiveness to sources in electronic news stories.

THE INTERNET AND U&G

Additionally, some media scholars argued that even the traditional audience concept must be radically amended because of novel informational characteristics of the Internet. Abrahamson (1998) envisioned the Internet moving from a mass-market medium to a "vehicle for the provision of very specific high-value information to very specific high-consumption audiences" (p. 15). Specifically, he theorized a mass Internet audience "fractionated" into smaller, more elite audiences, such as occurred with consumer magazines in the 1960s. Ha and James (1998) believed the medium will evolve from a mass-produced and mass-consumed commodity to an "endless feast of niches and specialties" (p. 2). Weaver (1993) forecasted a tiered communication system emerging, with some messages reaching the masses (presidential speeches, war coverage), others reaching a significant segment of society (business news, some sporting events), and others reaching relatively small, special-interest groups (music, art, and hobbies). Dicken-Garcia (1998) envisioned common interests rather than geographic space defining much of the Internet audience. Yet, she asserted, the Internet, unlike other media, has no targeted community as a primary audience or as a result of its function.

Other scholars have insisted that the traditional audience concept must be modified because of the interpersonal potential of the Internet. Ironically, interpersonal relationships, one of the two mediating variables of the early persuasion model (selectivity being the other), and the forerunner of diffusion of innovations, is reemerging as a serviceable U&G variable. This concept of "personalness," social presence, or the degree of salience in interpersonal relationships is being explored increasingly by U&G researchers, particularly in relation to interactivity. Cowles (1989) found that interactive media (teletext and videotext) possessed more personal characteristics than noninteractive electronic media. She predicted media gratifications theory is ripe for future research involving new media and that such research "might best occur within the context of an individual's total media environment" (p. 83). Dicken-Garcia (1998) contended that the Internet places stronger emphasis on informal, interpersonal conversation than has been true of earlier media. A notable and novel characteristic of Internet audience behavior according to Dicken-Garcia lies in the phenomenon that users communicate electronically what they might never say in person or on the phone. Internet users sometimes take on new personalities, ages, and genders, all of these exemplified by less inhibited behavior. She also noted that Internet talk more resembles word of mouth than newspapers and television, and that, often, "users unquestionably accept information via the Internet that they would not accept so readily from another medium" (p. 22).

The Internet may also have important ramifications for the communication gratifications traditionally sought by consumers of news information. The news, particularly as provided by traditional media institutions, has been linked with the creation of an informed electorate in areas including politics and international events, and to the perpetuation of a democratic society (Wenner, 1985).

What Dunleavy and Weir (1998) called *open-book government* could also form a significant part of a new era of electronic democracy. Not only does the Internet have the potential to improve access to the government, it could also invigorate representative democracy:

> Electronic advances could make public consultation and participation wider, easier and more diverse; and provide new media opportunities which could both focus and diversify the information people receive and obtain for themselves, as the old media

fragment into more and more apolitical and specialised forms—sports channels, gardening channels, fashion channels, golf channels and so on. (p. 72)

As an example, Dunleavy and Weir (1998) cited the British Broadcasting Company's Election 97 Web site, which on election night recorded more than 1.5 million hits. During the election, the Web site not only provided far more reliable basic information than any conventional mass media source, it also allowed individuals to e-mail queries and get answers. Political experts were shocked by the quality of the questions submitted, the insights they contained, and the appetite for information. Party policies, opinion polls, electoral trajectories, and key issues were clarified and debated in depth.

The Internet may also greatly benefit in the creation of a vibrant "discursive democracy" (Dunleavy & Weir, 1998). Government departments, local councils, and other public bodies can clarify how they sculpt their policies and request interested citizens and specialists to participate directly in determining them.

> Interactive question-and-answer sessions, policy forums, panels and discussion groups, planning consultations, chat-lines, even tabloid-style votes can all generate a great deal more information that policymakers should consider. They could also give far more in-depth information more cheaply and conveniently, respond to people's questions and ideas and encourage the public to submit proposals for action. (p. 2)

Newhagen and Rafaeli (1996) also attempted to theoretically position the Internet as a legitimate subject of mass communication and social science research and they called for a U&G approach to investigate the medium. They suggested that because a tradition in mass communication research of studying U&G already exists, that approach may be useful in laying out a taxonomy of cyberspace. Newhagen and Rafaeli focused on five defining characteristics of communication on the Internet: multimedia, packet switching, hypertextuality, synchroneity, and interactivity.

Besides synchroneity and interactivity, which have already been discussed, the other three properties deserve closer explanation. *Multimedia* is the use of computers to present text, graphics, video, animation, and sound in an integrated way. Long extolled as the future revolution in computing, multimedia applications were, until the mid-1990s, scarce due to the costly hardware required. With increases in performance and decreases in price, multimedia is now ubiquitous. Nearly all current personal computers are capable of displaying video, although the resolution available depends on the power of the computer's video adapter and central processing unit. Because of the storage demands of multimedia applications, the most effective media are CD–ROMs, and now Zip™ disks, which both contain far greater memory capacity than traditional floppy disks.

Packet switching refers to protocols in which messages are divided into packets before they are sent. Each packet is then transmitted individually and can even follow different routes to its destination. Once all the packets forming a message arrive at the destination, they are recompiled into the original message. In contrast, normal telephone service is based on a circuit-switching technology, in which a dedicated line is allocated for transmission between two parties. Circuit switching is ideal when data must be transmitted quickly and must arrive in the same order in which it is sent. This is the case with most real-time data, such as live audio and video. Packet switching is more efficient and robust for data that can withstand some delays in transmission, such as e-mail messages and Web pages (Newhagen & Rafaeli, 1996).

Hypertextuality, which constitutes the core of Internet documents, is created by the simple hypertext markup language (HTML), so that the text represents not a fixed linear sequence, but performs as a network to be actively composed (Sandbothe, 1996). Every building block of text (node) contains an abundance of keywords, pictograms, and pictures, which can be clicked on with a mouse; these are the links. Sandbothe (1996) predicted that hypertext technology already is having profound effects on the use of electronic texts:

> Every reader lays his own trail in the text whilst reading. Or rather, every reader composes the object he reads through the active selection of the links provided. The individual reception perspective determines the succession of text building blocks. Reading is no longer a passive process of reception, but rather becomes a process of creative interaction between reader, author, and text. (p. 2)

Additionally, many contemporary communication researchers seek to legitimize the Internet as a subject of research by framing a theoretical construct of the Internet as a continuum between mass and interpersonal communication. Similar questions appear to exist in the literature for both U&G and interpersonal communication. In both cases, the focus is on the biological, psychological, and sociological motivations behind people taking part in receiving or exchanging messages (Newhagen & Rafaeli, 1996). For example, Rice and Williams (1984) argued that interactive new media have the ability to "co-locate with the interpersonal sources on one or both of the personal dimensions" (p. 65). Garramone, Harris, and Anderson (1986) suggested that social presence mediates the relation between the interactive use and noninteractive use of political computer bulletin boards. Garrison (1995) adopted U&G to quantify a number of important questions about how and why journalists do computer-assisted reporting. Eighmey and McCord (1995) drew on the U&G perspective to examine the audience experience associated with Web sites. Thus, U&G research may well play a major role in answering initial Web-use questions of prurience, curiosity, profit seeking, and sociability. U&G also holds the prospect for understanding the Internet's mutability, or its broad range of communication opportunities, by "laying out a taxonomy of just what goes on in cyberspace" (Newhagen & Rafaeli, 1996, p. 11).

U&G AND QUALITATIVE METHODOLOGIES

Leeds-Hurwitz (1992) suggested that a revolution was occurring in all the fields that study human behavior, including communication. She cited specifically "cultural studies, critical theory, postmodernism, semiotics, phenomenology, structuralism, hermeneutics, naturalistic inquiry, ethnography and social communication" (p. 131). This led Weaver (1993) to sound a note of caution about dismissing quantitative methods. Weaver argued that many communication researchers have spent decades applying quantitative methods and statistical analysis. These methods have told us much about general patterns, trends, and relationships, and "can enable us to generalize with far more accuracy than can our own personal experiences and impressions" (p. 213). Additionally, Dobos (1992) concluded that the U&G approach should prove effective in ascertaining the importance of social context as a factor in the communication experience. Significantly, the way that individuals choose to use media differs accordingly with their position in the social structure (Roe, 1983; Rosengren & Windahl, 1989).

Thus, it is important to remember that U&G theory continues to offer more than a methodological perspective. Dervin (1980) advocated that media planners and those conducting information campaigns should begin with the study of the potential information user and the questions that person is attempting to answer to make sense of the world. After all, Pool (1983) noted that when a medium is in the early stages of development, predictions are often inaccurate. Thus, the U&G approach may serve as the vanguard of an eventual thorough quantitative and qualitative analysis of new media technologies.

This is not to relegate qualitative or interpretive methodologies to a subordinate role. On the contrary, Jensen and Jankowski (1991) suggested that quantitative methodologies could be used quite effectively to inform the more commonly used qualitative audience methodologies of interpretive media research. Different levels of analysis, including individual, small group, organizational, societal, and cultural, may require the use of multiple methods in single studies. Thus, communication researchers should be encouraged to employ U&G more frequently in conjunction with qualitative methodologies in a holistic approach. One case of this is Schaefer and Avery's (1993) study of audience conceptualizations of the *Late Night With David Letterman* television show. The study used both questionnaires and interviews to "combine the strengths of survey data with the richness of depth interviews" (p. 271). Additionally, Massey (1995) used a ninefold U&G typology to operationalize her qualitative study of audience media use during the 1989 Loma Prieta earthquake disaster.

Newhagen and Rafaeli (1996) suggested that in time, questions at cultural and societal levels may offer the greatest contribution to communications research. For example, Morley's (1980, 1986, 1992) studies of family TV viewing and domestic power in the working class, Radway's (1984) account of female empowerment linked to reading romance novels, I. Ang's (1985) analysis of Dutch women's interpretations and use of the international television series *Dallas,* Liebes and Katz's (1990) analysis of ethnic and cultural variation in *Dallas* audiences, and Lull's (1991) study of Chinese viewers' resistive engagements with television all document culturally and historically specific ways in which audiences actively interpret and use mass media (Lull, 1995). However, to truly understand new media technologies, critical scholars should learn to embrace multiple levels of analysis. Empiricists, on the other hand, Newhagen and Rafaeli argued, "will have to show a greater, more eclectic tolerance for experimental science" (p. 9).

THEORETICAL SYNOPSIS OF U&G

More than a decade ago, after reviewing the results of approximately 100 U&G studies, Palmgreen (1984) proclaimed that a complex theoretical structure was emerging. Palmgreen's statement has significance for contemporary and future mass communication researchers in at least two ways. First, he was proposing an integrative gratifications model that suggested a multivariate approach (Wimmer & Dominick, 1994); that is, a commitment for researchers to investigate the relation between one or more independent variables and more than one dependent variable. He noted emergent research techniques such as hierarchical regression, canonical correlation, multiple classification analysis, and structural equation modeling to control for media exposure and other intervening variables (Rayburn, 1996). Second, Palmgreen was answering critics who had long argued that the U&G perspective was more a research strategy or heuristic orientation than a theory (Elliott, 1974; Swanson, 1977; Weiss, 1976). He suggested that audience GS and GO were associated with a broad variance of media effects including knowledge, dependency, attitudes, perceptions of social reality, agenda setting, discussion, and politics (Rayburn, 1996).

Thus, if anything, one of the major strengths of the U&G perspective has been its capacity to develop over time into a more sophisticated theoretical model. Historically, the focus of inquiry has shifted from a mechanistic perspective's interest in direct effects of media on receivers to a psychological perspective that stresses individual use and choice (Rubin, 1994b). U&G researchers have also moved from a microperspective toward a macroanalysis. Thus, although the microunit of data collection has primarily remained the individual, the focus of inquiry has been transformed over time. Interpretation of the individual's response by researchers has shifted from the sender to the receiver, from the media to the audience. The primary unit of data collection of U&G continues be the individual, but that individual's activity is now analyzed in a plethora of psychological and social contexts including media dependency, ritualization, instrumental, communication facilitation, affiliation or avoidance, social learning, and role reinforcement. U&G research continues to typologize motivations for media use in terms of diversion (i.e., as an escape from routines or for emotional release), social utility (i.e., to acquire information for conversations), personal identity (i.e., to reinforce attitudes, beliefs, and values), and surveillance (i.e., to learn about one's community, events, and political affairs).

Furthermore, previous U&G researchers have primarily concentrated on choice, reception, and manner of response of the media audience. A key assumption has been that the audience member makes a conscious and motivated choice among media channel and content (McQuail, 1994). Yet, recent U&G researchers have even begun to question stock assumptions about the active audience concept. Although researchers continue to regard audience members as universally active, some now suggest that all audience members are not equally active at all times (Rubin, 1994b). This assertiveness of U&G researchers to continuously critique basic assumptions suggests a dynamic and evolving theoretical atmosphere, especially as we depart the industrial era for the postindustrial age.

U&G AS LEGITIMATE THEORY

Perhaps endlessly, scholars will continue to debate which prevailing theories should be acknowledged as "legitimate" communication theories. U&G detractors may well continue to label it as an approach rather than an authentic theory. Skeptics may question the theory for a lack of empirical distinction between needs and motivations and the obstacles of measuring the gratification of needs. They may argue that the theory posits a rigid teleology within a functionalist approach (Cazeneuve, 1974). Or, as Carey and Kreiling (1974) argued, the utilitarianistic audience-centered interpretations will not suffice to decode popular culture consumption because "an effective theory of popular culture will require a conception of man, not as psychological or sociological man, but as cultural man" (p. 242). Finally, Finn (1997) questioned the ability of U&G researchers to solve the enigma of "linking personality traits to patterns of mass media use without accounting for alternative sources of gratification in the interpersonal domain" (p. 11). Yet, even critical scholars recognize that U&G research, chiefly pioneered by postwar social psychologists, has brought to the forefront the concept that the audience's perceptions of media messages may be altogether different from the meanings intended by their producers (Stevenson, 1997).

For its advocates, however, U&G is still touted as one of the most influential theories in the field of communication research (Lin, 1998). Furthermore, the concept of *needs,* which most U&G theorists embrace as a central psychological concept, is nearly irreproachable in more established disciplines. Within psychology, need is the bedrock of some of the discipline's most important theoretical work, including cognitive dissonance theory, social exchange theory, attribution theory, and some types of psychoanalytic theory (Lull, 1995). Samuels (1984) suggested physiological and psychological needs such as self-actualization, cognitive needs (such as curiosity), aesthetic needs, and expressive needs are inherent in every individual and central to human experience. Additionally, human needs are influenced by culture, not only in their formation but in how they are gratified. "Thus, culturally situated social experience reinforces basic biological and psychological needs while simultaneously giving direction to their sources of gratification" (Lull, 1995, p. 99). Lull further suggested that the study of how and why individuals use media, through U&G research, may offer clues to our understanding about exactly what needs are, where they originate, and how they are gratified.

Unfortunately, the polemic over whether U&G satisfies the standard of a full-fledged theory continues. In part it may be due to the antiquated perception that any communication theory is inherently deficient to the traditional disciplines of sociology and psychology. Even more acrimonious is continued criticism by critical and cultural scholars that the perspective embodies a functionalist approach. Certainly, early U&G emanated from a functionalist theoretical framework; a sociological theory that theorized patterned social phenomena leading to specific social consequences. However, Lin (1996) argued that this functionalist approach provides the "means–ends orientation [for the perspective and] opens up a world of opportunities for studying mediated communication as a functional process that is purposive and leads to specific psychological or social consequences" (p. 2). Additionally, Massey (1995) contended that qualitative communication scholars may find it difficult to advance the "illumination of audience interaction with the media" (p. 17) if they reject the questions, methods, and determinist results of U&G research. Newhagen and Rafaeli (1996) suggested that mass media scholars will eventually have to address profound societal ramifications of new media. However, U&G theory offers researchers the ability to examine challenges and barriers to access that individual users are currently experiencing.

U&G: A CUTTING-EDGE THEORY

By and large, U&G has always provided a cutting-edge theoretical approach in the initial stages of each new mass communications medium: newspapers, radio, television, and now the Internet. It may be argued that the timely emergence of computer-mediated communication has only bolstered the theoretical potency of U&G by allowing it to stimulate productive research into a proliferating telecommunications medium. Lin (1996) argued that the primary strength of U&G theory is its ability to permit researchers to investigate "mediated communication situations via a single or multiple sets of psychological needs, psychological motives, communication channels, communication content, and psychological gratifications within a particular or cross-cultural context" (p. 574). For example, the use of personal computers has been linked to individuals' motivations to use the Internet for communication purposes linked to the fulfillment of gratifications such as social identity, interpersonal communication, parasocial interaction, companionship, escape, entertainment, and surveillance. As new communication technologies rapidly materialize, the range of possible topics for U&G research also multiplies. This flexibility is particularly important as we enter an information age in which computer-mediated communication permeates every aspect of our individual and social lives.

U&G AND ITS ROLE IN THE 21ST CENTURY

The Internet lies at the locus of a new media ecology that has "altered the structural relations among traditional media such as print and broadcast and unites them around the defining technologies of computer and satellite" (Carey, 1998, p. 34). This convergence makes the old print–electronic and verbal–nonverbal distinctions, so long the focus of communication researchers, less relevant in light of messages that combine writing, still and animated images, and voices and other sounds (Weaver, 1993). For users, text, voice, pictures, animation, video, virtual reality motion codes, and even smell have already become part of the Internet experience (Newhagen & Rafaeli, 1996). Communication on the Internet travels at unparalleled velocity. The Internet offers its audience an immense range of communication opportunities. Networks are always "up," allowing 24-hour asynchronous or synchronous interactions and information retrieval and exchange among individuals and groups (Kiesler, 1997). Fortuitous for U&G researchers, communication on the Internet also leaves a trail that is easily traceable. Messages have time stamps, accurate to one hundredth of a second. Content is readily observable, recorded, and copied. Participant demography and behaviors of consumption, choice, attention, reaction, and learning afford extraordinary research opportunities (Newhagen & Rafaeli, 1996). James et al. (1995) suggested Internet forums such as electronic bulletin boards fulfill many expectations of both mass and interpersonal communication. Hence, if the Internet is a new dominion of human activity, it is also a new dominion for U&G researchers.

If the Internet is a technology that many predict will be genuinely transformative, it will lead to profound changes in media users' personal and social habits and roles. The Internet's growth rates are exponential. The number of users has doubled in each of the last 6 years. If this development continues at the same rate, the Internet will soon be as widely disseminated a medium in daily usage as television or the telephone (Quarterman & Carl-Mitchell, 1993). Thus, electronic communication technology may sufficiently alter the context of media use that current mass communication theories do not yet address. Some foresee, for example, that soon the novelty of combining music, video, graphics, and text will wane, and more natural methods will be created for Web users to interact in, such as data "landscapes" (Aldersey-Williams, 1996). Others predict a move beyond studying single users, two-person ties, and small groups, to analyzing the computer-supported social networks that flourish in areas as diverse as the workplace and in virtual communities (Garton, Haythornthwaite, & Wellman, 1997). Gilder (1990) argued that the new media technologies like the Internet will empower individuals by "blowing apart all monopolies, hierarchies, pyramids, and power grids of established society" (p. 32). Others caution that the Internet is becoming more institutionally and commercially driven and is beginning to be "less the egalitarian cyberspace of recent memory than it does a tacky, crowded-with-billboards freeway exit just before any major tourist destination in the U.S." (Riley, Keough, Christiansen, Meilich, & Pierson, 1998, p. 3).

Theoretically and practically, for U&G scholars, however, the basic questions remain the same. Why do people become involved in one particular type of mediated communication or another, and what gratifications do they receive from it? Although we are likely to continue using traditional tools and typologies to answer these questions, we must also be prepared to expand our current theoretical models of U&G to include concepts such as interactivity, demassification, hypertextuality, asynchroneity, and interpersonal aspects of mediated communication. Then, if we are able to situate a "modernized" U&G theory within this new media ecology, in an evolving psychological, sociological, and cultural context, we should be able to anticipate a highly serviceable theory for the 21st century.

REFERENCES

Abrahamson, D. (1998). The visible hand: Money, markets, and media evolution. *Journalism and Mass Communication Quarterly, 75,* 14–18.
Aldersey-Williams, H. (1996). Interactivity with a human face. *Technology Review, 99,* 34–40.
Anderson, D. R., Collins, P. A., Schmitt, K. L., & Jacobvitz, R. S. (1996). Stressful life events and television viewing. *Communication Research, 23,* 243–260.
Anderson, J. A. (1996). *Communication theory: Epistemological foundations.* New York: Guilford.
Anderson, K. J., & Revelle, W. (1995). Personality processes. *Annual Review of Psychology, 46,* 295–328.
Ang, I. (1985). *Watching Dallas: Soap opera and the melodramatic imagination.* London: Routledge.
Ang, S., & Cummings, L. L. (1994). Panel analysis of feedback-seeking patterns in face-to-face, computer-mediated, and computer-generated communication environments. *Perceptual and Motor Skills, 79,* 67–73.
Anonymous. (1989). Functional displacement of traditional TV viewing by VCR owners. *Journal of Advertising Research, 29*(2), 18–23.
Armstrong, C. B., & Rubin, A. M. (1989). Talk radio as interpersonal communication. *Journal of Communication, 39*(2), 84–94.
Atkin, D. (1993). Adoption of cable amidst a multimedia environment. *Telematics & Informatics, 10,* 51–58.

Ball-Rokeach, S. (1985). The origins of individual media-system dependency: A sociological framework. *Communication Research, 12,* 485–510.
Bantz, C. R. (1982). Exploring uses and gratifications: A comparison of reported uses of television and reported uses of favorite program type. *Communication Research, 9,* 352–379.
Barwise, T. P., Ehrenberg, A. S. C., & Goodhardt, G. J. (1982). Glued to the box. *Journal of Communication, 32*(4), 22–29.
Berelson, B. (1949). What "missing the newspaper" means. In P. F. Lazarsfeld & F. N. Stanton (Eds.), *Communication research 1948–1949* (pp. 111–129). New York: Harper.
Berelson, B., Lazarsfeld, P. F., & McPhee, W. N. (1954). *Voting: A study of opinion formation in a presidential campaign.* Chicago: University of Chicago Press.
Bergeron, B. P., & Bailin, M. T. (1997). The contribution of hypermedia link authoring. *Technical Communication, 44,* 121–128.
Blumler, J. G. (1979). The role of theory in uses and gratifications studies. *Communication Research, 6,* 9–36.
Blumler, J. G. (1985). The social character of media gratifications. In K. E. Rosengren, L. A. Wenner, & P. Palmgreen (Eds.), *Media gratifications research: Current perspectives* (pp. 41–59). Beverly Hills, CA: Sage.
Bryant, J., & Zillman, D. (1984). Using television to alleviate boredom and stress. *Journal of Broadcasting, 28,* 1–20.
Cantril, H. (1940). *The invasion from Mars: A study in the psychology of panic.* Princeton, NJ: Princeton University Press.
Cantril, H. (1942). Professor quiz: A gratifications study. In P. F. Lazarsfeld & F. Stanton (Eds.), *Radio research 1941* (pp. 34–45). New York: Duell, Sloan & Pearce.
Cantril, H., & Allport, G. (1935). *The psychology of radio.* New York: Harper.
Carey, J. W. (1998). The Internet and the end of the National Communication System: Uncertain predictions of an uncertain future. *Journalism and Mass Communication Quarterly, 75*(1), 28–34.
Carey, J. W., & Kreiling, A. L. (1974). Popular culture and uses and gratifications: Notes toward an accommodation. In J. G. Blumler & E. Katz (Eds.), *The uses of mass communications: Current perspectives on gratifications research* (pp. 225–248). Beverly Hills, CA: Sage.
Cattell, R. B., Edger, H. W., & Tatsuoka, M. M. (1970). *Handbook for the Sixteen Personality Factor Questionnaire.* Champaign, IL: Institute of Personality and Ability Testing.
Cazeneuve, E. (1974). Television as a functional alternative to traditional sources of need satisfaction. In J. G. Blumler & E. Katz (Eds.), *The uses of mass communications: Current perspectives on gratifications research* (pp. 213–224). Beverly Hills, CA: Sage.
Chamberlain, M. A. (1994). New technologies in health communication. *American Behavioral Scientist, 38,* 271–284.
Cohen, A. A. (1981). People without media: Attitudes and behavior during a general media strike. *Journal of Broadcasting, 25,* 171–180.
Cooper, R. (1996). The status and future of audience duplication research: An assessment of ratings-based theories of audience behavior. *Journal of Broadcasting & Electronic Media, 40,* 96–116.
Cooper, R. (1997). Japanese communication research: The emphasis on macro theories of media in an information based environment. *Journal of Broadcasting & Electronic Media, 41,* 284–288.
Cowles, D. (1989). Consumer perceptions of interactive media. *Journal of Broadcasting & Electronic Media, 33,* 83–89.
de Bock, H. (1980). Gratification frustration during a newspaper strike and a TV blackout. *Journalism Quarterly, 57,* 61–66, 78.
December, J. (1996). Units of analysis for Internet communication. *Journal of Communication, 46*(1), 14–37.
DeFleur, M. L., & Ball-Rokeach, S. (1982). *Theories of mass communication* (4th ed.). New York: Longman.

Dervin, B. (1980). Communication gaps and inequities: Moving toward a reconceptualization. In B. Dervin & M. J. Voight (Eds.), *Progress in communication sciences* (Vol. 2, pp. 73–112). Norwood, NJ: Ablex.

Dicken-Garcia, H. (1998). The Internet and continuing historical discourse. *Journalism and Mass Communication Quarterly, 75,* 19–27.

Dobos, J. (1992). Gratification models of satisfaction and choice of communication channels in organizations. *Communication Research, 19,* 29–51.

Donohew, L., Finn, S., & Christ, W. G. (1988). The nature of news revisited: The roles of affect, schemas, and cognition. In L. Donohew, H. E. Sypher, & E. T. Higgins (Eds.), *Communication, social cognition and affect* (pp. 195–218). Hillsdale, NJ: Lawrence Erlbaum Associates, Inc.

Donohew, L., Palmgreen P., & Rayburn, J. D., II. (1987). Social and psychological origins of media use: A lifestyle analysis. *Journal of Broadcasting & Electronic Media, 31,* 255–278.

Dorsher, M. (1996, August). *Whither the public sphere: Prospects for cybersphere.* Paper presented at the Media, Technology, and Community Conference, Grand Forks, ND.

Dozier, D. M., & Rice, R. E. (1984). Rival theories of electronic newsgathering. In R. E. Rice (Ed.), *The new media: Communication, research, and technology* (pp. 103–128). Beverly Hills, CA: Sage.

Dunleavy, P., & Weir, S. (1998). How to freshen up democracy. *New Statesman, 11,* 535, 571–572.

Dutton, W. H., Rogers, E. M., & Jun, S. (1987). Diffusion and social impact of personal computers. *Communication Research, 14,* 219–249.

Dyson, E. (1993). Interactivity means "active" participation. *Computerworld, 27*(50), 33–34.

Eastman, S. T. (1979). Uses of television viewing and consumer life styles: A multivariate analysis. *Journal of Broadcasting, 23,* 491–500.

Eighmey, J. (1997). Profiling user responses to commercial Web sites. *Journal of Advertising Research, 37*(3), 59–66.

Eighmey, J., & McCord, L. (1995, November). *Adding value in the information age: Uses and gratifications of the World-Wide Web.* Paper presented at the Conference on Telecommunications and Information Markets. Newport, RI.

Elliott, P. (1974). Uses and gratifications research: A critique and a sociological alternative. In J. G. Blumler & E. Katz (Eds.), *The uses of mass communications: Current perspectives on gratifications research* (pp. 249–268). Beverly Hills, CA: Sage.

Eysenck, H. J. (1991). Dimensions of personality: 16, 5, or 3?—Criteria for a taxonomic paradigm. *Personality and Individual Differences, 12,* 773–790.

Ferguson, D. A. (1992). Channel repertoire in the presence of remote control devices, VCRs and cable television. *Journal of Broadcasting & Electronic Media, 36,* 83–91.

Ferguson, D. A., & Perse, E. M. (1994, March). *Viewing television without a remote: A deprivation study.* Paper presented at the annual meeting of the Research Division, Broadcast Education Association, Las Vegas, NV.

Finn, S. (1997). Origins of media exposure: Linking personality traits to TV, radio, print, and film use. *Communication Research, 24,* 507–529.

Fishbein, M., & Ajzen, I. (1975). *Belief, attitude, and behavior.* Reading, MA: Addison-Wesley.

Fredin, E. S., & David, P. (1998). Browsing and the hypermedia interaction cycle: A model of self-efficacy and goal dynamics. *Journalism and Mass Communication Quarterly, 75,* 35–54.

Fry, D. L., & McCain, T. A. (1983). Community influentials' media dependency in dealing with a controversial local issue. *Journalism Quarterly, 60,* 458–463.

Fulk, J., Flanagin, A. J., Kalman, A. E., Monge, P. R., & Ryan, T. (1996). Connective and communal public goods in interactive communication systems. *Communication Theory, 6,* 60–87.

Funk, J. B., & Buchman, D. D. (1996). Playing violent video and computer games and adolescent self-concept. *Journal of Communication, 46*(2), 19–32.

Galloway, J. J., & Meek, F. L. (1981). Audience uses and gratifications: An expectancy model. *Communication Research, 8,* 435–449.

Gandy, O. H., Jr., Matabane, P. W., & Omachonu, J. O. (1987). Media use, reliance, and active participation. *Communication Research, 14,* 644–663.

Garramone, G. (1984). Audience motivation effects: More evidence. *Communication Research, 11,* 79–96.

Garramone, G. (1985). Motivation and selective attention to political information formats. *Journalism Quarterly, 62,* 37–44.

Garramone, G. M., Harris, A. C., & Anderson, R. (1986). Uses of political computer bulletin boards. *Journal of Broadcasting & Electronic Media, 30,* 325–339.

Garrison, B. (1995). Online services as reporting tools: Daily newspaper use of commercial databases in 1994. *Newspaper Research Journal, 16*(4), 74–86.

Garton, L., Haythornthwaite, C., & Wellman, B. (1997). Studying online social networks. *Journal of Computer-Mediated Communication, 3*(1). Retrieved May 1999 from the World Wide Web: http://jcmc.huji/ vol3/issue1/garton.html#ABSTRACT

Geiger, S., & Newhagen, J. (1993). Revealing the black box: Information processing and media effects. *Journal of Communication, 43*(4), 42–50.

Gerson, W. (1966). Mass media socialization behavior: Negro–Whites differences. *Social Forces, 45,* 40–50.

Gilder, G. (1990). *Life after television.* Knoxville, TN: Whittle Direct.

Goodhardt, G. J., Ehrenberg, A. S. C., & Collins, M. A. (1987). *The television audience: Patterns of viewing* (2nd ed.). Aldershot, England: Gower.

Grant, A. E., Guthrie, K. K., & Ball-Rokeach, S. (1991). Television shopping: A media dependency perspective. *Communication Research, 18,* 773–798.

Greenberg, B. S. (1974). Gratifications of television viewing and their correlates for British children. In J. G. Blumler & E. Katz (Eds.), *The uses of mass communications: Current perspectives on gratifications research* (pp. 71–92). Beverly Hills, CA: Sage.

Greenberg, B. S., & Dominick, J. (1969). Race and social class differences in teenager's use of television. *Journal of Broadcasting, 13*(4), 331–344.

Grunig, J. E. (1979). Time budgets, level of involvement and use of the mass media. *Journalism Quarterly, 56,* 248–261.

Ha, L. (1995). Subscriber's behavior in electronic discussion groups: A comparison between academics and practitioners. In *Proceedings of the first annual conference on telecommunications and information markets* (pp. 27–36).

Ha, L., & James, E. L. (1998). Interactivity reexamined: A baseline analysis of early business Web sites. *Journal of Broadcasting & Electronic Media, 42,* 457–474.

Hawkins, R. P., & Pingree, S. (1981). Uniform messages and habitual viewing: Unnecessary assumptions in social reality effects. *Human Communication Research, 7,* 291–301.

Heeter, C. (1989). Implications of new interactive technologies for conceptualizing communication. In J. L. Salvaggio & J. Bryant (Eds.), *Media use in the information age: Emerging patterns of adoption and consumer use* (pp. 217–235). Hillsdale, NJ: Lawrence Erlbaum Associates, Inc.

Heeter, C., & Greenberg, B. (1985). Cable and program choice. In D. Zillman & J. Bryant (Eds.), *Selective exposure to communication* (pp. 203–224). Hillsdale, NJ: Lawrence Erlbaum Associates, Inc.

Herzog, H. (1940). Professor quiz: A gratification study. In P. F. Lazarsfeld & F. N. Stanton (Eds.), *Radio and the printed page* (pp. 64–93). New York: Duell, Sloan & Pearce.

Herzog, H. (1944). What do we really know about daytime serial listeners? In P. F. Lazarsfeld & F. N. Stanton (Eds.), *Radio research 1942–1943* (pp. 3–33). New York: Duell, Sloan & Pearce.

Horna, J. (1988). The mass media as leisure: A western-Canadian case. *Society and Leisure, 11,* 283–301.

Jackson, M. H. (1997). Assessing the structure of communication on the World Wide Web. *Journal of Computer-Mediated Communication, 3.* Retrieved May 1999 from the World Wide Web: http://jcmc.huji.ac. il/vol3/issue1/jackson.html#ABSTRACT

Jacobs, R. (1995). Exploring the determinants of cable television subscriber satisfaction. *Journal of Broadcasting & Electronic Media, 39,* 262–274.
James, M. L., Wotring, C. E., & Forrest, E. J. (1995). An exploratory study of the perceived benefits of electronic bulletin board use and their impact on other communication activities. *Journal of Broadcasting & Electronic Media, 39,* 30–50.
Jensen, K. B., & Jankowski, N. W. (1991). *A handbook of qualitative methodologies for mass communication research.* New York: Routledge.
Katz, E. (1960). The two-step flow of communication. In W. Schramm (Ed.), *Mass communications* (pp. 346–365). Urbana: University of Illinois Press.
Katz, E. (1987). Communication research since Lazarsfeld. *Public Opinion Quarterly, 51,* 525–545.
Katz, E., Blumler, J., & Gurevitch, M. (1974). Utilization of mass communication by the individual. In J. Blumler & E. Katz (Eds.), *The uses of mass communication: Current perspectives on gratifications research* (pp. 19–34). Beverly Hills, CA: Sage.
Katz, E., & Foulkes, D. (1962). On the use of mass media as escape: Clarification of a concept. *Public Opinion Quarterly, 26,* 377–388.
Katz, E., Gurevitch, M., & Haas, H. (1973). On the use of the mass media for important things. *American Sociological Review, 38,* 164–181.
Katz, E., & Lazarsfeld, P. F. (1955). *Personal influence: The part played by people in the flow of mass communications.* Glencoe, IL: Free Press.
Kiesler, S. (Ed.). (1997). *Culture of the Internet.* Mahwah, NJ: Lawrence Erlbaum Associates, Inc.
Kimball, P. (1959). People without papers. *Public Opinion Quarterly, 23,* 389–398.
Klapper, J. T. (1960). *The effects of mass communication.* New York: Free Press.
Klapper, J. T. (1963). Mass communication research: An old road resurveyed. *Public Opinion Quarterly, 27,* 515–527.
Kubey, R. (1986). Television use in everyday life: Coping with unstructured time. *Journal of Communication, 36*(3), 108–123.
Kubey, R., & Csikszentmihalyi, M. (1990). *Television and the quality of life.* Hillsdale, NJ: Lawrence Erlbaum Associates, Inc.
Kuehn, S. A. (1994). Computer-mediated communication in instructional settings: A research agenda. *Communication Education, 43,* 171–182.
LaRose, R., & Atkin, D. (1991). An analysis of pay-per-view versus other movie delivery modalities. *Journal of Media Economics, 4,* 3–17.
Lazarsfeld, P. F., Berelson, B., & Gaudet, H. (1948). *The people's choice* (2nd ed.). New York: Columbia University Press.
Lazarsfeld, P. F., & Stanton, F. (1942). *Radio research, 1942–1943.* New York: Duell, Sloan & Pearce.
Lazarsfeld, P. F., & Stanton, F. (1944). *Radio research, 1941.* New York: Duell, Sloan & Pearce.
Lazarsfeld, P. F., & Stanton, F. (1949). *Communication research 1948–1949.* New York: Harper & Row.
Leeds-Hurwitz, W. (1992). Social approaches to interpersonal communication. *Communication Theory, 2,* 131–139.
Lemish, D. (1985). Soap opera viewing in college: A naturalistic inquiry. *Journal of Broadcasting & Electronic Media, 29,* 275–293.
Levy, M. R., & Windahl, S. (1984). Audience activity and gratifications: A conceptual clarification and exploration. *Communication Research, 11,* 51–78.
Lichtenstein, A., & Rosenfeld, L. B. (1983). Uses and misuses of gratifications research: An explication of media functions. *Communication Research, 10,* 97–109.
Liebes, T., & Katz, E. (1990). *The export of meaning.* New York: Oxford University Press.
Lin, C. A. (1993). Exploring the role of the VCR use in the emerging home entertainment culture. *Journalism Quarterly, 70,* 833–842.
Lin, C. A. (1996). Looking back: The contribution of Blumler and Katz's uses and mass communication to communication research. *Journal of Broadcasting & Electronic Media, 40,* 574–581.

Lin, C. A. (1998). Exploring personal computer adoption dynamics. *Journal of Broadcasting & Electronic Media, 42,* 95–112.
Lind, R. A. (1995). How can TV news be improved?: Viewer perceptions of quality and responsibility. *Journal of Broadcasting & Electronic Media, 39,* 360–375.
Loges, W. E., & Ball-Rokeach, S. (1993). Dependency relations and newspaper readership. *Journalism Quarterly, 70,* 601–614.
Lometti, G. E., Reeves, B., & Bybee, C. R. (1977). Investigating the assumptions of uses and gratifications research. *Communication Research, 4,* 321–328.
Lowery, S., & DeFleur, M. L. (1983). *Milestones in mass communication research.* New York: Longman.
Lull, J. (1991). *China turned on: Television, reform and resistance.* London: Routledge.
Lull, J. (1995). *Media, communication, culture: A global approach.* New York: Columbia University Press.
Markus, M. L. (1994). Finding a happy medium: Explaining the negative effects of electronic communication on social life at work. *ACM Transactions on Information Systems, 14,* 119–149.
Massey, K. B. (1995). Analyzing the uses and gratifications concept of audience activity with a qualitative approach: Media encounters during the 1989 Loma Prieta earthquake disaster. *Journal of Broadcasting & Electronic Media, 39,* 328–342.
McGuire, W. J. (1974). Psychological motives and communication gratifications. In J. G. Blumler & E. Katz (Eds.), *The uses of mass communications: Current perspectives on gratifications research* (pp. 167–196). Beverly Hills, CA: Sage.
McIlwraith, R. D. (1998). "I'm addicted to television": The personality, imagination, and TV watching patterns of self-identified TV addicts. *Journal of Broadcasting & Electronic Media, 42,* 371–386.
McLeod, J. M., & Becker, L. (1981). The uses and gratifications approach. In D. Nimmo & K. Sanders (Eds.), *Handbook of political communication* (pp. 67–100). Beverly Hills, CA: Sage.
McLeod, J. M., Bybee, C. R., & Durall, J. A. (1982). On evaluating news media performance. *Political Communication, 10,* 16–22.
McQuail, D. (1994). The rise of media of mass communication. In D. McQuail (Ed.), *Mass communication theory: An introduction* (pp. 1–29). London: Sage.
McQuail, D., Blumler, J., & Brown, J. (1972). The television audience: A revised perspective. In D. McQuail (Ed.), *Sociology of mass communications* (pp. 135–165). Middlesex, England: Penguin.
Mendelsohn, H. (1964). Listening to the radio. In L. A. Dexter & D. M. White (Eds.), *People, society and mass communication* (pp. 239–248). New York: Free Press.
Merton, R. K. (1949). Patterns of influence: A study of interpersonal influence and communications behavior in a local community. In P. F. Lazarsfeld & F. N. Stanton (Eds.), *Communication research, 1948–1949* (pp. 180–219). New York: Harper.
Morley, D. (1980). *The nationwide audience.* London: Film Institute.
Morley, D. (1986). *Family television: Cultural power and domestic leisure.* London: Routledge.
Morley, D. (1992). *Television, audiences, and cultural studies.* London: Routledge.
Morris, M., & Ogan, C. (1996). The Internet as mass medium. *Journal of Communications, 46*(1), 39–50.
Nelson, T. H. (1990). The right way to think about software design. In B. Laurel (Ed.), *The art of human–computer interface design.* Reading, MA: Addison-Wesley.
Newhagen, J., & Rafaeli, S. (1996). Why communication researchers should study the Internet: A dialogue. *Journal of Communications, 46*(1), 4–13.
Nisbett, R., & Wilson, T. (1977). Telling more than we can know: Verbal reports on mental processes. *Psychological Review, 84,* 231–259.
Ostman, R. E., & Jeffers, D. W. (1980, June). *The relationship of life-stage to motives for using television and the perceived reality of TV.* Paper presented at the International Communication Association convention, Acapulco, Mexico.

Palmgreen, P. (1984). Uses and gratifications: A theoretical perspective. In R. Bostrom (Ed.), *Communication Yearbook 8* (pp. 20–55). Beverly Hills, CA: Sage.
Palmgreen, P., & Rayburn, J. D., II. (1979). Uses and gratifications and exposure to public television. *Communication Research, 6,* 155–180.
Palmgreen, P., & Rayburn, J. D., II. (1982). Gratifications sought and media exposure: An expectancy value model. *Communication Research, 9,* 561–580.
Palmgreen, P., & Rayburn, J. D., II. (1985). A comparison of gratification models of media satisfaction. *Communication Monographs, 52,* 334–346.
Perse, E. M., & Courtright, J. A. (1993). Normative images of communication research. *Human Communication, 19,* 485–503.
Perse, E. M., & Dunn, D. G. (1998). The utility of home computers and media use: Implications of multimedia and connectivity. *Journal of Broadcasting & Electronic Media, 42,* 435–456.
Perse, E. M., & Rubin, A. M. (1988). Audience activity and satisfaction with favorite television soap opera. *Journalism Quarterly, 65,* 368–375.
Pool, I. D. (1983). *Technologies of freedom.* Cambridge, MA: Harvard University Press.
Quarterman, J. S., & Carl-Mitchell, S. (1993). The computing paradigm shift. *Journal of Organizational Computing, 3,* 31–50.
Radway, J. (1984). *Reading the romance: Feminism, and the representation of women in popular culture.* Chapel Hill: University of North Carolina Press.
Rafaeli, S. (1986). The electronic bulletin board: A computer-driven mass medium. *Computers and the Social Sciences, 2,* 123–136.
Rayburn, J. D. (1996). Uses and gratifications. In M. B. Salwen & D. W. Stacks (Eds.), *An integrated approach to communication theory and research* (pp. 97–119). Mahwah, NJ: Lawrence Erlbaum Associates, Inc.
Rayburn, J. D., & Palmgreen, P. (1984). Merging uses and gratifications and expectancy-value theory. *Communication Research, 11,* 537–562.
Reagan, J. (1996). The "repertoire" of information sources. *Journal of Broadcasting & Electronic Media, 40,* 112–119.
Rice, R. E., & Williams, F. (1984). Theories old and new: The study of the new media. In R. E. Rice (Ed.), *The new media: Communication, research, and technology* (pp. 55–80). Beverly Hills, CA: Sage.
Riley, P., Keough, C. M., Christiansen, T., Meilich, O., & Pierson, J. (1998). Community or colony: The case of online newspapers and the Web. *Journal of Computer-Mediated Communication, 4.* Retrieved May 1999 from the World Wide Web: http://jcmc.huji.ac.il/vol4/issue1/keough.html#ABSTRACT
Roe, K. (1983). *Mass media and adolescent schooling: Conflict or co-existence?* Stockholm, Sweden: Almqvist & Wiksell.
Rogers, E. (1986). *Communication technology: The new media.* New York: Free Press.
Rosengren, K. E. (1974). Uses and gratifications: A paradigm outlined. In J. G. Blumler & E. Katz (Eds.), *The uses of mass communications: Current perspectives on gratifications research* (pp. 269–286). Beverly Hills, CA: Sage.
Rosengren, K. E., Johnsson-Smaragdi, U., & Sonesson, I. (1994). For better and for worse: effects studies and beyond. In K. E. Rosengren (Ed.), *Media effects and beyond: Culture, socialization and lifestyles* (pp. 302–315). New York: Routledge.
Rosengren, K. E., & Windahl, S. (1989). *Media matter: TV use in childhood and adolescence.* Norwood: NJ: Ablex.
Rosenstein, A. W., & Grant, A. E. (1997). Reconceptualizing the role of habit: A new model of television audience. *Journal of Broadcasting & Electronic Media, 41,* 324–344.
Rubin, A. M. (1981). An examination of television viewing motivations. *Communication Research, 8,* 141–165.

Rubin, A. M. (1983). Television uses and gratifications: The interactions of viewing patterns and motivations. *Journal of Broadcasting, 27,* 37–51.

Rubin, A. M. (1984). Ritualized and instrumental television viewing. *Journal of Communication, 34*(3), 67–77.

Rubin, A. M. (1986). Uses, gratifications, and media effects research. In J. Bryant & D. Zillmann (Eds.), *Perspectives on media effects* (pp. 281–301). Hillsdale, NJ: Lawrence Erlbaum Associates, Inc.

Rubin, A. M. (1994a). Audience activity and media use. *Communication Monographs, 60,* 98–105.

Rubin, A. M. (1994b). Media uses and effects: A uses and gratifications perspective. In J. Bryant & D. Zillmann (Eds.), *Media effects: Advances in theory and research* (pp. 417–436). Hillsdale, NJ: Lawrence Erlbaum Associates, Inc.

Rubin, A. M., & Windahl, S. (1986). The uses and dependency model of mass communication. *Critical Studies in Mass Communication, 3,* 184–199.

Samuels, F. (1984). *Human needs and behavior.* Cambridge, MA: Schnenkman.

Sandbothe, M. (1996). Interactivity—hypertexuality—transversality: A media-philosophical analysis of the Internet. Retrieved May 1999 from the World Wide Web: http://www.uni-jena.de/ms/tele/part2.html

Schaefer, R. J., & Avery, R. K. (1993). Audience conceptualizations of "Late night with David Letterman." *Journal of Broadcasting & Electronic Media, 37,* 253–273.

Schramm, W. (1949). The nature of news. *Journalism Quarterly, 26,* 259–269.

Schramm, W., Lyle, J., & Parker, E. (1961). *Television in the lives of our children.* Stanford, CA: Stanford University Press.

Severin, W. J., & Tankard, J. W. (1997). *Communication theories: Origins, methods, and uses in the mass media* (4th ed.). New York: Longman.

Singer, J. B. (1998). Online journalists: Foundations for research into their changing roles. *Journal of Computer-Mediated Communication, 4.* Retrieved May 1999 from the World Wide Web: http://jcmc.huji.ac.il/vol4/issue1/smith.html#ABSTRACT

Smith, C. B. (1997). Casting the net: Surveying an Internet population. *Journal of Computer-Mediated Communication, 3.* Retrieved May 1999 from the World Wide Web: http://jcmc.huji.ac.il/vol3/issue1/singer.html#ABSTRACT

Stanford, S. W. (1983). Comments on Palmgreen and Rayburn: Gratifications sought and media exposure. *Communication Research, 10,* 247–258.

Stevenson, N. (1997). Critical perspectives within audience research. In T. O'Sullivan & Y. Jewkes (Eds.), *The media studies reader.* New York: St. Martin's.

Stolz, C. (1995). *Silicon snake oil: Second thoughts on the information highway.* New York: Doubleday.

Stone, G., & Stone, D. (1990). Lurking in the literature: Another look at media use habits. *Mass Communications Review, 17,* 25–33.

Sundar, S. S. (1998). Effect of source attribution on perception of online news stories. *Journalism and Mass Communication Quarterly, 75,* 55–68.

Swanson, D. L. (1977). The uses and misuses of uses and gratifications. *Human Communication Research, 3,* 214–221.

Swanson, D. L. (1987). Gratification seeking, media exposure, and audience interpretations. *Journal of Broadcasting & Electronic Media, 31,* 237–254.

Trevino, L. K., & Webster, J. (1992). Flow in computer-mediated communication: Electronic mail and voice mail evaluation and impacts. *Communication Research, 19,* 539–573.

Thomas, P. J. (1995). Introduction: The social and interactional dimensions of human–computer interfaces. In P. J. Thomas (Ed.), *The social and interactional dimensions of human–computer interfaces* (pp. 1–10). Cambridge, England: Cambridge University Press.

Walker, J. R. (1990). Time out: Viewing gratifications and reactions to the 1987 NFL players' strike. *Journal of Broadcasting & Electronic Media, 34,* 335–350.

Walker, J. R., & Bellamy, R. V. (1991). Gratifications of grazing: An exploratory study of remote control use. *Journalism Quarterly, 68,* 422–431.
Waples, D., Berelson, B., & Bradshaw, F. R. (1940). *What reading does to people.* Chicago: University of Chicago Press.
Weaver, D. H. (1993). Communication research in the 1990s. In P. Gaunt (Ed.), *Beyond agendas: New directions in communication research* (pp. 199–220). Westport, CT: Greenwood.
Webster, J., & Wakshlag, J. (1983). A theory of television program choice. *Communication Research, 10,* 430–446.
Weiss, W. (1976). Review of the uses of mass communications. *Public Opinion Quarterly, 40,* 132–133.
Wenner, L. A. (1985). The nature of news gratification. In K. E. Rosengren, L. A. Wenner, & P. Palmgreen (Eds.), *Media gratifications research: Current perspectives* (pp. 171–194). Beverly Hills, CA: Sage.
White, R. A. (1994). Audience interpretation of media: Emerging perspectives. *Communication Research Trends, 14*(3), 3–36.
Williams, F., Phillips, A. F., & Lum, P. (1985). Gratifications associated with new communication technologies. In K. E. Rosengren, L. A. Wenner, & P. Palmgreen (Eds.), *Media gratification research: Current perspectives* (pp. 241–252). Beverly Hills, CA: Sage.
Williams, F., Rice, R. E., & Rogers, E. M. (1988). *Research methods and the new media.* New York: Free Press.
Wimmer, R. D., & Dominick, J. R. (1994). *Mass media research: An introduction.* Belmont, CA: Wadsworth.
Windahl, S. (1981). Uses and gratifications at the crossroads. *Mass Communication Review Yearbook, 2,* 174–185.
Windahl, S., Hojerback, I., & Hedinsson, E. (1986). Adolescents without television: A study in media deprivation. *Journal of Broadcasting & Electronic Media, 30,* 47–63.
Young, K. (1996, August). *Internet addiction: The emergence of a new addictive disorder.* Poster presented at the annual meeting of the American Psychological Association, Toronto, Canada.
Zillman, D., & Bryant, J. (1985). *Selective exposure to communication.* Hillsdale, NJ: Lawrence Erlbaum Associates, Inc.
Zillman, D., & Bryant, J. (1994). Entertainment as media effect. In J. Bryant & D. Zillman (Eds.), *Media effects: Advances in theory and research* (pp. 437–461). Hillsdale, NJ: Lawrence Erlbaum Associates, Inc.

Ethnic Media in the United States: An Essay on Their Role in Integration, Assimilation, and Social Control

K. Viswanath
School of Journalism and Communication
Ohio State University

Pamela Arora
Hillard Fleishman
Toronto, Canada

Hundreds of thousands of immigrants have entered the United States in the last 2 decades and even more are expected to do so in the coming years. This increasing presence of members from diverse ethnic identities is leading to what some have characterized as a permanently unfinished American society. Ethnic groups have grown active and have established institutions to sustain their ethnicity and ease their transition into American society with varying degrees of success. One such institution with a significant role in assimilation and integration is the ethnic mass media. This article is a theoretical exegesis on the role of ethnic media from a functional conflict perspective. Drawing from the literature on immigration, the sociology of the community press, social conflict, and postindustrial theories, we speculate on the functions of ethnic media and how that may manifest in their news content. Finally, propositions are offered for a more systematic study of ethnic media and their roles given their importance to current debates on American identity and multiculturalism raging in the country.

America is a nation of immigrants. Ever-increasing numbers of immigrants have been coming into the country as a result of successive reforms in the nation's immi-

---

Requests for reprints should be sent to K. Viswanath, School of Journalism and Communication, 3026 Derby Hall, 154 North Oval Mall, Ohio State University, Columbus, OH 43210. E-mail: visht@osu.edu

gration laws in 1965, 1985, and 1990. According to Portes and Rumbaut (1990), an average of 600,000 immigrants and refugees a year were legally admitted to the United States in the 1980s, leading to what some have characterized as a permanently unfinished American society.[1] In fact, a recent report from the U.S. Census Bureau (1999) suggested that about 9.3% of the current U.S. population is foreign born.

Earlier theories of immigration argued that America is a melting pot where immigrants will eventually assimilate into the mainstream (Park, 1950, 1970). Subsequent work has cast doubts on this theory and in fact has argued that ethnicity has grown stronger among both newer and older immigrant groups in the United States (Blauner, 1982; Glazer & Moynihan, 1970; Hirschman, 1983). Whatever the argument, the increasing ethnic pluralism of the United States is undeniable.

The growing ethnic diversity and pluralism has led to increasing competition for resources—housing, jobs, assistance, and business. Furthermore, among certain groups and politicians, the diversity has led to an anxiety and alarm over the seeming threat to the "mainstream" of American culture and the English language. Calls have been made to restrict immigration (Lamm & Imhoff, 1985) and actions taken either at the federal or the state level to restrict welfare benefits or assistance to the immigrants and in some case, declare English as an official language.

Ethnic groups have grown active and have established institutions to sustain their ethnicity and ease their transition into American society with varying degrees of success. The ethnic media are a product of these groups' attempts to organize, communicate, and facilitate their transition into American society (Park, 1922/1970; Subervi-Velez, 1986). Given the rising levels of immigration into the United States, increasing tensions and questions about immigration, and the growing importance of media, it is worthwhile to systematically examine and explore the role of the ethnic press in the United States. Drawing from the literature on community press in the United States and the works of scholars on ethnicity and immigration, this article is a theoretical analysis on the nature and potential function of the ethnic press in the United States.[2] What are the functions of the ethnic press? What is the degree of similarity and differences between the mainstream community press and the ethnic press? What role does ethnic community structure play in the coverage by the ethnic news medium? We attempt to elucidate these questions drawing on our current research program on the role of Asian Indian press in the United States.

---

[1]This figure does not include illegal immigration.

[2]This theoretical examination is an extension of recent work on minorities and media by such scholars as Rubin (1980), Greenberg, Michael, Burgoon, and Korzenny (1983), Wilson and Gutierrez (1985), and Miller (1987), among others. Much of this earlier work, although comprehensive in one sense, also is bereft of any work on the press of the new ethnics such as the Asian Indians, the Pakistanis, and the Filipinos.

IMMIGRATION: THE RECENT TREND

The new immigrants to America, as a result of reforms in the immigration law in 1965, are mostly from non-European nations, unlike the earlier immigration waves. Among them, there has been a trend to preserve their ethnic heritage, in contrast to the anxiety of earlier ethnics to assimilate, expressed in the phrase *melting pot* (Glazer & Moynihan, 1970; Hirschman, 1983).[3] In fact, Glazer and Moynihan argued that among the more recent immigrants, there has been a tendency to revive their ethnicity and maintain their cultural identity.[4] Aided with the modern means of communication, the new immigrants are able to maintain their links to the homeland relatively more easily than the earlier waves of immigrants.

Furthermore, the range of variation along language, ethnic, class, and linguistic lines is impressive. For example, immigrants from Asia are generally likely to hold professional jobs or have small businesses (see Kitano & Daniels, 1988; Portes & Rumbaut, 1990). Most settle down in highly industrial areas or cities with high-tech industry, and near major academic institutions. On the other hand, migrant farm workers may or may not have legal status and may be itinerant, facing great odds in assimilation. Given the influx and diversity and the associated tensions, a number of these groups have been increasingly concerned with their rights and have become more active politically, supporting candidates of both political parties, working on campaigns, and even running for office. Immigrant media function as one of the principal vehicles of socialization and communication within immigrant communities.

COMMUNITY PRESS IN THE UNITED STATES

The role of mass media in the community has been a recurrent question in mass communication research. Scholars examining media from a macrosocial perspective have posited that media are a critical subsystem of the total community system and product of the environment from which they emanate. Media reflect, refract, and amplify the concerns of power groupings in the social system, thus performing a central integrative function (Tichenor, Donohue, & Olien, 1980). Their primary function is social control, in the interest of system maintenance, which they perform by drawing attention to what is acceptable and not acceptable within the domi-

---

[3]The term *melting pot* was used to legitimize the idea that America is a land of opportunity: A place where no religion, race, or national origin can impede social mobility (Hirschman, 1983). Assimilation theory has been criticized by scholars for (a) being untestable, as it does not specify when changes will occur (Lyman, 1968); (b) its assumption that change is nonlinear; and (c) its ideological overtones.

[4]Glazer and Moynihan (1970) rejected the idea of assimilation as unreal. They suggested that "historical experiences, cultures, skills, and times of arrival" (p. 14) developed unique economic, political, and cultural patterns for each group. The complete identity of the immigrants with the mainstream American culture has been inhibited by a subtle system of identification.

nant norms and values of the community (Demers, 1996; Gitlin, 1978; Paletz & Entman, 1981; Tichenor et al., 1980; Viswanath & Demers, 1999).[5] These include the functions of environmental surveillance, transmission of cultural heritage, correlation of different segments, mobilization, and entertainment (Lasswell, 1948; Wright, 1960).

Although all media perform the social control function, the way in which the function is performed is influenced by the structure of the community, otherwise termed *community pluralism* (Donohue, Tichenor, & Olien, 1984; Olien, Donohue, & Tichenor, 1968; Olien, Tichenor, & Donohue, 1986; Tichenor et al., 1980).

Community Pluralism: Relevance and Application to an Ethnic Press

Community pluralism or heterogeneity can be defined as the degree of differentiation in the system with potential for organized sources of power.[6] The study of system complexity or the lack of it has a distinguished history in social sciences, occupying the attention of a long line of scholars including Comte, Toennies, Maine, Spencer, and Durkheim, among many others. In media studies, the notion of complexity draws extensively from Durkheim's (1964) ideas on the *Division of Labor in Society*. He identified two types of social integration: mechanical and organic solidarity. Communities with mechanical solidarity are characterized by a "strong collective conscience" (p. 79), present among individuals who are relatively similar to each other. There is a greater degree of commonality in beliefs, norms, interpretations, and values among members of a community. On the other hand, a predominant feature of organic solidarity, present in a highly differentiated society, is that social integration or solidarity is based on contractual relationships (Applebaum, 1970; Giddens, 1971). Differentiation, in Durkheim's view, is correlated with size and density of the social system where greater density could lead to greater interactions (Tiryakian, 1978).

In media studies, the Minnesota Community Studies Team used pluralism as the principal contextual variable in examining news coverage by the community press

---

[5]The arguments of Tichenor, Donohue, and Olien (1980) are often misconstrued to mean that they are in favor of the status quo and that power is not considered. On the contrary, their propositions suggest sensitivity to the power differentials in the system. They argued that the dominant values and norms of a system are functional to the groups interested in the status quo and dysfunctional to those groups that try to change the power relations. In general, mainstream media function as a guard dog of the power structure rather than as a watchdog (Donohue, Tichenor, & Olien, 1995).

[6]In this article, such terms as *pluralism, complexity, heterogeneity,* and *homogeneity* are being used interchangeably with the acknowledgment that they could be conceptually different. Furthermore, pluralism does not necessarily imply a uniform or equal distribution of power among all subgroups. We make the assumption that power is always unequally distributed even though it is somewhat more decentralized in more pluralistic systems.

(Tichenor et al., 1980). They used such indicators as population size, number of jobs in the nonagricultural sector, distance from the metropolitan areas, and number of groups and institutions. To these indicators, Viswanath, Finnegan, Hertog, Pirie, and Murray (1994) added the number of media systems as an additional indicator. Given the increasing ethnic diversity of American communities, others have incorporated differentiation along ethnic lines as yet another indicator of pluralism (Gandy, 1998; Hindman, Littlefield, Preston, & Neumann, 1999; Melwani et al., 1994).

Given the current wave of immigration and the postindustrial nature of the society, pluralism as a variable requires careful and rigorous conceptualization. Size will continue to be a critical indicator. The number of immigrants into the United States from any given part of the world will be small to begin with. As the size of the group increases because of increasing immigration, there is likely to be a shift in reliance from primary to secondary channels of communication. Increasing size is also likely to bring in increasing complexity within the ethnic community, adding to its heterogeneity.

Other indicators will have to be reevaluated closely depending on the ethnic group and their mode of entry into the country. Class, ethnicity or ethnic subdivisions, occupation, and income are predictable indicators.

There are, however, additional considerations that must be taken into account. For example, immigrants from India may all be from one geographical part of the world but may have different mother tongues. Similarly, people from mainland China may be able to speak one language but in actuality may have different mother tongues depending on the region that they come from in China.

Some indicators could be unique to certain groups. Caste may be a significant factor in India, given that it correlates highly with social class and influences occupational mobility in India.

Pluralism: Primacy of Indicators

The previous section described the various indicators that could potentially be used to conceptualize and measure pluralism. The question is whether all indicators are equal or whether some matter more than others. For example, one reason that size matters is because of increasing interaction density and how it affects interaction among primary and secondary groups (Durkheim, 1984). However, this is based on the conceptualization of a community in spatial terms where members of the ethnic group are congregated in close proximity. In general, however, an ethnic community could be a community without propinquity (Webber, 1963). Such a condition demands a reevaluation of how conventional assumptions about the usual indicators are valid. That is, are the assumptions one makes about the reliability and validity of some indicators in certain conditions valid when applied to different conditions?

Let us discuss this further using the Asian Indian ethnic community as an exemplar. The Indian ethnic community in the United States in terms of size is about 1 million strong. It is, however, geographically widely dispersed with the largest concentrations of tens of thousands in major urban centers. Most of them speak English and enjoy high formal education, most are in professional occupations, and they have one of the highest average household incomes of any ethnic group in the United States (Portes & Rumbaut, 1990). Furthermore, it is conceivable that the traditional power structures such as gender (being male), class, and caste enjoy dominance and even hegemony defining the culture of the community and what it means to be an Asian Indian. These assumptions lead one to characterize the Indian ethnic community as relatively homogeneous.

On the other hand, if one were to take the linguistic dimension, the Asian Indian ethnic community could not be more diverse. In India, there are more than 14 official languages and almost 1,000 dialects. Many of these languages are represented within the Asian Indian immigrant community in varying numbers. Given the proximity of culture or subculture to language, one might imagine the diversity within the community. Also, there is considerable subcultural as well as religious variation within the Asian Indian ethnic group, where tensions among the groups are not uncommon. A good indicator of the diversity of the community is the number of Indian cultural organizations formed along linguistic lines and the number of different religious centers.

Therefore in terms of pluralism, the Asian Indian ethnic community press in the United States should share commonalities with both a small-town community press as well as the press from a heterogeneous system.[7] The question is, what is the impact of such an ambiguous pluralistic condition on the way the medium covers the issues?

Community Press and Social Conflict

As suggested earlier, the central integrative role of the media means that they play an active role in covering or not covering social conflict. Much social conflict is generally over distribution of scarce resources and differential distribution in authority or power (Coleman, 1957; Dahrendorf, 1959; Wallace & Wolf, 1986) over which there are likely to be "excess claimants" (Coser, 1967). Coser (1956, 1967) suggested that conflicts establish group identities and strengthen group consciousness. External conflicts can result in the *Simmel effect*, an increase in integration and cohesion of group members (Simmel, 1955). Internal conflicts define group

---

[7]As mentioned earlier, the concept of community is being used in a much broader sense here. One definition of community may deal with geographic and spatial limitations. However, another definition could be a group of people that shares some commonality of interest, ethnicity, or occupation. It is this latter definition that is being adopted here.

identity, norms of behavior, group cohesion, and stability. Conflicts are intense, according to Coser (1956, 1967), when they involve fundamental values and beliefs of a system. However between groups, conflicts can lead to withering away of relationships and groups that become increasingly polarized (Coleman, 1957, p. 11).

News media are disseminators of information that there is potential for conflict or even the existence of disagreement or dispute (Coleman, 1957). Media coverage of conflict, however, is a function of the complexity of the system with system maintenance as the ultimate goal. In large, complex communities, media perform the feedback function, alerting the system to problems existing in the subsystems, a function akin to that of a community sentinel. Conflict coverage in heterogeneous systems is routine as there are competing groups with organized power (Tichenor et al., 1980).

In more homogenous systems, on the other hand, conflict coverage is less emphasized. In homogeneous communities, power is relatively more centralized and decision making is seldom public and usually is run on the basis of consensus. The reason noted by some scholars is that no one really wants to stir up trouble (Vidich & Bensman, 1958). Editors are likely to be a part of the community elite and the reporting in the newspaper is more likely to be distributive rather than feedback in orientation. Ties between the political elite and the media elite are likely to be closer in smaller, less complex, or more homogeneous communities (Tichenor et al., 1980). Edelstein and Schulz (1963) reported that a majority of the community leaders proposed that controversies should be publicized only when it is unavoidable. A community newspaper is seen by the audience as a resource and as an agent of progress and not as a partisan actor (Janowitz, 1952).

This does not mean that news media do not cover conflict in small, homogeneous systems. News media do enter conflict situations based on certain conditions. Tichenor et al. (1980) identified three types of newspaper entry into a conflict situation. The first type is "presentation of a local interest based upon surveillance of the external environment" (p. 115). Newspapers take their watchdog function seriously and may act as lookouts for the community. Another type of newspaper entry is follow-up reporting in nonlocal media. The third type of entry is the reporting of an internal issue by the newspaper.

Therefore a newspaper is rarely likely to initiate conflict but will accelerate and publicize it to a wider audience. Once the controversy develops, however, newspapers may seize the initiative. Media then define, albeit within power and structural limitations, the issues, strategies, actions, and positions of groups.

Ethnic Press and Conflict Coverage

The question then is to what extent these findings are applicable to the ethnic newspapers. Based on community press literature reviewed in the previous section, one might expect conflict news coverage to be directly related to the pluralism of the community about which and to which the media are reporting. This, in turn, is also related to the issue of whether the reporting of conflict poses a threat to the stability of the community.

If the ethnic community is relatively small and homogenous, it is likely that the community elite are likely to be reluctant to wash their dirty laundry in the press. They may want to maintain their image as hard-working ethnics who are trying to succeed in the "new world" and may see any coverage of internal conflict as harmful to the long-term interests and stability of the community. On the other hand, if the ethnic community is pluralistic, its role may be analogous to that of news medium in a more heterogeneous system. For example, the Asian Indian ethnic press in the United States will be reporting on a polyglot society such as India with diverse castes, classes, and linguistic, religious, and subcultural groups. The press is in a unique position where it has to perform both informational and feedback functions. In addition, it must report on a pluralistic system such as India to a homogeneous Asian Indian ethnic community in the United States.

This puts the medium in an ambiguous, if not countervailing pluralistic condition. Given this dual role of social control and strengthening of ethnic identity, and the reporting on and in a pluralistic system, one might expect the ethnic newspaper to give high attention to conflict. At the same time, it might pay attention to conflicts that do not threaten the fundamental stability of the system in which it operates. Our preliminary analyses of an Indian ethnic newspaper support this proposition. Our data indicate that the Indian ethnic press appears to have adopted itself well to its ambiguous roles covering conflicts that could be of interest to the readers, but at the same time paying relatively less attention to conflict that may threaten the local community's stability (Viswanath & Arora, 1997).

Based on the foregoing review, one might offer the following propositions:

H1: As long as the community remains small, ethnic community press is less likely to cover controversial issues.

H2: Even when conflict is covered, relatively more attention is likely to be paid to issues that do not threaten the community's stability (i.e., external conflicts) rather than to issues that threaten the system.

H3: As a corollary, as the size of the community increases, the coverage of conflict is also likely to increase in the ethnic community press.

H4: Although size is an important criterion, at some point size is likely to matter relatively less than other indicators of pluralism such as language, social class, and subculture.

Social Control and the Ethnic Community Press: A Functional Analysis

In the literature on media sociology, there appears to be a broad consensus that media are indeed agents of social control, whose operations and functions are determined by the power groupings in the society (Gitlin, 1978; Glasgow Media Group, 1976; Tichenor et al., 1980; Tuchman, 1978; Viswanath & Demers, 1999).

Social control is concerned with the internalization of norms and values by the individual, where the individual's values and behavior conform to group norms and that of the social structure (Coser, 1982; Ross, 1969). A vital resource in the exercise of social control by those in power is the control over information or knowledge. Some have attributed such power to the media, as they are one of the principal forums in which potential social problems are identified, defined, and articulated. To the extent that power is understood as an ability to influence others (Mott, 1970; Weber, 1958), news media could be said to possess *conditioning power, power to win submission without coercion* (Galbraith, 1983).

In general, social control function in the media is performed through two types of information control processes (Tichenor et al., 1980): feedback and distributive control processes. Reports of feedback control are published with the aim of drawing attention to a potential problem in the system. They may result in audience reaction in the form of protest, mobilization, or flak. Newspapers may act as forums for community groups and institutions in setting the public agenda for discussion but may also play an active role in defining the issues for the public. The consequence of a feedback control function could be an effort by some community members or groups to resolve the problem and restore system stability. On the other hand, distributive function is served when media casually report routine events.

However, as discussed earlier, the reportage is influenced by the nature of the social structure in which the newspapers operate. Newspapers are more likely to serve a feedback function in heterogeneous communities and a distributive function in relatively homogeneous societies. These functions may manifest accordingly in the ethnic community press. When the community is small and relatively homogeneous, one might expect the primary mechanism of control by ethnic press to be that of distributive control. As the community size and diversity increase, more of the content may be classified as feedback control process. Within this social control framework, there are specific functions that an ethnic press might serve.

Cultural transmission. A transparent way a community press might serve the distributive function is by publishing information on community events, programs, schedules, calendars, and so on, information that does not primarily question the established community institutions and powerful groups within the community. For example, reports about festivals, community celebrations, and local government and associational meetings fall under this category. These reports do not threaten the system in any way and strengthen the feeling that the system is functioning well. This is particularly true in homogeneous community newspapers, which are considered as extensions of personal communication channels.

In the Asian Indian ethnic community, for example, the news media may carry information on cultural and religious celebrations including a plethora of India religious festivals, cultural programs, and visits by cultural artists from India. Such coverage is likely to serve several manifest and latent functions:

- It has the unintended consequence of "reviving the ethnicity," strengthening the ethnic identity of the community. Whether it will inhibit assimilation is an empirical question.
- Continued and celebratory coverage maintains and strengthens the ethnic identity among the second generation, children. A sense of cultural identity, of belonging to a different heritage, is most likely to be initiated and developed within the family and at home. Community institutions and the media are likely to reinforce that sense of identity.

Ethnic newspaper as a community booster. A community newspaper is also a local booster. Local newspaper coverage of most issues strives to present the community in a positive light, projecting an image of wholesomeness, success, and achievement. The community looks to the press to portray a positive image of itself to the external public as well as to the members within the community (Janowitz, 1952; Kaniss, 1991).[8]

For example, local newspapers usually cover local developments such as urban renewal programs in a positive light, seldom focusing on the downside of the issues. Close ties between local reporters and editors and the community elite in relatively homogeneous systems means a general reluctance by the newspapers to stir up trouble or draw attention to issues that may affect the community image.

An immigrant newspaper may focus on such themes as the following:

- human interest features and profiles,
- success stories of immigrants, and
- volunteer work being done by the immigrants either in the United States or in their native land demonstrating their contribution to society.

Furthermore, as is the case with neighborhood press, much reporting is taking place within the commercial, consumerist context. The ethnic press is likely to rely on merchants and businesses such as groceries, banks, travel agencies, and insur-

---

[8]This does not mean that newspapers do not cover negative events. They, in fact, do. Most often, however, particularly in homogeneous communities, there is a greater degree of consensus and closer structural ties between the news media and the local elite, which generally engenders coverage that "helps" the community. In heterogeneous communities, in contrast, newspaper coverage of community "problems" is functional in that it draws attention to the problems that need resolution in the interest of stability. Most local newspapers, as Kaniss (1991) observed, are sensitive to the fact that negative coverage may affect the economic investment environment of a community, particularly the central city.

ance agencies targeting the ethnic group and may not be inclined to offer a radical voice.

At the same time, relatively less attention is likely to be paid to stories that portray the ethnic community and its members in a negative light. Such categories may include stories on crimes by members of the community or any behavior that could be considered deviant from the dominant norms and values of the host culture and country (Viswanath & Arora, 1997).

Community newspaper as a sentinel. Functional theorists such as Lasswell (1948) and Wright (1960), among others, argued that media often work as community sentinels, acting as both radars and early warning systems against external threats. It is a function that seems to be well suited for an ethnic community press. An ethnic group is potentially vulnerable to discrimination from other groups particularly if they are "different" from the mainstream and are perceived as a threat to the mainstream culture. Given the recent negative reactions in the United States toward immigration by certain groups, it is most likely that the role of a watchdog may become an important function for the immigrant press. To perform its role as a community sentinel against external threat, the newspaper may present stories affecting the legal rights of the ethnic community: civil rights violations, changes in immigration laws, and crime against immigrants.

The amount of attention a community and its press pays such a subject is, however, dependent on at least three factors: the social status of the group, the mode of entry of the group, and the subsequent experiences of members of the group. The first two, mode of entry and social status, influence the third, the group's experience in America subsequent to their emigration.

Blauner (1982) drew two ideal types of entry into the United States: colonization and immigration. *Colonization* refers to the process of involuntary entry into the United States, as has been the case with Blacks and Chicanos and to an extent, Puerto Ricans. On the other hand, White European entry has been more voluntary, characterized by greater freedom of movement and assimilation. As most ideal types go, experiences of immigrants from China, Japan, and Philippines, among others, fall somewhere between colonialism and voluntary immigration. In case of immigrants from South Asia, it is safe to characterize it as voluntary with a greater degree of freedom of movement.

Second, if the community, in general, enjoys a relatively higher status, as is the case with certain Asian ethnic groups, it is most likely that the press will be assertive in terms of protecting the rights of the immigrants. The question is the extent to which the ethnic community and the ethnic press identify and work with other groups in protecting their legal rights.

This is also a part of the mobilizing function of the press. This is most likely witnessed in times of disasters in the immigrants' native countries. It is not unusual to see the media volunteering to collect donations to be sent to the homeland to aid the needy or those affected. Much depends on how the elite and press define the issues.

For example, our preliminary analyses of the Asian Indian ethnic press revealed considerable coverage of impending changes in immigration laws that were likely to directly impinge on the Asian Indians. On the other hand, little attention was paid to civil rights in general, presumably because the community and the press chose not to define the issue as important (Viswanath & Arora, 1997). Similarly, the coverage on welfare reform as it affected immigrants might have received differential coverage in various ethnic presses depending on the proportion of ethnic community members affected by the issue.

Assimilatory function. One unique role of an ethnic newspaper that differentiates it from a community newspaper is its role in promoting assimilation. Whatever the mode of entry, the greatest struggle of an immigrant is survival in a new country and a new culture that is alien. In an effort to fit in, immigrant groups adopt outward symbols of assimilation: language (especially the idiom), dress, food, and behavior. Their success in the country partly depends on their degree of assimilation and learning the ropes of the system. Second, the success of the group as whole and the way it is received depends on the extent to which it is perceived by the host culture and country as having been assimilated and as a part of the mainstream.

It is here that the ethnic press may play a critical role. Coverage could focus on such stories as the community's involvement in local politics, promotion of positive feelings between the ethnic groups' homelands and their adopted country, and the demonstration of patriotism by the ethnic group members.[9]

Informational function. A critical function of media is to offer information and mobilize the community. In fact, one might argue that the ethnic community press begins with the purpose of informing the community about events occurring not only within the community, but also in their native homeland. Given the limited coverage of international news in mainstream American news media, the immigrants are more likely to rely on ethnic media to fill that gap.

---

[9]The involvement of the ethnic groups in politics is a function of at least three factors: their mode of entry, the size of the community, and the socioeconomic status (SES) of the group. Taking off on Blauner's (1982) description, if the group's entry is involuntary, then the forces that combined to forcibly bring the group into the country are also likely to keep them from acquiring power. On the other hand, a voluntary entry may coincide with fewer overt barriers. However, this depends on the size and the status of the community. A certain minimum size is necessary for the numbers to matter for political actors and political parties to pay attention to the ethnic group. Similarly, the ethnic group's SES, which may influence its ability to mobilize funds, may be an important motivator in attracting attention from the mainstream political parties and actors.

INFORMATION SOCIETY AND ETHNIC COMMUNICATIONS

A predominant characteristic of the postindustrial society is the importance of knowledge and information in serving as community resources (Bell, 1976; Kumar, 1995). A benign variation of the information society argument suggests that the usual barriers of cost, time, geography, and social status are likely to become less important as new communication technologies make access and usage easier (Pool, 1983; for a detailed and interesting discussion on the information society, see Kumar, 1995; Hindman, 1999). On the other hand, others argued that the ability to generate and transmit information quickly and cheaply differentiates and reinforces the existing power differentials among social groups given the wide disparities in access to new information technologies among different social strata (Viswanath, 1997; Viswanath, Lavrakas, & Wei, 1998).

For the ethnic audience in particular, as a result of the new communication technologies such as the Internet and the World Wide Web, geographical and temporal barriers indeed may become less important, allowing different groups to obtain information from and about distant areas. Will that, however, mean that other barriers such as social class, ideology, and power cease to matter? Does the content and focus of the information available in cyberspace differ from the traditional media? Our theoretical analysis briefly addresses both questions.

Even a casual, exploratory analysis of the Web reveals an extensive list of newspapers and magazines available, targeting various ethnic groups and special interests.[10] With the emergence of the Web and other new communication technologies, immigrants now have an array of choices to gather information on their homelands. Internet news services located in the United States, in home countries, or even a third country, are increasingly offering news about developments in the home countries and the diaspora. Interestingly enough, such offerings include both established press from the homelands as well as alternative press, products of efforts by a small group of people. Furthermore, such "Webzines" are from countries in both the developing and the developed world. A question for future research is whether that part of the informational function that covers the immigrants' native countries is likely to change with competition from the newspapers from those countries.

The profile of the ethnic community is likely to play a role in the extent to which the Web emerges as an alternative communication medium. This is critical, as a

---

[10]A complete and a more extensive analysis of the role of the Internet on ethnic communications, in particular, and communication, in general, is beyond the scope of this article. Furthermore, it is a brave and a foolish soul indeed who makes predictions about the information environment on the World Wide Web. The environment is changing so fast that it is hazardous to one's credibility to make any predictions. What can best be done, in the words of Bell (1976), is to identify the broad propensities that allow one to speculate on the likely trajectories the media on the Web may take.

major characteristic of the information society is the emergence and importance of a professional class, the knowledge worker, which decidedly is likely to be different in training, skills, and social status from workers engaged in other sectors. For example, some immigrant group organizations in the Asian Indian community are already using e-mail and Web sites to communicate with their members. Given the large proportion of workers from the Asian Indian community employed in the high-tech sector, it is functional and efficient for the Asian Indian ethnic organizations to use the Web. The acceptance of the Web and the use of the Internet for communications is a reciprocal process that ultimately influences press coverage.

The content on the Web at the moment reflects the hard-copy versions of the news media. This could, however, potentially change and emerge into more progressive versions in two ways. First, more progressive and controversial themes or subjects that might not otherwise garner attention could be covered. For example, progressive topics on feminism and women's issues have established a presence in the case of Indian media as exemplified in sites such as Manushi (www.freespeech.org/manushi). Second, in the future, magazines catering exclusively to the second generation of immigrants, focusing principally on their concerns, may emerge. They could potentially focus more on civil rights, political issues, and cultural identity rather than ethnic identity.

In summary, then these remain empirical questions:

1. Will the Web indeed allow for the breach of geographical and temporal barriers?
2. Will the nature of the coverage of online media, which also have hard-copy versions, be less likely to be different from each other?
3. Will media produced exclusively online be different from conventional media with or without Web presence?
4. Is there potential for alternative press to reach a much wider audience and a play a more activist role, including providing links to other activist groups?

If the Web offers news content from native country newspapers, then one might question the nature of the impact it is likely to have on the local ethnic press. Given the competition, is it likely to shift away from its informational function of covering the homeland to pay more attention to local community affairs? Will the local ethnic press pay more attention to alternative viewpoints? These are some of the issues that warrant attention in future research of the ethnic press.

CONCLUSIONS

Two major trends occurring in American society served as a background for this article. One has to do with the increasing flow of immigrants into the United States. According to the latest estimates by the U.S. Census Bureau, between 1990 and

1998, the growth in the foreign-born population in the United States was four times that of the native population. The number of foreign-born residents is now around 25 million, constituting about 9.3% of the U.S. population (U.S. Government, 1999).

This influx is already having a profound influence on American society, culture, and politics at federal, state, and local levels. This is evident from the recent debates on such politically charged issues as welfare benefits for immigrants, quotas on the "model minority" Asians, and the boom in diversity in cultural and culinary fares that are available in U.S. cities.

As mentioned in the introduction, historically immigrants have built several institutions to facilitate their survival and to assist them in assimilating into the mainstream. As Glazer and Moynihan (1970) pointed out, increasingly, the characteristic of the new immigrants is to maintain their cultural identity even while assimilating into the American mainstream. This selective assimilation raises interesting theoretical and practical questions on the role played by the ethnic media. Historically, ethnic media have played a great role in promoting assimilation and aiding the immigrants (Park, 1922/1970). We have recast the question in more theoretical terms to ask how the ethnic media serve the triple functions of information, assimilation, and ethnic identity reinforcement. Specifically, our assumptions are that ethnic media are facing two seemingly contradictory expectations that might affect performance. One is the fact that it is reporting in a heterogeneous or pluralistic system, the United States. At the same time, most immigrant presses serve a relatively small, less diverse audience. How do they perform or behave in the face of such countervailing trends? This is the question we pose in this article.

A second trend that served as a background to our study is the changing information environment. Ethnic community groups are now served not only by print and electronic media, but also by new communication technologies such as the Web. A wide array of information sources is available from cyberspace. It is too early to assess the impact of the cyberspace media on conventional media, we raise certain preliminary questions about the Web and how it will influence ethnic groups' communication behaviors and the ethnic media themselves.

The ethnic news medium is one of the most important and vital institutions, along with religious and cultural organizations, that sustain the ethnicity of immigrants. They are even more important when it comes to ever-increasing groups of immigrants who are seeking information on issues that interest and affect them. It plays a very complex role, sharing many characteristics and features of coverage with the community press in the United States, rather than newspapers in large, heterogeneous communities.

Two developments in the United States make it necessary that we continue to observe and see if the role may change over time. First, as the size of the immigrant populations increase, heterogeneity within the immigrant community is also likely to increase. As a result, it is possible that coverage in the ethnic press may change from that similar to a community press in a homogeneous system to coverage that is closer to the press in a more pluralistic system. Second, it is also possible that the press may become even more like a community press, leaving the informational function behind because of the changing information and communication environment, including new technologies such as the Web. That is, with the emergence of ethnic media online, the ethnic press may prefer to serve exclusively cultural transmission and assimilatory functions. Yet again, the ethnic press is facing an uncertain situation with countervailing forces.

In summary, based on our theoretical analyses, the following propositions may be offered about the role of an ethnic community newspaper in the United States:

1. An ethnic news medium is likely to perform a social control function, one manifestation of which is to report relatively more stories on conflict that do not threaten the stability of the ethnic community here.

2. An ethnic news medium is likely to perform a cultural transmission function by providing stories of a distributive nature; that is, information about meetings, festivals, celebrations, and so on. We are not, however, suggesting that the cultural transmission function is exclusive of the social control function.

3. In line with assimilatory function, the ethnic newspaper may provide more information on involvement of ethnic community members in American politics and more coverage of the relationship between ethnic groups' native homelands and the their adopted country.

4. An ethnic news medium is likely to act as a community sentinel, identifying threats from the external environment.

5. The ethnic news medium will act as a community booster, providing information on community members' success in American society and their contribution to it in an effort to show the community in a positive light.

ACKNOWLEDGMENTS

We gratefully acknowledge the support of grants from the Miller Research Fund, School of Journalism and Communication, the Ohio State University Research Foundation, and the Ohio State University College of Social and Behavioral Sciences. We also thank Dave Demers and the reviewers for their insightful comments.

REFERENCES

Applebaum, R. C. (1970). *Theories of social change.* Chicago: Markham.
Bell, D. (1976). *The coming of post-industrial society.* New York: Basic Books.
Blauner, R. (1982). Colonized and immigrant minorities. In A. Giddens & D. Held (Eds.), *Classes, power and conflict* (pp. 501–519). Berkeley: University of California Press.
Coleman, J. S. (1957). *Community conflict.* New York: Macmillan.

Coser, L. (1956). *The functions of social conflict.* New York: Free Press
Coser, L. (1967). *Continuities in the study of social conflict.* New York: Free Press.
Coser, L. A. (1982). The notion of control in sociological theory. In J. Gibbs (Ed.), *Social control: Views from social sciences* (pp. 13–22). Beverly Hills, CA: Sage.
Dahrendorf, R. (1959). *Class and conflict in the industrial society.* Palo Alto, CA: Stanford University Press.
Demers, D. P. (1996). *The menace of corporate newspaper: Fact or fiction?* Ames: Iowa State University Press.
Donohue, G. A., Tichenor, P. J., & Olien, C. N. (1984). Media evaluations and established power. In A. Arno & W. Dissanayake (Eds.), *The news media in national and international conflict* (p. 214). Boulder, CO: Westview.
Donohue, G. A., Tichenor, P. J., & Olien, C. N. (1995). A guard dog perspective on the role of media. *Journal of Communication, 45*(2), 115–132.
Durkheim, E. (1964). *The division of labor in society.* New York: Free Press.
Edelstein, A., & Schulz, J. B. (1963). The weekly newspaper's leadership role as seen been by community leaders. *Journalism Quarterly, 40,* 565–574.
Galbraith, J. K. (1983). *The anatomy of power.* Boston: Houghton Mifflin.
Gandy, O., Jr. (1998). *Communication and race: A structural perspective.* London: Arnold.
Giddens, A. (1971). *Capitalism and modern social theory.* Cambridge, England: Cambridge University Press.
Gitlin, T. (1978). *The whole world is watching: The mass media in the making and the unmaking of the new left.* Berkeley: University of California Press.
Glasgow Media Group. (1976). *Bad news.* London: Routledge & Kegan Paul.
Glazer, N., & Moynihan, D. P. (1970). *Beyond the melting pot* (2nd ed.). Cambridge, MA: MIT Press.
Greenberg, B. S., Michael, B., Burgoon, J. K., & Korzenny, F. (1983). *Mexican Americans and the mass media.* Norwood, NJ: Ablex.
Hindman, D. B. (1999). Community pluralism, mass society, and the information society: Constraints on local media. In D. Demers & K. Viswanath (Eds.), *Mass media, social control and social change: A macrosocial perspective* (pp. 99–116). Ames: Iowa State University Press.
Hindman, D. B., Littlefield, R., Preston, A., & Neumann, D. (1999). Structural pluralism, ethnic pluralism, and community newspapers. *Journalism & Mass Communication Quarterly, 76,* 250–263.
Hirschman, C. (1983). America's melting pot reconsidered. *Annual Review of Sociology, 9,* 397–423.
Janowitz, M. (1952). *The community press in an urban setting.* Chicago: University of Chicago Press.
Kaniss, P. (1991). *Making local news.* Chicago: University of Chicago Press.
Kitano, H. L., & Daniels, R. (1988). *Asian Americans: Emerging minorities.* Englewood Cliffs, NJ: Prentice-Hall.
Kumar, K. (1995). *From post-industrial to post-modern society: New theories in contemporary world.* Oxford, England: Blackwell.
Lamm, R. D., & Imhoff, G. (1985). *The immigration time bomb: The fragmenting of America.* New York: Truman Talley.
Lasswell, H. (1948). The structure and function of communication in society. In L. Bryson (Ed.), *The communication of ideas* (pp. 37–51). New York: Harper.
Lyman, S. (1968). The race relation cycle of Robert E. Park. *Pacific Sociological Review, 11,* 16–22.
Melwani, G., Viswanath, K., Becker, L. B., & Kosicki, G. M. (1994). *Community complexity and knowledge gaps: A longitudinal study of one community.* Paper presented to the annual conference of the Midwest Association for Public Opinion Research, Chicago.
Miller, S. M. (1987). *History of the ethnic press in the United States.* Westport, CT: Greenwood.
Mott, P. E. (1970). Power, authority and influence. In M. Aiken & P. E. Mott (Eds.), *The structure of community power* (pp. 3–16). New York: Random.
Olien, C. N., Donohue, G. A., & Tichenor, P. J. (1968). The community editor's power and reporting of conflict. *Journalism Quarterly, 45,* 243–252.

Olien, C. N., Tichenor, P. J., & Donohue, G. A. (1986, November). *Structure, editor characteristics and reporting of conflict: 1965–1985*. Paper presented at the annual conference of the Midwest Association for Public Opinion Research, Chicago.

Paletz, D. L., & Entman, R. M. (1981). *Media power politics*. New York: Free Press.

Park, R. E. (1950). *Race and culture*. Glencoe, IL: Free Press.

Park, R. E. (1970). *The immigrant press and its control*. St. Clair Shores, MI: Scholarly. (Original work published 1922)

Pool, I. (1983). *Technologies of freedom*. Cambridge, MA: Harvard University Press.

Portes, A., & Rumbaut, R. G. (1990). *Immigrant America: A portrait*. Berkeley: University of California Press.

Ross, E. A. (1969). *Social control: A survey of the foundations of order*. Cleveland, OH: The Press of Case Western Reserve University.

Rubin, B. (1980). *Small voices and great trumpets: Minorities and the media*. New York: Praeger.

Simmel, G. (1955). *Conflict and the web of group affiliations*. New York: Macmillan.

Subervi-Velez, F. A. (1986). Mass media and ethnic assimilation: A review and research proposal with special focus on Hispanics. *Communication Research, 13,* 71–79.

Tichenor, P. J., Donohue, G. A., & Olien, C. N. (1980). *Community conflict and the press*. Beverly Hills, CA: Sage.

Tiryakian, E. A. (1978). Emile Durkheim. In T. Bottomore & R. Nisbet (Eds.), *A history of sociological analysis* (pp. 187–236). New York: Basic Books.

Tuchman, G. (1978). *Making news: A study in the construction of reality*. New York: Free Press.

U.S. Government. (1999). *Nearly 1 in 10 U.S. residents are foreign-born*. Washington, DC: U.S. Department of Commerce, Bureau of Census. Retrieved September 17, 1999 from the World Wide Web: http://www.census.gov/population/estimates/nation/nativity/fbtab001.txt

Vidich, A. J., & Bensman, J. (1958). *Small town in mass society*. Princeton, NJ: Princeton University Press.

Viswanath, K. (1997, July). *Communication inequities in the post-industrial society: Enduring questions for communication research*. Paper presented at the annual meeting of the Association for Education in Journalism and Mass Communication, Chicago.

Viswanath, K., & Arora, P. (1997, July). *Indian ethnic media in the United States: Integration, assimilation and social control*. Paper presented at the annual conference of the Association for Education in Journalism and Mass Communication, Chicago.

Viswanath, K., & Demers, D. (1999). Mass media from a macrosocial perspective. In D. Demers & K. Viswanath (Eds.), *Mass media, social control and social change: A macrosocial perspective*. Ames: Iowa State University Press.

Viswanath, K., Finnegan, J. R., Hertog, J., Pirie, P., & Murray, D. (1994). Community type and the diffusion of campaign information. *Gazette, 54,* 39–59.

Viswanath, K., Lavrakas, P. J., & Wei, C. (1998, May). *"New wine in an old bottle?" New media, opinion holding and perceptions of media coverage*. Paper presented at the annual conference of the American Association for Public Opinion Research, St Louis, MO.

Wallace, R. A., & Wolf, A. (1986). *Contemporary sociological theory: Continuing the classical tradition* (2nd ed.). Englewood Cliffs, NJ: Prentice-Hall.

Webber, M. (1963). Order in diversity: Community without propinquity. In L. Wingo, Jr. (Ed.), *Cities and space: The future use of urban land* (pp. 23–54). Baltimore: John Hopkins University Press.

Weber, M. (1958). *From Max Weber: Essays in sociology* (H. H. Gerth & C. Wright Mills, Eds.). New York: Oxford University Press.

Wilson, C. C., II, & Gutierrez, F. (1985). *Minorities and the media*. Newbury Park, CA: Sage.

Wright, C. R. (1960). Functional analysis and mass communication. *Public Opinion Quarterly, 24,* 606–620.

The Third-Person Effect: A Meta-Analysis of the Perceptual Hypothesis

Bryant Paul
Department of Communication
University of California at Santa Barbara

Michael B. Salwen and Michel Dupagne
School of Communication
University of Miami

In this study, we report the results of a meta-analysis concerning the third-person effect's perceptual hypothesis. The hypothesis predicts that people judge the media to exert greater persuasive influence on other people than on themselves. Thirty-two published and unpublished studies with 121 separate effect sizes were examined. The overall effect size between estimated media effects on self and on others was r = .50. *Among the 8 moderators investigated (source, method, sampling, respondent, country, desirability, medium, and message), 3 (sampling, respondent, and message) yielded significant effect size variations. Third-person perception in nonrandom and college student samples was significantly larger than in random and noncollege student samples. From a theoretical perspective, these findings may have been due to student participants perceiving themselves to be smarter than other people. A more disturbing explanation would attribute these findings to researchers relying on student samples.*

Research on the social effects of mass communication has advanced markedly by examining individuals' perceptions of media messages and public opinion (Davison, 1983; Fields & Schuman, 1976; Glynn, Ostman, & McDonald, 1995; Mutz & Soss, 1997; Noelle-Neumann, 1974; O'Gorman & Garry, 1976; Sears & Freedman, 1967; Tyler & Cook, 1984; Vidmar & Rokeach, 1974). Among these

---

Requests for reprints should be sent to Bryant Paul, Department of Communication, University of California at Santa Barbara, Santa Barbara, CA 93106–4020. E-mail: long_time@msn.com

approaches, Davison's (1983) third-person effect has generated considerable research (for reviews, see Lasorsa, 1992; Perloff, 1993, 1996). The third-person effect's perceptual hypothesis, also known as third-person perception (Davison, 1996; Perloff, 1993; Salwen, 1998), predicts that people will perceive a persuasive media message to have greater effects on others than on themselves.[1] Although the perceptual hypothesis has yielded robust empirical findings, research has yet to adequately explain how people perceive themselves as smarter and less resistant to media messages than others. Research has also failed to identify the contingent factors that might enhance or diminish the perception. The failure of predictive models to provide a clear explanation led one scholar to declare the third-person effect "a phenomenon without a clear process explanation" (Mason, 1995, p. 612).

In addition, despite the robustness of the effect, many individuals fail to exhibit the perception. In reviewing the literature, Lasorsa (1992) reported that about 50% of the members of a particular sample are susceptible to the third-person effect. This underscores the need to understand why the other 50% do not exhibit third-person perception, and in some instances display a reverse first-person effect to estimate greater effects on themselves (Gunther & Mundy, 1993; Innes & Zeitz, 1988). Perloff (1993) identified a number of conditions that mediate the third-person effect, such as message topic and demographics, adding that the effect may be "a function of the situation, and is more likely to show up in certain situations than in others" (p. 172). However, as research studies accumulate, the number of contingent conditions becomes imposing and daunting. This underscores the need to summarize the findings in a systematic manner.

In this study, we perform a meta-analysis to ferret out methodological and content variables that moderate the third-person effect.[2] Eight moderators are exam-

---

[1]The third-person effect also posits a behavioral hypothesis that predicts that perceiving others as more influenced than oneself will lead to increased support for restrictions on messages (Davison, 1983). The behavioral hypothesis has received mixed or qualified support (Gunther, 1995; Lee & Yang, 1996; McLeod, Eveland, & Nathanson, 1997; Rojas, 1994; Rojas, Shah, & Faber, 1996; Rucinski & Salmon, 1990; Salwen, 1998; Salwen, Dupagne, & Paul, 1998). Unfortunately, most behavioral results cannot be aggregated using meta-analytic procedures because these studies use multiple regression with different control variables (e.g., media use, self-knowledge, demographics). Cumulation of regression weights for the purpose of a meta-analysis is only appropriate when the predictors are the same across studies (Hunter, Schmidt, & Jackson, 1982). Of the 62 third-person effect studies we located, 13 tested the behavioral hypothesis. Of those 13, only 5 reported a correlation coefficient between third-person perception and support for restrictions. Eight studies used multiple regression and quantified the relationship between third-person perception and restrictions using beta weights without reporting zero-order correlations between the predictor and the criterion variables.

[2]With most social-structural variables, such as gender, age, and education, a moderator analysis cannot be carried out unless studies report statistics for each category of these variables (e.g., effect sizes for male and female respondents in the case of gender) or focus on a single variable category that can be compared to another variable category (e.g., the effect size of a study using a sample of male respondents can be compared to the effect size of another study using a sample of female respondents).

ined: source, method, sampling, respondent, country, desirability, medium, and message. Meta-analysis, which has become increasingly popular in mass communication research (e.g., Allen, D'Alessio, & Brezgel, 1995; Glynn, Hayes, & Shanahan, 1997; Kim & Hunter, 1993; Morgan & Shanahan, 1997; Paik & Comstock, 1994; Ware & Dupagne, 1994), enables researchers to draw generalizations concerning a hypothesis and make sense of diverse empirical findings. Before formulating the research questions and describing the methodology, we review the theoretical foundations of the third-person effect.

THEORETICAL FOUNDATIONS

Researchers have drawn on a variety of psychological theories to justify the third-person effect. Few, however, explicitly linked these theories to the third-person effect. Some researchers have used ego involvement (e.g., Perloff, 1989; Vallone, Ross, & Lepper, 1985), the elaboration likelihood model (e.g., Stenbjerre & Leets, 1998; White, 1995, 1997), and social categorization theory (e.g., Stenbjerre, 1997), but most have relied on attribution theory (e.g., Gunther, 1991; Hoffner et al., 1997; Rucinski & Salmon, 1990) and biased optimism (e.g., Brosius & Engel, 1996; Gunther & Mundy, 1993; Rucinski & Salmon, 1990) to explain the theoretical underpinnings of the third-person effect. In a reflective and candid essay, Davison (1996), a sociologist, writing 13 years after his seminal study and expressing surprise at the number of studies generated by his 1983 piece, confessed he originally viewed the third-person effect as "an interesting phenomenon ... but of minor theoretical significance" (p. 114).

Attribution Theory

In its broadest sense, attribution theory refers to the study of processes used by people to infer causes of behavior. Heider (1958) argued that people act like "naive psychologists" who seek to understand actions and events that are relevant to them and form beliefs based on observations. Attribution theory has four major assumptions:

1. People perceive behavior as being caused and intentional.
2. People possess dispositional properties (e.g., traits, abilities, intentions).
3. People assess behavior as being caused by a combination of internal or dispositional (e.g., motivations, knowledge, attitudes, moods, needs, opinions of others) and external or situational (e.g., task difficulty, luck) factors.
4. People perceive that others have similar characteristics as themselves.

Heider's principle of similarity appears to contradict the basic theoretical premise of the third-person effect, which posits that people perceive others to be different, not similar, to themselves and more vulnerable to media influences.

However, Heider (1958) recognized that there are situations in which attributions to self and others can differ: "The person tends to attribute his own reactions to the object world, and those of another, when they differ from his own, to personal characteristics in *o* [the other]" (p. 157). Jones and Nisbett (1972) removed Heider's phrase "when they differ from his own" and amplified his statement as a formal proposition about actor and observer differences. They postulated that "there is a pervasive tendency for actors to attribute their actions to situational requirements, whereas observers tend to attribute the same actions to stable personal dispositions" (p. 80; see also Zimbardo, 1972). For instance, a student (actor) who turns in an assignment late might explain to the professor that this tardiness was out of character and caused by an unusual computer problem (external or situational factor). On the other hand, the professor (observer) might believe that this tardiness was not due to the student's environment but instead the student's laziness or ineptitude (internal or dispositional factor). These actor–observer differences in causal attributions are to be interpreted in the context of the so-called fundamental attribution error, defined as "the tendency for attributers to underestimate the impact of situational factors and to overestimate the role of dispositional factors in controlling behavior" (Ross, 1977, p. 183; see also Zebrowitz, 1990). It is this nonmotivational source of bias in attribution theory that has attracted the attention of third-person effect researchers (e.g., Gunther, 1991; Rucinski & Salmon, 1990; Standley, 1994).

Applied to a media message, attribution theory explains why a person may think he or she understands the underlying persuasive aspects of the message, whereas others' dispositional flaws (e.g., gullibility, naiveté, lack of intelligence, etc.) make them incapable of perceiving message persuasiveness. Because this explanation deals with circumstances and situations, attributions may vary based on message content. Gunther (1991) described the relevance of attribution theory to third-person perception:

> Attribution theory is pertinent to the third-person effect simply because of the consistent bias in estimating the situational response. There may or may not be specific dispositional attributes assigned to the greater persuasability of others, but the relevant point is that observers see others as less responsive to the situation. (p. 357)

In a rare empirical test of attribution theory applied to the third-person effect, Standley (1994) found support for the proposition that people attribute their own actions to situational factors, whereas they attribute others' actions to dispositional factors. Using a series of in-depth interviews, she reported that respondents were more likely to cite situational reasons than dispositional ones when asked to assess the effects of television on themselves. When asked to determine the effects of television on the audience, respondents were more likely to cite dispositional reasons than situational ones.

Biased Optimism

Another commonly used framework has been called *biased optimism* (Gunther, 1995; Gunther & Mundy, 1993), variations of which are also known as *impersonal impact* (Brosius & Engel, 1996; Glynn & Ostman, 1988; Tyler & Cook, 1984), *unrealistic optimism* (Glynn & Ostman, 1988; Weinstein, 1980; Weinstein & Lachendro, 1982), and *personal optimism* or *societal pessimism* (Culbertson & Stempel, 1985; Weinstein, 1980). This explanation holds that people judge themselves less likely than others to experience negative consequences. Biased optimism explains why people believe they are better drivers than others (Svenson, 1981), receive better health care than others (Culbertson & Stempel, 1985), or are better off than others in a myriad of ways (Whitman, 1996). Biased optimism has two underlying assumptions: that people can distinguish between societal-others and personal-self level effects and that media messages influence people's perceptions of risk or harm (Tyler & Cook, 1984).

People's optimism has been explained by their attempts to reinforce self-esteem. People reinforce their self-esteem by estimating themselves to be smart enough to disbelieve media messages whereas others believe the messages. However, the process is not that simple. Some media messages that advocate beneficial outcomes may be desirable to believe. As Gunther and Mundy (1993) stated, "The concept of harmful vs. beneficial outcome is a central one in theoretical research on the 'optimistic bias' phenomenon—the tendency for people to think they are less likely to have negative or undesirable experiences than others" (p. 60).

Biased optimism assumes the existence of a self-serving bias—that people evaluate themselves more favorably than they evaluate others and that they believe they are less likely than others to experience negative events (Weinstein & Klein, 1996). This bias is rooted in several social-psychological theories, such as social comparison theory and social evaluation theory (Brown, 1986). Central to biased optimism is the issue of event desirability. Weinstein (1980) described event desirability as involving two hypotheses: "[a] People believe that negative events are less likely to happen to them than to others, and [b] they believe that positive events are more likely to happen to them than to others" (p. 807). Weinstein's first hypothesis describes the third-person effect and the second describes the first-person effect, the tendency to appraise oneself as more affected by desirable-to-believe media messages than others.

Third-person effect research overwhelmingly supports Weinstein's (1980) first hypothesis (see Perloff, 1993, 1996). Third-person effect research pertaining to Weinstein's second hypothesis suggesting a first-person effect is equivocal. Hoorens and Ruiter (1996) and Duck, Terry, and Hogg (1995) found individuals to be more strongly influenced by desirable messages than others, as Weinstein's second hypothesis posits. Other studies, however, indicate that desirable messages either diminish third-person perception or result in no perceptual difference (Brosius

& Engel, 1996; Gunther & Mundy, 1993; Gunther & Thorson, 1992; Innes & Zeitz, 1988). These findings suggest that whereas a first-person effect may manifest itself with extremely desirable-to-believe messages, third-person perception is the norm. Furthermore, it seems reasonable to assume that absent any message desirability, the general undesirability associated with believing a media message will result in third-person perception.

RESEARCH QUESTIONS

In summary, there has been much recent research on the third-person effect. Almost all findings have supported the perceptual hypothesis. However, what is the magnitude of the effect? This led to our first research question:

RQ1: What is the overall level of support for the third-person effect's perceptual hypothesis?

In addition to determining overall level of support for third-person perception, it is necessary to map out the conditions that enhance or diminish third-person perception to make inferences about the underlying process. Therefore, a second research question was advanced:

RQ2: What study characteristics and content variables moderate the third-person effect's perceptual hypothesis?

METHOD

Following the methodological procedures of Hunter, Schmidt, and Jackson (1982), Wolf (1986), and Rosenthal (1984), we describe the five major steps of meta-analysis: locating and searching the literature, selecting a common metric, computing an average effect size and testing for variance homogeneity across studies, identifying moderators, and computing a fail-safe N. Statistically, this meta-analysis involves two basic procedures: averaging zero-order correlation coefficients of studies weighted by their respective sample sizes and determining whether there is a significant difference in effect size across studies. If the test of homogeneity is statistically significant, then a moderator analysis is warranted to identify the source of this variation.

Literature Search

To locate published and unpublished third-person effect studies, three computer databases were searched: Educational Resources Information Center (ERIC), 1968 to 1997; Dissertation Abstracts International, 1861 to 1998; and Periodical Abstracts, 1982 to 1998. In addition, the following online databases were also used: PapersFirst, 1993 to 1998; Article1st, 1990 to 1998; and Social Science Abstracts, 1983 to 1998. Print copies of *Communication Abstracts* starting with Volume 1 were also consulted. The reference sections of all located studies were scrutinized for relevant citations. Finally, several scholars with an interest and publication record in third-person effect research were contacted to locate studies they had or knew of that might have been overlooked. In some cases, they supplied unpublished papers, theses, dissertations, and citations. In all, 62 empirical studies were found using these resources.

Common Metric

All studies included in the meta-analysis were converted to a common statistical metric for comparison. We used the Pearson's product–moment correlation coefficient r, the most widely used metric in meta-analysis (e.g., Glynn et al., 1997; Kim & Hunter, 1993; Morgan & Shanahan, 1997; Paik & Comstock, 1994; Ware & Dupagne, 1994). The data were coded so that a positive r indicated a third-person effect (i.e., greater perceived effects on others than on oneself), whereas a negative r indicated a first-person effect (i.e., greater perceived effects on oneself than on others).

Third-person effect studies typically report the difference between individuals' estimations of the mean level of influence of media messages on themselves and their perceptions of influence on others. The discrepancy between these perceptions (known as third-person perception, perceptual discrepancy, perceptual bias, and self–others difference in the literature) is then assessed using t or F statistics. Studies that provide ts or Fs can usually be converted to r using Wolf's (1986) t-to-r conversion formula in Equation 1:

$$r = \sqrt{\frac{t^2}{t^2 + df}}, \qquad (1)$$

where t^2 is the value of a t statistic squared and df is the degrees of freedom for the t test.

Equation 2 was used for the F-to-r conversion:

$$r = \sqrt{\frac{F}{F + df}}, \qquad (2)$$

where F is the value of an F statistic and df is the degrees of freedom for the F test.

Two criteria were used to determine inclusion of studies in this meta-analysis: A study had to include effect measures of the media on oneself and others and report the self–others difference in a manner that permitted conversion to r. Therefore, studies reporting only perceived self–others effects means without standard deviations (or other measures of dispersion that could be converted to standard deviations) as well as studies reporting only the percentages of self and others effects, could not be included in the meta-analysis.

Effect Size and Test of Homogeneity

After the study results were converted to a common metric, the effect size across studies was computed. According to Hunter et al. (1982):

> If the population correlation is assumed to be constant over studies, then the best estimate of that correlation is not the simple mean across studies but a weighted average in which each correlation is weighted by the number of persons in that study. (pp. 40–41)

Hunter et al.'s formula for computing the mean correlation across studies is provided in Equation 3:

$$r_{Ave} = \frac{\sum(N_i r_i)}{\sum N_i}, \qquad (3)$$

where N_i is the sample size in Study i and r_i is the correlation in Study i.

Before undertaking a moderator analysis, data were analyzed to determine whether the variance in effect size across studies is greater than would be expected by chance. Should this be the case, the effect size can be said to be heterogeneous and a moderator analysis is warranted. A test of homogeneity was performed using a chi-square (χ^2) statistic with degrees of freedom $K - 1$ (Hunter et al., 1982):

$$\chi^2_{K-1} = \frac{\sum N_i}{(1 - r_{Ave}^2)^2} s_r^2, \qquad (4)$$

where N_i is the sample size in Study i, r_{Ave} is the mean correlation coefficient across all studies, and s_r^2 is the observed variance of the mean correlation coefficient obtained from Equation 5.

$$s_r^2 = \frac{\sum[N_i(r_i - r_{Ave})^2]}{\sum N_i}, \qquad (5)$$

where N_i is the sample size in Study i, r_i is the correlation coefficient in Study i, and r_{Ave} is the mean correlation coefficient across all studies. Hunter and Schmidt

(1990) noted that if a meta-analysis includes many studies, this statistic will have "very high statistical power and will therefore reject the null hypothesis, given even a trivial amount of variation across studies" (p. 112). Therefore, a nonsignificant chi-square value is a strong indication that there is indeed little variation in effect size across studies.

Moderator Analysis

Eight moderators culled from the literature were examined: source, method, sampling, respondent, country, message desirability, medium, and message. Moderating variables were investigated to determine whether there was a statistically significant difference (at the $p < .05$ level) between the average effect sizes (in terms of r) and whether the mean variance of effect sizes was less than that of the overall mean effect size. Should both of these criteria be satisfied, the variable can be said to be a significant moderator (Hunter et al., 1982).

Regarding the second condition, Hunter et al. (1982) and Hunter and Schmidt (1990) suggested correcting the across-studies variance for sampling error. They argued that because the observed variance is confounded by two factors—actual variation in sample correlations and variation in sample correlations produced by sampling error—an estimate of variance in population correlations must be obtained by correcting the observed variance s^2 for sampling error. Therefore, we first computed the observed variance using Equation 5 and then we calculated the sampling error using Equation 6 (Hunter et al., 1982):

$$\sigma_e^2 = \frac{(1 - r_{Ave}^2)^2 K}{\sum N_i}, \quad (6)$$

where r_{Ave} is the mean correlation coefficient across all studies, K is the number of studies, and N_i is the sample size in Study i. Once the sampling error was computed, we subtracted it from s_r^2 as shown in Equation 7.

$$s_r^{2 \text{ corrected}} = s_r^2 - \sigma_e^2. \quad (7)$$

The result of Equation 7 represents what can be called the true or corrected variance of r.

Coding. The first author coded all the studies. Nine studies were randomly selected and recoded by a trained graduate student. Across the combined nine studies, which included 25 effect sizes, the overall intercoder reliability, computed as the simple percentage of agreement between the two coders (Holsti, 1969), was 0.94. Intercoder reliability figures for individual moderators are reported below.

Source. Studies were coded to determine whether significant differences in the reported level of third-person perception existed between published and unpublished studies. Glynn et al. (1997) used this moderator in an effort to examine the possible impact of the file drawer problem in a meta-analysis of spiral of silence studies. The file drawer problem, an enduring concern in meta-analysis, refers to the charge that journals are more likely to publish studies that report significant results than nonsignificant results. If this were the case, it would suggest that published research leaves an overly optimistic impression of support for a body of research. Glynn et al. did not find source to be a significant moderator. Journal articles were coded as published, whereas theses, dissertations, and conference papers or proceedings were coded as unpublished (intercoder reliability = 1.00).

Method. Third-person effect studies have used either surveys or experimental methods. In theory, findings should not be attributable to the method. If survey and experimental research are in general agreement regarding a body of research, that would provide confidence in the findings. However, in an influential essay, Hovland (1963) reported the tendency of experiments to isolate variable relationships and to thereby increase the likelihood of finding significant outcomes. Paik and Comstock (1994) found that the average effect size for the relationship between exposure to television violence and antisocial behavior was larger for experiments than for surveys. To determine whether the third-person effect is moderated by research methods, studies were coded as either survey or experiment (intercoder reliability = 0.95). Studies that met inclusion criteria did not use other methods.

Sampling. For reasons of cost and tradition, survey and experimental researchers often use convenience samples of college students. Potter, Cooper, and Dupagne (1993) reported that 51% of quantitative mass communication articles selected from a sample of eight communication journals between 1965 and 1989 used nonprobabilistic sampling. However, nonprobabilistic samples, such as convenience samples, may vary from other populations in unknown and unanticipated ways. In their meta-analysis investigating the impact of U.S. television programs on foreign audiences, Ware and Dupagne (1994) found that using a random sample produced a larger effect size than using a nonrandom sample, although the difference failed to attain statistical significance. To determine whether third-person perception is affected by sampling procedures, study samples were coded as random or nonrandom (intercoder reliability = 0.93).

Respondent. It is often, but not always, the case that nonprobabilistic samples consist of college students and probabilistic samples consist of noncollege students; hence, the importance of considering type of respondent as a separate moderator. In our meta-analysis, one probabilistic study used college student respondents (Hoffner et al., 1997), and three nonprobabilistic studies used general population respondents

(Faber, Shah, Hanyoun, & Rojas, 1997; Shah, Faber, Hanyoun, & Rojas, 1997; Youn, Faber, & Shah, 1998). Still, the majority of nonprobabilistic studies relied on student samples ($n = 11$). Third-person effect research suggests a reason to expect differences in perceptions among college students. Research examining respondents' self-assessed knowledge indicates that respondents with high levels of self-assessed knowledge, such as college students, might exhibit greater third-person perception than others (Driscoll & Salwen, 1997; Lasorsa, 1989). In fact, it may be that student respondents' status as college students is the factor that allows them to assess themselves as smarter than other people. Studies were coded as using either college students or noncollege students (intercoder reliability = 0.93).

Country. Several studies have investigated the third-person effect in nations other than the United States. For example, Gunther and Ang (1996) examined the third-person effect in Singapore to study the effect in an authoritarian society. If the third-person effect is solely a psychological effect attributable to human perception, then country and cultural variations should not moderate the effect. However, if sociological factors influence people's perceptions of media influence, then social–political factors associated with different countries may moderate the effect. For example, it may be that respondents in authoritarian Singapore perceive media effects differently because of severe government restrictions on the media. Because few third-person effect studies have been conducted outside the United States, studies were dichotomously coded as conducted in the United States or other countries (intercoder reliability = 1.00).

Desirability. Message desirability has received considerable attention. It is believed that messages perceived as undesirable to believe will enhance third-person perception because these are precisely the types of messages that vulnerable others will believe. On the other hand, the perceiver views himself or herself clever enough to see the foolishness in believing an undesirable-to-believe message (Bereck & Glynn, 1993; Cohen, Mutz, Price, & Gunther, 1988; Duck et al., 1995; Gunther & Mundy, 1993; Gunther & Thorson, 1992; Innes & Zeitz, 1988; Ognianova, Meeds, Thorson, & Coyle, 1996; Thorson & Coyle, 1994). Desirable-to-believe messages may result in reduced third-person perception, no perceptual difference, or even a reverse first-person effect to estimate greater effects on oneself (Gunther & Mundy, 1993; Gunther & Thorson, 1992; Innes & Zeitz, 1988). Studies were coded as socially undesirable, socially desirable, or neither desirable nor undesirable.

The socially undesirable category included messages or issues that the study authors expressly stated were socially undesirable to be believed. Socially undesirable messages also included issues selected because of their obvious undesirability, even if not directly stated. The undesirable messages included pornography, television violence, political scandals, and cultural taboos such as extramarital affairs and sexual deviancy. Socially desirable messages were those that the researchers expressly stated would be desirable to be believed. Socially desirable messages also included messages and issues selected because of their obvious desirability. The desirable issue was public service announcements. Finally, neither desirable nor undesirable messages were those that the researchers stated were neither desirable nor undesirable to believe or neither obviously desirable nor undesirable messages (intercoder reliability = 0.93). We recognize that it is of dubious validity to operationally define issues as desirable or undesirable based on researchers' assumptions, even if this definition appeared to achieve reasonable face validity. A more valid definition would have respondents evaluate message desirability.

Medium. Research indicates that mass media effects can vary according to the type of medium (Jeffres, 1997). Salwen (1998) reported that newspaper reading was associated with greater third-person perception of presidential election news than was local and network news viewing. He claimed that newspaper readers saw this medium as closely associated with news and public affairs. As a result, newspaper readers were more confident than nonnewspaper readers in their superior news and public affairs knowledge. Medium categories included media in general (used when respondents were asked to estimate the perceived influence on self and others of no medium in particular or all media in general, such as "the media"), television, radio, newspapers, and other (intercoder reliability = 0.94).

Message. Related to message desirability is message content. Third-person effect studies have examined messages concerning a variety of issues and contexts, including commercial product advertisements (Thorson & Coyle, 1994), television violence (Hoffner et al., 1997), pornography (Gunther, 1995), and political news (Hu & Wu, 1996; Salwen, 1998). In their meta-analysis of television violence effects on antisocial behavior, Paik and Comstock (1994) found differences in average correlation coefficients by program type, with cartoons and fantasies producing the largest effect sizes. Message type in this study included seven coding categories selected from third-person effect studies: media messages in general (referring to the influence of the media without reference to specific message content), pornography, television violence, commercial ads, politics (when studies involved noncommercial political news, political debates, and political advertisements for political candidates and issues), nonpolitical news (when studies involved noncommercial news messages that did not relate to politics), and other (used when an issue did not fit into any of the other coding categories; intercoder reliability = 0.97).

Fail-Safe *N*

The file drawer problem refers to a retrievability bias inherent in all research. It can be especially acute when computing aggregated statistical findings in meta-analysis (Rosenthal, 1984). The file drawer problem posits that journals are more likely to publish studies that report significant results than nonsignificant results. As a result of this bias, generalizations made from published research are thought to be more affirmative than is warranted. Support for the file drawer problem appears to be based more on common sense than empirical evidence. Nevertheless, because results of published studies alone might provide an overly optimistic picture of the state of the research, the meta-analyst must use procedures to address the file drawer problem.

Hunter and Schmidt (1990) suggested the calculation of a fail-safe N to address this availability bias. The fail-safe N represents the number of studies with null results needed to render the average effect size statistically insignificant. The equation for this calculation originates from Rosenthal (1984):

$$x = \frac{K(KZ_{Ave}^2 - 2.706)}{2.706}, \tag{7}$$

where x is the number of studies needed to reduce the effect size to nonsignificance, K is the number of studies, and Z_{Ave} is the value of the mean correlation coefficient r after it has been converted to Z.

FINDINGS

A total of 32 published and unpublished studies that met a priori standards for inclusion in the meta-analysis were examined. From these, 121 separate effect sizes were computed. When combined, a total of 45,729 respondents were included in the meta-analysis (see Table 1).

To address the issue of statistical nonindependence of effect sizes,[3] a t test was performed to determine whether a significant difference existed between the mean

---

[3]Many third-person effect studies examine the perception of media influence on self and on others for a number of different media messages using the same sample of respondents. Each such effect score cannot be assumed to be independent. Hunter and Schmidt (1990) suggested two approaches to handle this problem. First, effect scores could be treated as independent, thereby contributing to a synthesis as separate values. Tracz (1984) conducted a statistical Monte Carlo simulation and found that the distribution of r was not affected by nonindependence when combining correlation coefficients in a meta-analysis (see also Allen, D'Alessio, & Brezgel, 1995). Second, these values could be averaged to contribute to an overall effect score. The first method is more commonly applied in meta-analyses (Hunter & Schmidt, 1990). However, to treat nonindependent data as independent, a meta-analyst must be assured that considering all effect scores separately will not produce results that would differ significantly from the averaging of scores. To avoid the risk of distortion attributable to nonindependence, Paik and Comstock (1994) compared the means of all combined hypothesis tests when each was treated as independent with the means of combined hypothesis tests when multiple effect scores from the same samples were averaged. The researchers found no significant difference between the two means, and hence decided to treat all effect scores as though they were independent. We used the same diagnostic approach in this study.

TABLE 1
Summary of the Third-Person Effect Studies and Moderators Included in the Meta-Analysis

Author	Source	Method	Sampling	Respondent	Country	Desirabilty	Medium	Message	N	r
Baldwin										
1991	U	Survey	R	NC	U.S.	Neither	Newspapers	Nonpolitical news	616	.51
1991	U	Survey	R	NC	U.S.	Neither	TV	Nonpolitical news	617	.52
1991	U	Survey	R	NC	U.S.	Neither	Radio	Nonpolitical news	606	.55
1991	U	Survey	R	NC	U.S.	Neither	Other	Nonpolitical news	606	.51
Driscoll & Salwen										
1997	P	Survey	R	NC	U.S.	Neither	All	Nonpolitical news	574	.41
1997	P	Survey	R	NC	U.S.	Neither	All	Nonpolitical news	553	.40
1997	P	Survey	R	NC	U.S.	Neither	All	Nonpolitical news	549	.04
Duck & Mullin										
1995	P	Experiment	NR	C	Other	Undesirable	All	Other	112	.70
1995	P	Experiment	NR	C	Other	Desirable	All	Other	112	.25
1995	P	Experiment	NR	C	Other	Desirable	All	Other	112	.24
Faber, Shah, Hanyoun, & Rojas										
1997	U	Survey	NR	NC	U.S.	Undesirable	All	Commercial ads	192	.50
1997	U	Survey	NR	NC	U.S.	Desirable	All	Commercial ads	192	.47
1997	U	Survey	NR	NC	U.S.	Desirable	All	Commercial ads	192	.35
1997	U	Survey	NR	NC	U.S.	Neither	All	Commercial ads	192	.17
Glynn & Ostman										
1988	P	Survey	R	NC	U.S.	Neither	All	Other	260	.01
Gunther										
1995	P	Survey	R	NC	U.S.	Undesirable	All	Pornography	648	.35
Gunther & Ang										
1996	P	Survey	R	NC	Other	Undesirable	TV	TV violence	506	.48
1996	P	Survey	R	NC	Other	Undesirable	TV	Other	506	.49
1996	P	Survey	R	NC	Other	Undesirable	TV	Other	506	.49
1996	P	Survey	R	NC	Other	Undesirable	TV	Other	506	.46
1996	P	Survey	R	NC	Other	Undesirable	TV	Other	506	.44
1996	P	Survey	R	NC	Other	Undesirable	TV	Other	506	.46

	1996	P	Survey	R	NC	Other	Undesirable	TV	All messages	506	.45
	1996	P	Survey	R	NC	Other	Desirable	TV	Other	506	.32
	1996	P	Survey	R	NC	Other	Desirable	TV	Other	506	−.29
	1996	P	Survey	R	NC	Other	Desirable	TV	Other	506	−.17
Hitchon, Chang, & Harris									
	1997	P	Experiment	NR	C	U.S.	Neither	TV	Politics	24	.72
	1997	P	Experiment	NR	C	U.S.	Neither	TV	Politics	24	.47
	1997	P	Experiment	NR	C	U.S.	Neither	TV	Politics	24	.79
Hoffner et al.									
	1997	U	Survey	R	C	U.S.	Undesirable	TV	All messages	253	.76
Hu & Wu									
	1996	U	Survey	R	NC	Other	Neither	TV	Politics	1,074	.63
	1996	U	Survey	R	NC	Other	Neither	Radio	Politics	1,074	.64
	1996	U	Survey	R	NC	Other	Neither	Newspapers	Politics	1,074	.61
	1996	U	Survey	R	NC	Other	Neither	Other	Politics	1,074	.62
	1998	U	Survey	R	NC	Other	Desirable	All	Other	1,075	.47
Innes & Zeitz									
	1988	P	Survey	R	NC	Other	NA	All	Other	171	.78
Kashima									
	1990	U	Survey	R	NC	U.S.	Neither	All	All messages	200	.42
	1990	U	Survey	R	NC	U.S.	Neither	All	All messages	200	.52
	1990	U	Survey	R	NC	U.S.	Neither	All	All messages	200	.32
	1990	U	Survey	R	NC	U.S.	Neither	All	All messages	200	.45
	1990	U	Survey	R	NC	U.S.	Neither	All	All messages	200	.61
	1990	U	Survey	R	NC	U.S.	Neither	All	All messages	200	.70
Lo & Paddon									
	1998	U	Survey	R	NC	Other	Undesirable	All	Pornography	1,842	.28
Matera & Salwen									
	1997	U	Survey	R	NC	U.S.	NA	All	Other	392	.53
	1997	U	Survey	R	NC	U.S.	NA	All	Other	127	.36
	1997	U	Survey	R	NC	U.S.	NA	All	Politics	399	.57

(continued)

TABLE 1 (Continued)

Author	Source	Method	Sampling	Respondent	Country	Desirabilty	Medium	Message	N	r
1997	U	Survey	R	NC	U.S.	NA	All	Politics	138	.60
1997	U	Survey	R	NC	U.S.	NA	All	Nonpolitical news	164	.56
1997	U	Survey	R	NC	U.S.	NA	All	Nonpolitical news	49	.39
1997	U	Survey	R	NC	U.S.	NA	All	Nonpolitical news	125	.46
1997	U	Survey	R	NC	U.S.	NA	All	Nonpolitical news	36	.89
McLeod, Eveland, & Nathanson										
1997	P	Survey	NR	C	U.S.	Undesirable	Other	Other	202	.83
1997	P	Survey	NR	C	U.S.	Undesirable	Other	Other	202	.58
Park										
1985	U	Survey	R	NC	U.S.	Neither	All	Politics	308	.62
1985	U	Survey	R	NC	U.S.	Neither	All	Politics	270	.57
1985	U	Survey	R	NC	U.S.	Neither	All	Politics	326	.59
1985	U	Survey	R	NC	U.S.	Neither	All	Politics	327	.51
Price, Huang, & Tewksbury										
1997	P	Survey	NR	C	U.S.	Neither	All	All messages	283	.51
1997	P	Survey	NR	C	U.S.	Neither	All	All messages	289	.57
1997	P	Survey	NR	C	U.S.	Neither	All	All messages	291	.65
Price & Tewksbury										
1996	P	Experiment	NR	C	U.S.	Neither	All	Politics	75	.57
1996	P	Experiment	NR	C	U.S.	Neither	All	Politics	34	.61
1996	P	Experiment	NR	C	U.S.	Neither	All	Politics	34	.67
1996	P	Experiment	NR	C	U.S.	Neither	All	Politics	75	.68
1996	P	Experiment	NR	C	U.S.	Neither	All	Politics	35	.75
1996	P	Experiment	NR	C	U.S.	Neither	All	Politics	35	.73
1996	P	Experiment	NR	C	U.S.	Neither	All	Politics	75	.70
1996	P	Experiment	NR	C	U.S.	Neither	All	Politics	34	.69
1996	P	Experiment	NR	C	U.S.	Neither	All	Politics	35	.77
1996	P	Experiment	NR	C	U.S.	Neither	All	Politics	75	.84
1996	P	Experiment	NR	C	U.S.	Neither	All	Politics	34	.59
1996	P	Experiment	NR	C	U.S.	Neither	All	Politics	35	.67

Price, Tewksbury, & Huang										
1996	U	Survey	NR	C	U.S.	Undesirable	Newspapers	Politics	107	.67
Rojas										
1994	U	Survey	NR	C	U.S.	Undesirable	All	Pornography	133	.68
1994	U	Survey	NR	C	U.S.	Undesirable	All	Pornography	133	.56
1994	U	Survey	NR	C	U.S.	Undesirable	TV	TV violence	131	.48
1994	U	Survey	NR	C	U.S.	Undesirable	TV	TV violence	131	.46
1994	U	Survey	NR	C	U.S.	Undesirable	TV	Other	131	.80
1994	U	Survey	NR	C	U.S.	Undesirable	TV	Other	131	.55
1994	U	Survey	NR	C	U.S.	Neither	All	Other	131	.76
1994	U	Survey	NR	C	U.S.	Neither	All	Other	131	.61
Rojas, Shah, & Faber										
1996	P	Survey	NR	C	U.S.	Neither	All	All messages	133	.76
1996	P	Survey	NR	C	U.S.	Neither	All	All messages	133	.61
1996	P	Survey	NR	C	U.S.	Undesirable	TV	TV violence	133	.64
1996	P	Survey	NR	C	U.S.	Undesirable	TV	TV violence	133	.80
1996	P	Survey	NR	C	U.S.	Undesirable	All	Pornography	133	.56
1996	P	Survey	NR	C	U.S.	Undesirable	All	Pornography	133	.68
Rucinski & Salmon										
1990	P	Survey	R	NC	U.S.	Neither	All	Politics	261	.49
1990	P	Survey	R	NC	U.S.	Neither	All	Politics	261	.66
1990	P	Survey	R	NC	U.S.	Undesirable	All	Politics	261	.65
1990	P	Survey	R	NC	U.S.	Neither	All	Politics	261	.46
1990	P	Survey	R	NC	U.S.	Neither	All	Other	261	.66
Salwen										
1998	P	Survey	R	NC	U.S.	Neither	Newspapers	Politics	485	.50
1998	P	Survey	R	NC	U.S.	Neither	TV	Politics	498	.57
1998	P	Survey	R	NC	U.S.	Neither	Radio	Politics	475	.47
1998	P	Survey	R	NC	U.S.	Neither	All	Politics	492	.55
Salwen, Dupagne, & Paul										
1998	U	Survey	R	NC	U.S.	Undesirable	TV	TV violence	721	.46
1998	U	Survey	R	NC	U.S.	Undesirable	TV	TV violence	721	.41
1998	U	Survey	R	NC	U.S.	Neither	TV	Other	721	.39
1998	U	Survey	R	NC	U.S.	Neither	TV	Other	721	.25

(continued)

TABLE 1 (Continued)

Author	Source	Method	Sampling	Respondent	Country	Desirability	Medium	Message	N	r
1998	U	Survey	R	NC	U.S.	Neither	TV	Politics	721	.38
1998	U	Survey	R	NC	U.S.	Neither	TV	Politics	721	.21
Shah, Faber, Hanyoun, Rojas										
1997	U	Survey	NR	NC	U.S.	Desirable	All	Politics	190	.39
1997	U	Survey	NR	NC	U.S.	Undesirable	All	Politics	192	.24
Stenbjerre										
1997	U	Experiment	NR	C	U.S.	NA	TV	Politics	45	.36
1997	U	Experiment	NR	C	U.S.	NA	TV	Politics	45	.44
Stenbjerre & Leets										
1997	U	Experiment	NR	C	U.S.	NA	Newspapers	Commercial ads	58	.35
1998	U	Experiment	NR	C	U.S.	NA	Newspapers	Commercial ads	59	.40
1998	U	Experiment	NR	C	U.S.	NA	Newspapers	Nonpolitical news	116	.59
Tiedge, Silverblatt, Havice, & Rosenfeld										
1991	P	Survey	R	NC	U.S.	Undesirable	All	Other	571	.82
Wang										
1995	U	Survey	R	NC	Other	Neither	TV	Politics	1,103	.63
1995	U	Survey	R	NC	Other	Neither	TV	Politics	1,103	.61
1995	U	Survey	R	NC	Other	Neither	TV	Politics	1,103	.64
1995	U	Survey	R	NC	Other	Neither	TV	Politics	1,103	.62
1995	U	Survey	R	NC	Other	Neither	TV	Politics	1,103	.64
1995	U	Survey	R	NC	Other	Neither	TV	Politics	1,103	.51
1995	U	Survey	R	NC	Other	Neither	TV	Politics	1,103	.65
1995	U	Survey	R	NC	Other	Neither	TV	Politics	1,103	.62
1995	U	Survey	R	NC	Other	Neither	TV	Politics	1,103	.68
Youn, Faber, & Shah										
1998	U	Survey	NR	NC	U.S.	Desirable	All	Commercial ads	190	.50
1998	U	Survey	NR	NC	U.S.	Desirable	All	Commercial ads	192	.53

Note. U = unpublished; R = random; NC = noncollege; P = published; NR = nonrandom; C = college. NA = not available.

r when all effect scores were treated as statistically independent (including multiple scores from the same sample) and the mean r when the average of multiple effect sizes coming from the same samples was considered (see Paik & Comstock, 1994). No significant difference was found between the two groups, $t(153) = .78$, ns. As such, nonindependence was not considered a threat to validity, and the larger set of data made possible by considering each hypothesis test as independent could be used. The unit of analysis was the hypothesis test, not the study, and accordingly K in the previous equations refers to the number of hypothesis tests (individual effect sizes).

Overall Effect Size

Overall, the mean r coefficient for the third-person effect's perceptual hypothesis weighted by sample size was .50 ($r^2 = .25$). This correlation had a fail-safe N of 1,519 (Rosenthal, 1984). This means that 1,519 additional nonsignificant effect sizes would be needed for the mean effect size to fail to attain statistical significance. The corrected (for sampling error) variance for this average correlation coefficient was .034. The correlations were found to be heterogeneous across studies, $\chi^2(120, N = 45,729) = 2,845.36, p < .001$. This finding suggests the presence of at least one moderator.

Moderator Analysis

In Table 2, K refers to the number of effect sizes considered in a group for a particular moderator. Therefore, a K of 25 indicates that 25 separate effect sizes were included in a group. N refers to the total number of respondents included in each group. As mentioned earlier, for a moderator to be statistically significant, there must be a significant difference in effect size between the moderator groups and the mean variance of effect sizes must be less than that of the overall mean effect size.

Source. Analysis of studies as published and unpublished indicated that this variable was not a significant moderator of third-person perception (Table 2). There was a significant difference in effect size between published studies and unpublished studies, $t(119) = 2.42, p < .05$, but the mean corrected variance (mean $s_r^{2 \text{ corrected}} = .039$; thereafter mean $s_r^{2 \text{ cor}}$) for the two groups was greater than that for the overall correlation coefficient of the perceptual hypothesis (.034).

Method. Analysis of the method indicated that this variable was not a significant moderator of third-person perception (Table 2). Although the mean corrected variance for the two groups was less than that for the overall r coefficient of the per-

TABLE 2
Summary of the Moderator Analyses

Moderator	Categories	Mean r	SD	Mean $s_r^{2\,corrected}$	N	K
Source	Published	.44	.24	.060	14,690	55
	Unpublished	.53	.13	.017	31,039	66
Method	Survey	.50	.18	.032	44,422	97
	Experiment	.56	.16	.027	1,307	24
Sampling	Random	.49	.18	.034	39,666	70
	Nonrandom	.56	.14	.021	6,063	51
Respondent	College students	.60	.14	.015	4,784	44
	Noncollege students	.49	.18	.033	40,945	77
Country	United States	.49	.15	.024	23,022	92
	Other countries	.51	.20	.041	22,707	29
Message desirability[a]	Undesirable	.47	.14	.020	10,888	30
	Desirable	.21	.29	.087	3,773	11
	Neither	.54	.14	.020	29,144	66
Medium	Media in general	.48	.17	.031	16,268	67
	TV	.50	.20	.040	22,707	40
	Radio	.56	.06	.004	2,155	3
	Newspapers	.55	.06	.004	2,515	7
	Other[b]	.56	.04	.002	2,084	4
Message	Media messages in general	.72	.05	.003	3,088	13
	Pornography	.37	.11	.013	3,022	6
	TV violence	.48	.08	.007	2,476	7
	Commercial ads	.42	.10	.010	1,267	8
	Politics	.58	.01	.001	21,654	49
	Nonpolitical news	.47	.17	.030	4,611	12
	Other[b]	.39	.07	.002	9,611	26

Note. Mean $s_r^{2\,corrected}$ = the mean variance of the mean r corrected for sampling error (see Equation 6 in the Method section).
[a]Fourteen of the 121 hypothesis tests could not be categorized for message desirability. [b]Not included in the F test.

ceptual hypothesis (mean $s_r^{2\,cor}$ = .030), no significant difference was found between mean correlations for the two groups, $t(119) = 1.39$, *ns*.

Sampling. Sampling was found to be a significant moderator of third-person perception (Table 2). There was a significant difference in effect size between the random sample and nonrandom sample groups, $t(119) = 2.33, p < .05$, and the mean variance (mean $s_r^{2\,cor}$ = .028) was less than that for the overall r of the perceptual hypothesis. On average then, third-person perception was larger in nonrandom samples ($r = .56, SD = .14$) than in random samples ($r = .49, SD = .18$).

Respondent. Comparison of effect sizes between college student samples and noncollege student samples indicated that this variable was a significant moderator (Table 2). A significant difference test, $t(119) = 3.63, p < .001$, as well as a mean variance (mean $s_r^{2\ cor} = .024$) less than that for the overall r of the perceptual hypothesis, supported this finding. On average, college student samples ($r = .60$, $SD = .14$) yielded a greater third-person effect than noncollege student samples ($r = .49, SD = .18$).

Country. Country was not a significant moderator of third-person perception (Table 2). Significant variation was not found across studies, $t(119) = 1.45, ns$, and the mean variance found across studies (mean $s_r^{2\ cor} = .035$) was greater than the variance for the overall self–others correlation.

Desirability. Message desirability was not a significant moderator of third-person perception (Table 2). We found a significant difference between groups, $F(2, 104) = 12.69, p < .001$; Levene statistic of homogeneity of variances $(2, 104) = 2.28, ns$. A Scheffé post hoc test revealed that the average effect size for undesirable to be influenced ($r = .47, SD = .14$) was significantly different from the average effect size for desirable to be influenced ($r = .21, SD = .29$) and that the average effect size for desirable for be influenced was significantly different from the average effect size for neither desirable nor undesirable to be influenced ($r = .54$, $SD = .14$). However, the mean variation for all three groups (mean $s_r^{2\ cor} = .042$) was greater than that for the overall mean correlation of the self–others discrepancy.

Medium. Medium was not a significant moderator of third-person perception (Table 2). Although the mean corrected variance for the category (mean $s_r^{2\ cor} = .016$) was less than that for the overall mean correlation of the self–others discrepancy, no significant variation was found across categories, $F(3, 113) = .53, ns$.

Message. Type of message was a significant moderator of third-person perception (Table 2). The mean combined variance across studies (mean $s_r^{2\ cor} = .018$) was less than that for the overall perceptual hypothesis correlation coefficient. Additionally, there was a significant difference across groups, $F(5, 88) = 2.75, p < .05$; Levene $(5, 88) = .93, ns$, although the Scheffé test failed to identify significant differences between pairs of effect sizes at the $p < .05$ level.

DISCUSSION

This study used meta-analytic procedures to investigate claims of robust support for the third-person effect's perceptual hypothesis. This study also examined whether eight moderators addressed in the literature enhanced or diminished third-person perception. Data from 32 studies affirmed claims of at least moderate support for third-person perception. The overall effect size between estimated media effects on self and on others was $r = .50$ ($r^2 = .25$), indicating a moderate relationship (Guilford, 1956). Compared to other meta-analyses in mass communication, this effect size is rather substantial. For instance, Paik and Comstock (1994) reported an r of .31 for the effect of television violence on antisocial behavior; Allen et al. (1995) reported an r of .13 for the effect of pornography on aggression; and Glynn et al. (1997), examining the spiral of silence, another perceptual theory, reported an r of .05 between perceptions of public opinion support and willingness to speak out.

The analyses yielded three significant moderators: type of sampling, type of respondent, and type of message. The findings that nonrandom samples and student samples yielded greater third-person perception than random samples and nonstudent samples are intriguing and perhaps disturbing. From a theoretical perspective, research suggests that respondents with high levels of self-assessed knowledge, such as college students who are often studied in nonrandom samples, might exhibit greater third-person perception because they evaluate themselves as smarter than other people. An intriguing explanation grounded in self-assessed knowledge (Driscoll & Salwen, 1997; Lasorsa, 1989) holds that college students may perceive that their educational status makes them smarter and less vulnerable to harmful media messages than others. It is also possible that the students' tendency to conform might make them especially more likely to express the desirable response that they are more resistant to media messages than others.

From a methodological perspective, a more disturbing explanation would be that greater third-person perception among college students is not a moderating variable at all. Instead it may be attributable to study designs relying on student samples. Some researchers have claimed that the use of nonprobabilistic samples, and of college students in particular, can skew findings and threaten external validity (Abelman, 1996; Courtright, 1996; Potter et al., 1993). Others have argued that there is a role for student samples in communication research and that randomization techniques can minimize or solve the nonprobabilistic sampling issue (Basil, 1996; Lang, 1996).

In this regard it is important to note that method, coded as survey or experiment, was not a significant moderator. This is important because experiments are more likely than surveys to use student samples. Thus, it may not be the method but rather the use of student samples in experiments and surveys that causes generalization problems. Survey studies that use student samples are especially problematic because in surveys, unlike experiments, the primary goal is to ensure external validity. Experimental researchers who often use student samples would argue that, despite problems associated with external validity, their goal is to secure internal validity and determine whether variables are causally related (Lang, 1996; Sparks, 1995).

Although message content was found to be a significant moderator, the importance of this finding is mitigated by the fact that the post hoc test produced nonsignificant differences between pairs of correlation coefficients. Therefore, this moderator is at best ambiguous. The related variable of message desirability was not a significant moderator. This was somewhat surprising because researchers believe that third-person perception is a function of desirability to be influenced (Gunther, 1995; Gunther & Thorson, 1992; Thorson & Coyle, 1994). It is possible that the desirable messages in the research were not perceived as desirable, or at least not perceived as desirable as the undesirable messages were perceived as undesirable. In fact, measurement of perceptions of messages as desirable or undesirable is problematic because message desirability is usually assumed without obtaining respondents' opinions. This underscores our earlier point about the need for researchers to directly obtain respondents' perceptions of issue or message desirability rather than ad hoc assume desirability.

What does this study imply regarding the other nonsignificant moderators? Third-person perception was not moderated by country, operationalized as studies conducted in the United States and other nations. Although the number of foreign studies is small, and perhaps differences by national settings may yet emerge as more studies in different countries are conducted, this finding suggests that third-person perception might be an enduring psychological characteristic that holds across national settings and social structures. As more studies are conducted in foreign countries, it will be necessary to move beyond a U.S.–non-U.S. dichotomy and distinguish among nations and aspects of national settings (e.g., democratic, authoritarian, First World, Third World, standard of living, amount of press freedom, availability of media, level of development, etc.) that may explain national differences.

Medium was also a nonsignificant moderator. In one sense this is surprising because it might be argued that the assumed ubiquity and pervasiveness of television makes this medium more influential and persuasive than print media. On the other hand, from a perceptual perspective, because consumers of print media might see themselves as smarter than nonprint users, they might exhibit greater third-person perception (Salwen, 1998).

The fact that source, coded as published or unpublished, was not a significant moderator casts doubt on the common wisdom associated with the file drawer problem. Perhaps too much is made of the file drawer problem. Certainly more research is needed to determine whether it is simply an untested truism in the academy. Perhaps journal editors are more open to well-designed studies than is often thought, even if results fail to attain significance. One would hope that this is the case. The publication of well-designed studies with nonsignificant findings can contribute to our knowledge. Likewise, perhaps unpublished studies remain unpublished simply because they are more likely to be written by students—especially theses and dissertations—who do not have as much of an interest and a career stake in journal publication as faculty do. Finally, in terms of coding this variable, a caveat is in order. Many unpublished studies become published studies, underscoring the variability of this moderator. During the course of data gathering we had to recode studies when unpublished conference papers were published in journals, and the recoding sometimes changed significance. We expect that several unpublished studies will be published by the time this article is in print.

A limitation of this study is that it did not examine the behavioral hypothesis due to the dearth of behavioral studies and because behavioral studies often fail to report statistics suitable for meta-analysis. Although it is important to study the perceptual hypothesis because perceptions precede behaviors, the behavioral hypothesis makes the third-person effect relevant to social researchers and media practitioners. For example, the behavioral hypothesis offers an intriguing explanation of public support for media censorship—people support censorship to "protect" others from harmful media messages (Rojas, Shah, & Faber, 1996; Salwen, 1998; Salwen & Driscoll, 1996). Another limitation associated with meta-analyses is that results are often based on small sample sizes of studies (not effect sizes). The relatively small number of studies means that the publication of even a few new studies can impact the overall findings and alter outcomes. As noted, we became especially aware of this limitation during the course of this study when we coded the source variable.

So what do our findings mean? They affirm that the third-person effect's perceptual hypothesis is a moderate to robust finding, not only in terms of the consistency of the findings but also in the overall effect size. They also affirm that moderators can affect third-person perception. The message moderator indicates that researchers need to be aware how issue characteristics might affect third-person perception. The fact that sampling and types of respondents might moderate the effect warns of the need to be cautious when deviating from traditional random sampling with a general population. The fact that these methodological moderators were significant warns third-person effect researchers to be extra careful because other methodological matters such as question wording or sample size might affect outcomes.

Although desirability was not a significant moderator, we noted dissatisfaction with past conceptualizations and operationalizations of message desirability. Desirability is still an important variable worth studying, although more creative ways of studying this variable are needed. Finally, although not part of our meta-analysis, we feel the need to comment on the use of theory in third-person effect research. Studies that drew on attribution theory, biased optimism, and other theories used them as theoretical rationales to gird third-person perception. Third-person effect research might profit if it went further and borrowed some of the operational measures and procedures in these theory-oriented bodies of research to more convincingly demonstrate the link between third-person perception and psychological theories.

We conclude with a comment of methodological nature regarding the use of meta-analysis. As Glynn et al. (1997) suggested, it would be helpful to meta-analysts if statistical data were reported in a manner that facilitated their combination.

In many cases this would simply entail reporting a mean and standard deviation for the groups being compared. As such, presenting empirical research results in a manner that enables the effective combination and comparison of equivocal findings seems essential.

ACKNOWLEDGMENT

We acknowledge the insightful comments of the anonymous reviewers of this article.

REFERENCES

References marked with an asterisk indicate studies included in the meta-analysis.

Abelman, R. (1996). Can we generalize from Generation X? Not! *Journal of Broadcasting & Electronic Media, 40,* 441–446.
Allen, M., D'Alessio, D., & Brezgel, K. (1995). A meta-analysis summarizing the effects of pornography: II. Aggression after exposure. *Human Communication Research, 22,* 258–283.
*Baldwin, T. M. (1991). Response to an earthquake prediction in Southeast Missouri: A study in pluralistic ignorance (Doctoral dissertation, Southern Illinois University, Carbondale, 1991). *Dissertation Abstracts International, 53,* 3025.
Basil, M. D. (1996). The use of student samples in communication research. *Journal of Broadcasting & Electronic Media, 40,* 431–440.
Bereck, S. R., & Glynn, C. J. (1993, May). *Interpersonal interaction and the third-person effect in potential first time presidential election voters.* Paper presented at the annual meeting of the American Association for Public Opinion Research, St. Charles, IL.
Brosius, H., & Engel, D. (1996). The causes of third-person effects: Unrealistic optimism, impersonal impact, or generalized negative attitudes towards media influence? *International Journal of Public Opinion Research, 8,* 142–162.
Brown, J. D. (1986). Evaluations of self and others: Self-enhancement biases in social judgments. *Social Cognition, 4,* 353–376.
Cohen, J., Mutz, D., Price, V., & Gunther, A. (1988). Perceived impact of defamation. *Public Opinion Quarterly, 52,* 161–173.
Courtright, J. A. (1996). Rationally thinking about nonprobability. *Journal of Broadcasting & Electronic Media, 40,* 414–421.
Culbertson, H. M., & Stempel, G. H. (1985). Media malaise: Explaining personal optimism and societal pessimism about health care. *Journal of Communication, 35*(2), 180–190.
Davison, W. P. (1983). The third-person effect in communication. *Public Opinion Quarterly, 47,* 1–15.
Davison, W. P. (1996). The third-person effect revisited. *International Journal of Public Opinion Research, 8,* 113–119.
*Driscoll, P. D., & Salwen, M. B. (1997). Self-perceived knowledge of the O. J. Simpson trial: Third-person perception and perceptions of guilt. *Journalism & Mass Communication Quarterly, 74,* 541–556.
*Duck, J. M., & Mullin, B. (1995). The perceived impact of the mass media: Reconsidering the third-person effect. *European Journal of Social Psychology, 25,* 77–95.
Duck, J. M., Terry, D. J., & Hogg, M. A. (1995). The perceived influence of AIDS advertising: Third-person effects in the context of positive media content. *Basic and Applied Social Psychology, 17,* 305–325.

*Faber, R. J., Shah, D., Hanyoun, S., & Rojas, H. (1997). *Advertising censorship: Factors accounting for a willingness to restrict commercial speech for legal products.* Manuscript submitted for publication.

Fields, J., & Schuman, H. (1976). Public beliefs about the beliefs of the public. *Public Opinion Quarterly, 40,* 427–448.

Glynn, C. J., Hayes, A. F., & Shanahan, J. (1997). Perceived support for one's opinions and willingness to speak out: A meta-analysis of survey studies on the "spiral of silence." *Public Opinion Quarterly, 61,* 452–463.

*Glynn, C. J., & Ostman, R. E. (1988). Public opinion about public opinion. *Journalism Quarterly, 65,* 299–306.

Glynn, C. J., Ostman, R., & McDonald, D. (1995). Opinions, perception, and social reality. In T. Glasser & C. Salmon (Eds.), *Public opinion and the communication of consent* (pp. 249–277). New York: Guilford.

Guilford, J. P. (1956). *Fundamental statistics in psychology and education.* New York: McGraw-Hill.

Gunther, A. (1991). What we think others think: Cause and consequence in the third-person effect. *Communication Research, 18,* 355–372.

*Gunther, A. (1995). Overrating the X-rating: The third person perception and support for censorship of pornography. *Journal of Communication, 45*(1), 27–38.

*Gunther, A. C., & Ang, P. H. (1996). Public perception of television influence and opinions about censorship in Singapore. *International Journal of Public Opinion Research, 8,* 248–265.

Gunther, A. C., & Mundy, P. (1993). Biased optimism and the third-person effect. *Journalism Quarterly, 70,* 58–67.

Gunther, A. C., & Thorson, E. (1992). Perceived persuasive effects of product commercials and public service announcements: Third-person effects in new domains. *Communication Research, 19,* 574–596.

Heider, F. (1958). *The psychology of interpersonal relations.* New York: Wiley.

*Hitchon, J. C., Chang, C., & Harris, R. (1997). Should women emote? Perceptual bias and opinion change in response to political ads for candidates of different genders. *Political Communication, 14,* 49–69.

*Hoffner, C., Plotkin, R. S., Buchanan, M., Schneider, S., Ricciotti, L. A., Kowalczyk, L., Silberg, K., & Pastorek, A. (1997, May). *The third-person effect in perceptions of the influence of television violence.* Paper presented at the annual meeting of the Association for Education in Journalism and Mass Communication, Montreal, Canada.

Holsti, O. R. (1969). *Content analysis for the social sciences and humanities.* Reading, MA: Addison-Wesley.

Hoorens, V., & Ruiter, S. (1996). The optimal impact phenomenon: Beyond the third-person effect. *European Journal of Social Psychology, 26,* 599–610.

Hovland, C. I. (1963). Reconciling conflicting results derived from experimental studies of attitude change. In E. P. Hollander & R. G. Hunt (Eds.), *Current perspectives in social psychology* (pp. 378–389). New York: Oxford University Press.

*Hu, Y. W., & Wu, Y. C. (1996, August). *Testing a theoretical model on the third person effect: Perceived impacts of election polls.* Paper presented at the annual meeting of the Association for Education in Journalism and Mass Communication, Anaheim, CA.

*Hu, Y. W., & Wu, Y. C. (1998, August). *The "critics," "believers," and "outsiders" of election polls: Comparing characteristics of the third-person effect, first-person effect and consensus effect.* Paper presented at the annual meeting of the Association for Education in Journalism and Mass Communication, Baltimore.

Hunter, J. E., & Schmidt, F. L. (1990). *Methods of meta-analysis: Correcting error and bias on research findings.* London: Sage.

Hunter, J. E., Schmidt, F. L., & Jackson, G. B. (1982). *Meta-analysis: Cumulating research findings across studies.* New York: Sage.
*Innes, J. M., & Zeitz, H. (1988). The public's view of the impact of the mass media: A test of the "third person" effect. *European Journal of Social Psychology, 18,* 457–463.
Jeffres, L. W. (1997). *Mass media effects* (2nd ed.). Prospect Heights, IL: Waveland.
Jones, E. E., & Nisbett, R. E. (1972). The actor and the observer: Divergent perceptions of the causes of behavior. In E. E. Jones, D. E. Kanouse, H. H. Kelley, R. E. Nisbett, S. Valins, & B. Weiner (Eds.), *Attribution: Perceiving the causes of behavior* (pp. 79–94). Morristown, NJ: General Learning.
*Kashima, Y. (1990). *Third-person effect of the mass media: A study in a community setting.* Unpublished master's thesis, University of Wisconsin, Madison.
Kim, M. S., & Hunter, J. E. (1993). Attitude–behavior relations: A meta-analysis of attitudinal relevance and topic. *Journal of Communication, 43*(1), 101–142.
Lang, A. (1996). The logic of using inferential statistics with experimental data from nonprobability samples: Inspired by Cooper, Dupagne, Potter, and Sparks. *Journal of Broadcasting & Electronic Media, 40,* 422–430.
Lasorsa, D. L. (1989). Real and perceived effects of "Amerika." *Journalism Quarterly, 66,* 373–378, 529.
Lasorsa, D. L. (1992). How media affect policymakers: The third-person effect. In J. D. Kennamer (Ed.), *Public opinion, the press and public policy* (pp. 163–175). New York: Praeger.
Lee, C., & Yang, S. (1996, August). *Third-person perception and support for censorship of sexually explicit visual content: A Korean case.* Paper presented at the annual meeting of the Association for Education in Journalism and Mass Communication, Anaheim, CA.
*Lo, V., & Paddon, A. R. (1998, August). *The third-person perception and support for restrictions of pornography: Some methodological problems.* Paper presented at the annual meeting of the Association for Education in Journalism and Mass Communication, Baltimore.
Mason, L. (1995). Newspaper as repeater: An experiment on defamation and the third-person effect. *Journalism & Mass Communication Quarterly, 72,* 610–620.
*Matera, F. R., & Salwen, M. B. (1997, May). *Issue salience and the third-person effect: Perceptions of illegal immigration.* Paper presented at the annual meeting of the International Communication Association, Montreal, Canada.
*McLeod, D. M., Eveland, W. P., Jr., & Nathanson, A. I. (1997). Support for censorship of violent and misogynic rap lyrics: An analysis of the third-person effect. *Communication Research, 24,* 153–174.
Morgan, M., & Shanahan, J. (1997). Two decades of cultivation research: An appraisal and meta-analysis. In B. R. Burleson (Ed.), *Communication yearbook 20* (pp. 1–45). Thousand Oaks, CA: Sage.
Mutz, D. C., & Soss, J. (1997). Reading public opinion: The influence of news coverage on perceptions of public sentiment. *Public Opinion Quarterly, 61,* 431–451.
Noelle-Neumann, E. (1974). The spiral of silence: A theory of public opinion. *Journal of Communication, 24*(2), 43–51.
Ognianova, E., Meeds, R., Thorson, E., & Coyle, J. (1996, August). *Political adwatches and the third-person effect.* Paper presented at the annual meeting of the Association for Education in Journalism and Mass Communication, Anaheim, CA.
O'Gorman, H., & Garry, S. (1976). Pluralistic ignorance—A replication and extension. *Public Opinion Quarterly, 40,* 449–458.
Paik, H., & Comstock, G. (1994). The effects of television violence on antisocial behavior: A meta-analysis. *Communication Research, 21,* 516–546.
*Park, J. S. (1985). Pluralistic ignorance and third-person effect of the mass media in the process of public opinion formation. (Doctoral dissertation, Ohio University, 1985). *Dissertation Abstracts International, 46,* 547.
Perloff, R. M. (1989). Ego-involvement and the third person effect of televised news coverage. *Communication Research, 16,* 236–262.

Perloff, R. M. (1993). Third-person effect research 1983–1992: A review and synthesis. *International Journal of Public Opinion Research, 5,* 167–184.
Perloff, R. M. (1996). Perceptions and conceptions of political media impact: The third-person effect and beyond. In A. N. Crigler (Ed.), *The psychology of political communication* (pp. 177–191). Ann Arbor: University of Michigan Press.
Potter, W. J., Cooper, R., & Dupagne, M. (1993). The three paradigms of mass media research in mainstream communication journals. *Communication Theory, 3,* 317–335.
*Price, V., Huang, L., & Tewksbury, D. (1997). Third-person effects of news coverage: Orientations toward media. *Journalism & Mass Communication Quarterly, 74,* 525–540.
*Price, V., & Tewksbury, D. (1996). Measuring the third-person effect of news: The impact of question order, contrast and knowledge. *International Journal of Public Opinion Research, 8,* 120–141.
*Price, V., Tewksbury, D., & Huang, L. N. (1996, May). *Denying the Holocaust: Third-person effects and decisions to publish a controversial advertisement.* Paper presented at the annual meeting of the American Association for Public Opinion Research, Salt Lake City, UT.
*Rojas, H. (1994). *Censorship and the third-person effect in mass communication.* Unpublished master's thesis, University of Minnesota, St. Paul.
*Rojas, H., Shah, D. V., & Faber, R. J. (1996). For the good of others: Censorship and the third-person effect. *International Journal of Public Opinion Research, 8,* 162–185.
Rosenthal, R. (1984). *Meta-analytic procedures for social research.* Beverly Hills, CA: Sage.
Ross, L. (1977). The intuitive psychologist and his shortcomings: Distortions in the attribution process. In L. Berkowitz (Ed.), *Advances in experimental social psychology* (pp. 173–220). New York: Academic.
*Rucinski, D., & Salmon, C. T. (1990). The "other" as vulnerable voter: A study of the third-person effect in the 1988 U.S. presidential campaign. *International Journal of Public Opinion Research, 2,* 343–368.
*Salwen, M. B. (1998). Perceptions of media influence and support for censorship: The third-person effect in the 1996 presidential election. *Communication Research, 25,* 259–285.
Salwen, M. B., & Driscoll, P. D. (1996, August). *Self-perceived knowledge and the third-person effect: Media influence during the O. J. Simpson trial.* Paper presented at the annual meeting of the Association for Education in Journalism and Mass Communication, Anaheim, CA.
*Salwen, M. B., Dupagne, M., & Paul, B. (1998, August). *Perceptions of media power and moral influence: Issue legitimacy and the third-person effect.* Paper presented at the annual meeting of the Association for Education in Journalism and Mass Communication, Baltimore.
Sears, D. O., & Freedman, J. L. (1967). Selective exposure to information: A critical review. *Public Opinion Quarterly, 31,* 194–213.
*Shah, D. V., Faber, R. J., Hanyoun, S., & Rojas, H. (1997, August). *Censorship of political advertising: A third-person effect.* Paper presented at the annual meeting of the Association for Education in Journalism and Mass Communication, Chicago.
Sparks, G. G. (1995). Comments concerning the claim that mass media research is "prescientific": A response to Potter, Cooper, and Dupagne. *Communication Theory, 5,* 273–280.
Standley, T. C. (1994). *Linking third-person effect and attribution theory.* Unpublished master's thesis, Southern Methodist University, Dallas, TX.
*Stenbjerre, M. N. (1997). *A social categorization model of the third-person effect in mass communication.* Unpublished master's thesis, Cornell University, Ithaca, NY.
*Stenbjerre, M., & Leets, L. (1997). *On the anatomy of the third-person effect.* Manuscript submitted for publication.
*Stenbjerre, M., & Leets, L. (1998, July). *Central and peripheral routes to the third-person effect: Media effects attribution to self and others as a function of message elaboration.* Paper presented at the annual meeting of the International Communication Association, Jerusalem.

Svenson, O. (1981). Are we all less risky and more skillful than our fellow drivers? *Acta Psychologica, 47,* 693–708.

Thorson, E., & Coyle, J. (1994). The third person effect in three genres of commercials: Product and greening ads, and public service announcements. In K. King (Ed.), *Proceedings of the American Academy of Advertising* (pp. 103–112). Athens: University of Georgia.

*Tiedge, J. T., Silverblatt, A., Havice, M. J., & Rosenfeld, R. (1991). Discrepancy between perceived first-person and perceived third-person mass media effects. *Journalism Quarterly, 68,* 141–154.

Tracz, S. M. (1984). The effect of the violation of the assumption of independence when combining correlation coefficients in a meta-analysis (Doctoral dissertation, Southern Illinois University, Carbondale, 1984). *Dissertation Abstracts International, 56,* 688.

Tyler, T. R., & Cook, F. L. (1984). The mass media and judgments of risk: Distinguishing impact on personal and societal level judgments. *Journal of Personality and Social Psychology, 47,* 693–708.

Vallone, R. P., Ross, L., & Lepper, M. R. (1985). The hostile media phenomenon: Biased perception and perceptions of media bias in coverage of the Beirut massacre. *Journal of Personality and Social Psychology, 49,* 577–585.

Vidmar, N., & Rokeach, M. (1974). Archie Bunker's bigotry: A study in selective perception and exposure. *Journal of Communication, 24*(1), 124–137.

*Wang, H. (1995). The third-person effect in Taiwan (Doctoral dissertation, University of Wisconsin, Madison, 1995). *Dissertation Abstracts International, 56,* 4598.

Ware, W., & Dupagne, M. (1994). Effects of U.S. television programs on foreign audiences: A meta-analysis. *Journalism Quarterly, 71,* 947–959.

Weinstein, N. (1980). Unrealistic optimism about future life events. *Journal of Personality and Social Psychology, 39,* 806–820.

Weinstein, N. D., & Klein, W. M. (1996). Unrealistic optimism: Present and future. *Journal of Social and Clinical Psychology, 15,* 1–8.

Weinstein, N. D., & Lachendro, E. (1982). Egocentrism as a source of unrealistic optimism. *Personality and Social Psychology Bulletin, 8,* 195–200.

White, H. A. (1995, August). *Issue involvement and argument strength as mediating factors in the third-person effect.* Paper presented at the annual meeting of the Association for Education in Journalism and Mass Communication, Washington, DC.

White, H. A. (1997). Considering interacting factors in the third-person effect: Argument strength and social distance. *Journalism & Mass Communication Quarterly, 74,* 557–564.

Whitman, D. (1996, December 16). I'm OK, you're not. *U.S. News & World Report, 121,* 24–30.

Wolf, F. M. (1986). *Meta-analysis: Quantitative methods for research synthesis.* London: Sage.

*Youn, S., Faber, R. J., & Shah, D. V. (1998). *Attitudes toward gambling advertising and the third-person effect.* Manuscript submitted for publication.

Zebrowitz, L. A. (1990). *Social perception.* Pacific Grove, CA: Brooks/Cole.

Zimbardo, P. (1972). The tactics and ethics of persuasion. In B. T. King & E. McGinnies (Eds.), *Attitudes, conflict and social change* (pp. 88–114). New York: Academic.

Rebellion and Ritual in Disciplinary Histories of U.S. Mass Communication Study: Looking For "The Reflexive Turn"

Karin Wahl-Jorgensen
Institute for Communication Research
Department of Communication
Stanford University

In this article, I take a fresh look at disciplinary histories of American communication study. Specifically, the discussion groups disciplinary histories into 2 different kinds of narratives, referred to as biographical and intellectual histories. The first group has as its method biography, and focuses on the achievement of central individuals and the methodology of their research. It is argued that these accounts constitute rituals of disciplinary affirmation. The second group has as its method intellectual history, and focuses on the theoretical foundations of ideas taken up by communication scholars, tracing the relations among ideology, culture, technology, and communication. These accounts, on the other hand, are read as polite rebellions against received understandings of communication history.

In this article, I explore whether disciplinary histories represent a space for a reflexive turn in communication studies. The notion of reflexivity is borrowed from the work of sociologist Pierre Bourdieu (e.g., 1990, 1991), who called for an examination of our stakes as producers of knowledge of the past, and the conditions that brought about this past.

The discussion shows that the genre of disciplinary histories, as a self-interested discourse, does not allow for reflexivity because it falls short of considering our stakes as producers of knowledge—whether it be of a historical or scientific nature.

Requests for reprints should be sent to Karin Wahl-Jorgensen, Institute for Communication Research, Department of Communication, Stanford University, McClatchy Hall, Stanford, CA 94030. E-mail: karinwj@leland.stanford.edu

It has become fashionable for communication scholars to turn to introspection. As our discipline has grown older and gained the dignity of an established past, we have become increasingly concerned with its history (cf. Robinson, 1996, p. 157; Wartella, 1996, p. 169). It seems that with age comes the realization of mortality, and with it, the need for reflection (for a comparison with similar claims, see Hardt, 1992, chap. 1). Since the 1983 special issue of *Journal of Communication* (Gerbner, 1983) on "Ferment in the Field" put intradisciplinary debate on the agenda, scholars have initiated more systematic efforts to identify the epistemological and institutional foundations of communication research. They have done so by publishing an array of books, articles, and chapters, and holding panels and symposia to ascertain and negotiate the state of communication research. In the accelerating introspection, communication study has been transformed into a polite intellectual battlefield. As the discipline undergoes construction, reconstruction, and deconstruction, its boundaries are hotly delineated and contested, and its territory fought over (e.g., see Dervin, Grossberg, O'Keefe, & Wartella, 1989; Gerbner, 1983). The debate circles around the problem of what communication study as a discipline is and what—if at all—it should be.

In this article, I seek to both contribute to and interrogate the assumptions of this debate by honing in on the manifestations of disciplinary anxiety in histories of U.S. mass communication research. Although a variety of epistemological and methodological approaches have been accommodated under the broad label of mass communication research, the disciplinary debates have focused on attempts from each of the competing camps at legitimating their own approach. To refashion Peters's (1986a) observation, the historical accounts have as their subtext the "transformation of communication research from an intellectual to an institutional entity" (p. 537). Frequently, the rhetoric of institutional consolidation has been rooted in the question of how communication research came about, and what it has been. In this article, I use disciplinary histories to explore the intellectual implications of a fundamental epistemological split within the discipline of mass communication study: that between scholars who locate themselves within a social scientific tradition, and those who work within the humanities—roughly speaking, an epistemological difference that can be traced back to the split between administrative and critical research that Lazarsfeld (1941) so aptly captured. It does so by analyzing and critiquing historical narratives produced with the ambition of telling the comprehensive history of mass communication research in the United States, and written by scholars within the discipline.[1] They are viewed as disciplinary artifacts, as political arguments about how we should conduct our research.

---

[1]Czitrom (1982), who wrote the rightfully prominent communication history *Media and the American Mind,* which links the development of technologies to the intellectual trajectory of communication study, is a historian and thus outside the field of mass communication, and his account is therefore not included in this study.

Although the accounts picked for this analysis are not the only ones to tell the history of mass communication research, they are picked because they provide the most fertile ground for an assessment of claims about where the discipline has been and where it is going. To be more specific, I focus on complete histories of mass communication research, covering the trajectory from its inception to the present. The histories picked for this analysis offer us a myth of origin as an organizing framework, an analysis of subsequent events, and a projection of the future of the field on this basis (cf. Novick, 1988, p. 4).

There is no doubt that this focus excludes a range of important histories of mass communication research. It leaves out sophisticated and compelling, but more narrow accounts, such as Simpson's (1994) work on the relation between the Cold War psychological warfare effort and mass communication research in the period between 1945 and 1960, which makes important contributions toward a nuanced understanding of the history and toward critiquing already-existing accounts. Histories that detail the evolution of particular research specialties, such as political communication (Chaffee & Hochheimer, 1985) or children and television (Wartella & Reeves, 1985), are excluded because they do not seek to carve out an identity for the whole of the discipline of mass communication research. A range of excellent articles, such as Carey's (1992, 1996) work on the Chicago School of Sociology, and Peters's (1986a, 1986b, 1993, 1995) intellectual-historical writings remind us of the complexities of history writing in outlining the evolution and continuity of ideas but look at specific moments in the history of mass communication research. Likewise, chronological literature reviews of specific periods of communication research, such as Delias's (1987) comprehensive and excellent "Communication Research: A History" that traces research in the period 1945 to 1970, are not analyzed here because they focus on a particular period of mass communication research. Although they tell us where we come from, these tales are not linked to claims about where we should be going. The histories examined here, on the other hand, point to desirable futures with reference to both the past and the present.[2] Finally, it is worth noting that the emphasis on histories that are concerned with the work of mass communication scholars excludes the history of speech communication—a diverse area with a longer and more complicated historical trajectory than that traced here (e.g., Benson, 1985).

The histories examined here take as their vantage points the assumption that mass communication research emerged as a discipline at major U.S. universities in the 1940s. They are often selected as undergraduate and graduate textbooks for courses on the history of mass communication research and are read by a broad range of scholars within the field. They are sold as the tools of socializing mass

---

[2]At the time of submission of this article, Peters's (1999) intellectual history of communication was just about to be released from the publisher, and therefore, regretfully, did not make it into this discussion.

communication scholars from within the discipline. In this regard, they are central to our self-understanding and self-definition.

Although these histories engage in the project of advancing unity in the messy field of mass communication study by providing a tale of coherence to describe it, this article seeks to investigate the histories as discourses of disparate theoretical perspectives and approaches, to understand which assumptions about mass communication, and about knowledge in general, separate them, and which unite them. Although these accounts, like those of all communication scholars, acknowledges the consequentiality of communication (Sigman, 1995), and see communication as a "fundamental mode of explanation" (Deetz, 1994, p. 568; see also Craig, 1999), they do not agree on what communication means and how it should be studied.

Specifically, the discussion groups disciplinary histories into two different kinds of narratives, referred to as *biographical* and *intellectual histories*. The first group, written by authors who primarily work in a social scientific tradition, has as its method biography and focuses on the achievement of central individuals and the methodology of their research.[3] The second group, coming out of scholarship within the humanities, has as its method intellectual history and focuses on the theoretical foundations of ideas taken up by communication scholars, emphasizing a philosophical mode of argument (cf. Hardt, 1992; Schiller, 1996). This simplified typology does not imply that biographical accounts are, by their very nature, devoid of intellectual history, and it does not imply that their intellectual counterparts have completely evacuated biography from their domain. Instead, the distinction is useful for the purposes of understanding the dominant mode of discourse characterizing each of the historical accounts examined here: It describes a particular way of telling our stories and justifying our existence, and one that seeks, implicitly or explicitly, to guide our inquiry.

The distinction is specific to our field: In general a biographical approach does not necessarily preclude a history of ideas, and vice versa. Disciplinary historians often blend together the two approaches and let each of them inform the other. Jay's (1993) lifelong preoccupation with the history of the Frankfurt School, Novick's (1988) account of the history of historical objectivity, and Ross's (1991) disciplinary history of the social sciences are all examples of work that easily move back and forth between biographical descriptions and the explication of ideas. These approaches seek to demonstrate how various influences of both an intellectual and a personal nature determine the development of disciplines within the academy. Nevertheless, in mass communication research, as we shall see, it happens so that the complete histories almost self-consciously place themselves in either camp (e.g., Hardt, 1992, pp. xi–xii; Rogers & Chaffee, 1994, p. 1; Schiller, 1996, p. xiii).

---

[3]In particular, as discussed later in more detail, Schramm and his students are often accredited with these accounts.

Their respective historiographic methods, in turn, are consequences of and have consequences for the mode of intellectual inquiry that they advance.

In this article, I investigate whether the production of historical accounts represents a possibility for a reflexive turn in communication studies, akin to that which has occurred in most other disciplines of the humanities and social sciences over the last 30 years.[4] The concept of reflexivity is used to understand the two different kinds of accounts already identified. The biographical accounts look back not primarily to reflect, but to provide us with a narrative of origins that we can celebrate and rally around as a ritual of disciplinary religion. They constitute, to put it in Novick's (1988) helpful term, history written to stabilize a field of inquiry. The intellectual histories, discussed synthetically toward the end of the article, represent a potential space for rebellious reflection on the conditions that gave rise to and shaped communication study. These histories, on the other hand, look at history as a way to mobilize a discipline (cf. Novick, 1988).

At the outset, it is worthwhile to stake out the nature and the limits of the claims made here. As a critical scholar, I enter into the scrutiny of historical accounts with my own set of predispositions: first of all, with a belief that looking at such stories from a politicized, reflexive approach is a useful activity; second, and perhaps most important, with a sympathy to projects that engage social, cultural, economic, and historical contexts in a critical fashion. The reading offered here should not be seen as an objective or authoritative package but rather as an attempt to raise some questions about what it means for a discipline to invent its own past, present, and future, and as an invitation to debate. I, then, reject the idea that there is such a thing as an epistemological view from nowhere, but I believe instead that all knowledge is situated and partial, and should be appreciated and critiqued with that in mind.

THE PLACE OF HISTORIES IN DISCIPLINARY DEBATES

Histories help us organize our activity by locating our roots. Our understanding of origins has led us, among other things, to current divisions into professional associations, to the naming of departments and journals, and the endowment of professorships (cf. Nothstine, Blair, & Copeland, 1994, pp. 21–22). More than that, debates among mass communication scholars have centered on legitimating and unifying the discipline. As universities experienced funding cuts throughout the 1980s, it became increasingly important for each discipline to justify its own existence, and in doing so, to define its core, its boundaries, and its unified and identifiable projects.[5]

---

[4]See, for example, Bernstein's (1976) introduction for a contextualization of the restructuring of social and political theory.

[5]Hardt (1992), for example, argued that the mission of communication studies "must be the integration of a number of disciplines and areas of intellectual endeavor under considerations like culture or society" (p. xiv). Similarly, Schramm (as cited in Chaffee & Rogers, 1997) argued that, in the face of the technological developments of the late 20th century, "there may now be especially good reason to re-

Adding to the strain of disciplinary neurosis, recent years have witnessed a shift in the priorities and interests of mass communication researchers: As the histories read here compellingly document, the discipline arose out of social and political concerns, in the hopes of addressing such urgent problems as those of disease epidemics, national security, news dissemination, and urban migration. The methods of empirical social science were uniquely suited for providing the answers that politicians, academics, and citizens alike were looking for, and mass communication was born as an instantaneously socially and politically relevant discipline, one whose central figures were also important contributors to policy decision making and consulting. Increasingly, as part of a larger shift away from positivism, mass communication researchers have turned to critical and cultural scholarship, located more firmly within a humanities tradition, and preoccupied with problems other than those of a policy-oriented or administrative nature (cf. Stripas, 1998). This development has engendered much richness and expansion in the scope of the field, but the move away from problems recognized as legitimate outside the academy has also increased the pressure to justify our existence and our interests, whether they be primarily social scientific or humanistic in shape.

Amid this ferment, histories carve out the lines of debate to justify particular versions of the field's mission. As Rosaldo (1993) wrote about intradisciplinary debates, the "material stakes in such battles variously include office space, funding for programs, curriculum development and faculty positions. More broadly at stake in the battle ... are competing political and intellectual visions" (p. 218). The debate between social scientists and humanities scholars within the field is as much a struggle for survival as it is an expression of intellectual and political views.

THE REFLEXIVE TURN

The production of disciplinary histories is here seen as a potential space for a reflexive turn in communication studies. The notion of reflexivity is borrowed from the work of Bourdieu (1991), who proposed that scholars of social theory should "uncover the social roots of [their] political and scientific dispositions, investments in the field, and even the purest of theoretical choices" (p. 385).[6] A commitment to self-critique, Bourdieu contended, is the bedrock of a socially responsible theory of

---

think our pattern of communication study in the direction of greater coherence and cohesiveness" (p. 119).

[6]Although sociology often parts ways with communication studies in terms of the research questions examined, it is assumed here that there are significant similarities between the concerns of sociology and those of communication that make relevant the "sociology of sociology" writing of Bourdieu (1991; Bourdieu & Wacquant, 1992): Both disciplines are broadly concerned with the study of human behavior, and like communication, sociology is a discipline that struggles with many of the same problems of epistemology that characterize our intradisciplinary debate.

knowledge, and strengthens the collective autonomy of the field of inquiry (Bourdieu, 1991, pp. 383–384). In particular, a reflexive approach to our disciplinary history is important because historical knowledge "releases us from the grip of an incorporated past" (Bourdieu, 1990, p. 184)—the unspoken limitations on our thought. As such, it can help us abandon false oppositions and divisions, and increase both the scope and the solidity of our knowledge (see also Bourdieu & Wacquant, 1992, pp. 17–39). More important, reflexivity interrogates the place of our scholarship in the field of practice—it moves toward asking the question of how research reflects or may translate into political action and commitment. At the level of disciplinary history, Bourdieu's argument calls for an examination of our stakes as producers of knowledge of the past and the conditions that brought about this past. Within our discipline, Carey (1992) poignantly called for an investigation of the "reflexive relationship of scholarship to society" (p. 94). He concocted a recipe for reflexivity in mass communication research in arguing that the:

> behavioral and cultural sciences should contain an analysis of ideology beyond the crude and reductive one they now have. But they should also make explicit their own ideological implications and persuasions and defend them on their own ground, not by pretending that "science says." (pp. 101–102)

The call for reflexivity lies at the heart of a revolution that has shaken the ground under the humanities and social sciences since the late 1960s. This revolution has turned the lens of academic inquiry inward, toward the scholar and his or her methods, and the political and social context of the academy.[7] As Bernstein (1976) convincingly showed, the ferment following the 1960s resulted in a rethinking of the basics of scholarly inquiry. Scholars began to raise questions "about the nature of human beings, what constitutes knowledge of society and politics, how this knowledge can affect the ways in which we shape our lives, and what is and ought to be the relation of theory and practice" (Bernstein, 1976, p. xiii). Across the disciplines, the grand narratives that had characterized academic inquiry were abandoned in favor of metacritique (Bernstein, 1976).[8] Among others, Rorty (1979) and Kuhn (1962) argued that scientific knowledge is located in scholarly communities defined by cultural and historical specificities, instead of coming out of nature or any metaphysical foundation. Kuhn pointed out that assent of the scientific community is the sine qua non of paradigm change. He saw truth as a constructed creature, born of discourse, and he placed the ultimate authority of epistemological debate with "the

---

[7]In other philosophical analyses of social theory, scholars such as Wittgenstein and Austin referred to this same tendency for reflection on literary production as the *linguistic turn*. For an overview, see Bernstein (1976, p. xvi).

[8]Consult also Marcus and Fischer (1986, chap. 2), where the authors argued that the recent years' upheaval in anthropology are part of a much larger crisis of representation in the humanities and social sciences.

techniques of persuasive argumentation effective within the quite special groups that constitute the community of scientists" (p. 94), or what Mohanty (1997) referred to as the "rhetorical and ideological underpinnings of scientific activity" (p. 167). The labor of knowledge maintenance and production takes place through the institution of the discipline. As Foucault (1979) and others argued, the idea of the discipline entails a notion of disciplining, of enforcement: an enforcement of boundaries of knowledge, a concerted effort at homogenizing and normalizing particular epistemological discourses, particular ways of knowing and translating ideas into research programs. To borrow Peters's (1993) observation, the idea of a discipline also calls for disciples, or for individuals devoted to the goals and assumptions of that tradition who can work toward its maintenance and perpetuation. Disciplinary histories play a central role in the maintenance and production of knowledge: They both hail disciples and enforce disciplinarity. In defining the canon in specific ways, the histories activate what Said (1983) referred to as "a blocking device for methodological and disciplinary self-questioning" (p. 22). Put differently, the disciplinary histories are weapons of epistemological policing and warfare, determining the way things should be based on they way they have been and are. Mass communication research is like a Rorschach test: It is whatever you see in it and make of it. The disciplinary boundaries are so poorly defined that the choices we make about what disciplinary territory to annex are profoundly political. As much as they represent a struggle for legitimacy within the discipline, such accounts also annex the territory of other disciplines, from political science, sociology, and psychology to cultural and critical studies and literary theory, in the quest to carve out an identity for mass communication research.

More than anything, disciplinary histories provide the leverage for particular understandings of rationality, or of what we understand as valid approaches to scholarly work (cf. Aronowitz, 1988, p. 8). They convince us to keep on doing what we are doing because it has been done that way for so long. The respective rationalities defended in the histories are exclusive ones that merely perpetuate the balkanization of the discipline. As we shall see, models of rationality are embedded in histories of communication study at two different levels: first, at the manifest, narrative level, where the stories told celebrate individuals and ideas belonging to the research tradition they advance; second, at the structural level, where the writers of the histories, in putting together their accounts, mimic the conventions of writing and the ways of knowing of the field in which they work and whose history they write. They adopt a form of historical discourse that serves as a stylistic legitimation of their own approach to communication study.

We should read the histories of communication research as disciplinary discourses that isolate certain aspects of the historical record by creating a model of what happened in the past through their representation of that past (cf. White, 1987, p. 2). In doing so, they justify and reproduce a particular version of the discipline's profile, whether it be one of behavioral social science, cultural studies, or critical scholarship. These texts, then, call for scholars to rally around their cause, and should be understood as arguments in the power struggle of mass communication research. Our disciplinary narratives are the products of a process of negotiating and mediating among what White called the historical field, the unprocessed historical record, other historical accounts, and an audience. Although the historical accounts examined here use as their raw material the same historical field and unprocessed historical record, and share some literature, they seek out very different audiences to legitimate their version of history.

ISSUES IN DISCIPLINARY HISTORY: UNCOVERING IDEOLOGY AND SUBJECTIVITY

Biographical Histories

The narrative level. The biographical histories of communication are Rogers's (1994) *A History of Communication Study*, and two works coauthored or edited by Rogers and Chaffee: the monograph "Communication and Journalism From 'Daddy' Bleyer to Wilbur Schramm" (Rogers & Chaffee, 1994) and *The Beginnings of Communication Study in America* (Chaffee & Rogers, 1997). *A History of Communication Study* links the thought that gave rise to the study of mass communication in the United States with the teachings of such scholars as Darwin, Marx, and Freud. Briefly put, the premise of this history is that Schramm was the founder of the field of social scientific communication study, and the book follows him "in this unique process of founding the new process of founding the new field of communication study and in gradually gaining its widespread acceptance in U.S. universities, initially in their schools of journalism" (Rogers, 1994, p. 445).

Rogers (1994) told his tale through the illustrative biographical anecdote. He showed the relevance of events, people, and places in the lives of individual scholars to their research projects, their careers, and the history of communication study. For example, Rogers explained the professional and life choices of Schramm by recounting, among other stories, how Schramm

> developed a severe stutter at age five due to an "amateurishly performed tonsillectomy." His speech difficulty was embarrassing to him and his family. ... Gradually Schramm learned to live with his stutter, which eventually became less pronounced. Nevertheless, his speech difficulty had an effect later in his life, eventually leading him into the field of communication for a second career. (p. 3)

The figure of Schramm as the catalyst of the field of communication stands at the center of what is both a personal biography and a narrative of disciplinary unity. The argument that Schramm "is ... the driving force behind the creation of communication study" (Rogers, 1994, p. 1) as a discipline within the social sciences, out of a tradition of journalism education, is elaborated in the *Journalism Monographs* volume "Communication and Journalism From 'Daddy' Bleyer to Wilbur Schramm," coauthored by Rogers and Chaffee (1994). This volume also uses a similar anecdotal and biographical approach to understanding the history of communication study. However, it stops short of offering a complete history of mass communication research, as its story comes to a close at around 1970. It is here seen as, first of all, one of the most elaborate attempts at offering an origins myth for our discipline. Second, and more important, it is treated as part of the elaborate historical narrative advanced in the other historical narratives crafted by the same authors.

The monograph traces the institutionalization of communication research in the United States, investigating the connections between Willard G. Bleyer, a Wisconsin journalism scholar, and a number of important figures in the early history of institutionalized communication research: Fred Siebert, Ralph Casey, Ralph Nafziger, Chilton Bush, and Wilbur Schramm. All of them were reporters early in life, and later on took up careers as journalism educators at large Midwestern universities. Rogers and Chaffee (1994) argued that these "linking figures, each an outstanding scholar in his own right, eventually institutionalized Schramm's vision of communication study within programs of journalism education built on the model they had learned from Bleyer" (p. 3). By telling stories of each individual scholar, Rogers and Chaffee drew conclusions about how particular events and relationships constituted the fabric of these men's personal and public lives to dispose them to pursue the particular career tracks and research interests that later were to define the field of mass communication research and, more broadly, communication studies.

A similar historiographic method characterizes *The Beginnings of Communication Study in America* (Chaffee & Rogers, 1997), the unfinished memoir of Wilbur Schramm. The first part of the book, written by Schramm, details the early history of mass communication research in the United States by mixing stories of institutional development at the University of Iowa, the University of Illinois, and Stanford University, with the personal biographies of the four "forefathers," Harold Lasswell, Paul Lazarsfeld, Kurt Lewin, and Carl Hovland. These forefathers of communication research, although educated and working before mass media began to interest social scientists, created its mold through their seminal work.[9] The second part of the book, written by Chaffee and Rogers, reenters Schramm into the equation of disciplinary history by telling his story as he had told those of the forefathers. The editors pointed out that Schramm's narrative had "left himself almost

---

[9]Schramm wrote about the forefathers that each of them

was extraordinarily prolific in the conduct of research and in the advancement of theory. Three of the four founded research and training institutes, and all four guided large numbers of students and exerted great influence on their colleagues. As many observers have said, they entered communication study at one stage of its development and left it at a new stage. (Chaffee & Rogers, 1997, p. 4)

completely out of his story of the beginnings of communication study in America" (Chaffee & Rogers, 1997, p. 125) except as a conversation partner of the forefathers. As a corrective, they set out to show that "Wilbur Schramm was the founder of communication study, not only in America but in the world" (p. 127). By a *founder*, Chaffee and Rogers (1997) referred to:

> the author of the first books to define the field; or the creator of the first university departments in the new field; or the teacher of the first generations of new scholars in the field (who then start new departments at other universities). (p. 129)

In other words, they concentrated on advancing the institution of mass communication research rather than simply the idea of it.

Disciplinary ritual and individual agency in biographical histories. A biographical metahistory of communication research hones in on how mass communication research has become an institutionalized part of the academy, having gained the territory of established departments in top universities over the last 50 years. It embarks on a search for origins, a move toward creating a disciplinary ritual. As Lipari (1999) suggested, a ritual is a "structured social and symbolic activity that invokes, demarcates, or celebrates a community's deepest and most closely held values, of what it holds to be sacred" (p. 88). Through rituals, we can strengthen communities by stressing "unity and similarity and minimize discord and differences" (p. 95). Durkheim (1971) observed that such rituals are central to the integration of individuals in a community, and therefore necessary for the health of that community. He argued that "there can be no society which does not feel the need of upholding and reaffirming at regular intervals the collective sentiments and collective ideas" (p. 89). At the same time, such rituals are inherently conservative and conformist in nature; they are designed to maintain and celebrate the status quo and hailing individuals to support it, rather than subvert it. As Knuf (1993) argued, "in the final analysis, sincere participation in a ritual amounts to a total submission of the individual to the external determinations of the larger social aggregate" (p. 92).

Thus, the search for a narrative of origins that can function as a disciplinary ritual is ultimately directed toward the naturalization, celebration, and maintenance of a unified epistemological vision, rather than an acknowledgment of difference and fragmentation. As Foucault (1972) argued in *The Archaeology of Knowledge*,

> In that field where we had become used to ... pushing back further and further the line of antecedents, to reconstituting traditions, to following evolutive curves, to projecting teleologies, and to having constant recourse to metaphors of life, we felt a particular repugnance to conceiving of difference, to describing separations and dispersions, to dissociating the reassuring form of the identical. (pp. 11–12)

The biographical accounts thus build the foundations for the kind of coherence needed for a field of inquiry to prosper (cf. Craig, 1999), but in doing so, they also inevitably gloss over differences, separations, and dispersions, all of which stand in the way of institutionalization.

As a result of the thematic orientation toward institutionalization, these accounts ground themselves in the spirit of particular times and places, re-creating the energy that brought about communication study. One can almost smell the chalk dust from the busy classrooms and sense the dynamism of narrow corridors crowded with important scholars who spent their hours oblivious to external concerns, sketching out the foundations of a new field. It is a folkloric tale that comes in a celebratory package—a ritual that attempts to create unity by building a sense of pride and collective memory of the achievements of the past.

In their closeness to the lives of people, the biographical histories are strongly individualistic in nature, and colored by a firm belief in human agency, to demonstrate how these individuals "entered communication study at one stage of its development and left it at a new stage. More accurately, the subjects entered the field before there was a field called communication research or communication study and they created one" (Schramm as cited in Chaffee & Rogers, 1997, p. 4). They tell the story of how the power of these outstanding individuals created the basis for the communication study as a discipline of behavioral science. By narrowing down history to the realm of individual action, the grounding of communication study in behavioral sciences is naturalized. Rogers (1994) spanned wide in his embrace of the European thinkers who were the forerunners to communication study to construct a narrative of origins that embraces the range of genius scholars who "changed the mind of the world with their revolutionary ideas about human behavior and society" (p. 33): Darwin, Marx, and Freud take center stage in this tale of "creative rebels in an intellectual sense, [who] violated the social norms of the European society in which they lived, and paid dearly for their intellectual radicalism" (p. 33).

Despite this inclusive gesture in embracing origins, Rogers's (1994) chapters on American communication study more narrowly describe the discipline as one of a positivist, empiricist science. Rogers spelled out his bias in his preface when he argued that the "history of communication study is the story of the social sciences, with important contributions also from biology, mathematics, and electrical engineering" (p. xiii). In pointing to these fields as the forebears of communication, Rogers put the premium on the scientificity of mass communication scholarship and its legitimate position within a long-standing system of research traditions. Rogers's discussion of critical scholarship fixes it outside the boundaries of communication inquiry, as a source of research questions for empirical scholars, rather than as a challenge to the dominance of social scientific scholarship:

> The tension between critical and empirical communication scholars in America poses a fruitful intellectual challenge; however, the conflict prevents the interesting leads

for communication study provided by the critical scholars from being investigated with the research methods and resources of the empirical school. (p. 125)

Schramm (as cited in Chaffee & Rogers, 1997) wrote, in explaining his pick of the four forefathers of communication studies that for "one thing, they emphasized the empirical approach to communication study more than did their predecessors. They borrowed from the intellectual tradition that had been growing up in the hard sciences and the social sciences" (p. 19). The passage offers a hint of the celebratory, rather than reflexive, mode of the biographical account. These accounts rightfully underscore and celebrate the social relevance of mass communication research in these early years, but there is little specific discussion of the fact that the rise of mass communication research was intrinsically tied to developments in American foreign policy, such as World War II and the Cold War.[10]

The convention of objectivity: Detachment as science. This tendency to stress science over politics, and consequently depoliticizing history, is but one manifestation of the workings of the convention of objectivity in the biographical stories. A central tenet of the objectivity that characterizes the behavioral paradigm within communication studies lies in the separation of science and history. As Bernstein (1976) pointed out, "social scientists came to view the history of their own disciplines through the spectacles of positivism" (p. 5). This belief, he argued, has led to a rejection of the history of ideas because "these traditional systems do not lend themselves to systematic, rigorous formulation by which they can be empirically tested" (p. 5). Social scientists are suspicious of connecting facts and values. The belief in the separation of communication theory from its political context undergirds the biographical histories and guides their configuration of the historical field in the direction of a decontextualized account of historical facts (for the intellectual historian's critique of the social science's strategy of ignoring the "structural underpinnings" of the media, see Robinson, 1988).

The decontextualization preserves the innocence and romanticism that makes for a good story, but sweeps away the factors that jumble a neat plot line. In his chronological literature review of communication research, Delia (1987) elaborated on the process of decontextualization inherent in what he referred to as the received

---

[10]In *Science of Coercion,* Simpson (1994) convincingly showed that "military, intelligence, and propaganda agencies ... helped bankroll substantially all of the post-World War II generation's research into techniques of persuasion, opinion measurement, interrogation, political and military mobilization, propagation of ideology, and related questions" (p. 4). Simpson pointed out that psychological warfare projects was one of the central themes of communication studies in the period between 1945 and 1960, and that Schramm, as a defining figure, played a particularly focal role in advancing government-directed research agendas (p. 5). For these reasons, he argued that communication researchers can essentially be seen as ideological workers. See chapter 8 for an in-depth discussion of Schramm's central role in the psychological warfare projects subsidized by the U.S. government.

history of communication study, by pointing to four parameters characterizing disciplinary canons, and perpetuated in historical accounts:

> (1) an identification of communication research with the study of the media of mass communication, (2) a presumption that the methods of communication research were the methods of social scientific research, (3) the treatment of communication research as an exclusively American research tradition, and (4) identification of the core concern of communication research as the processes by which communication messages influence audience members. (p. 21)

One way to naturalize a tale of these parameters is by packaging it in the history of individuals who, although they, too, are products of historical circumstances, embody these elements and explain how they came about.

As a result of the social scientific persuasion of these accounts, knowledge becomes a tangible, accessible commodity in the form of research procedures. Rogers and Chaffee (1994) explained that their

> approach to historiography assumes that great ideas are carried by people, and that biography is a useful way to understand the founding of an academic field. We find ideas in people, and we find ideas traveling between key people—those who originated them, those who refined them, and those who put them into practice. (p. 3)

It is the connections and continuities between these founding fathers and today's scholars that define the field of communication study. This theory of history presumes that only ideas carried by particular individuals and found in the documented contacts and connections between and among scholars qualify as history. This approach creates a parsimonious, manageable, and chartable understanding of the direction and linearity of historical forces, where the institutionalization of communication study can be adequately mapped onto flowcharts, graphs, and tables.[11] Although it represents a discussion and representation of history, it falls short of reflection. Instead, it advances a good story that can be told and retold. The myth becomes a way of constructing a language of powerful images and metaphors; a language that recalls the comforting and empowering stories of creation with which we make sense of the world or communication research (for a brief discussion of the role of myth in contemporary culture, see Barthes, 1995). This language shapes the tales of great men to suggest the victory of individual agency in the struggle for social scientific dominance.

The dimension of subjectivity: Personal experience as authority. In the biographical narratives, the ideal of an objective, empirically factual history is

---

[11]Both Rogers (1994) and Rogers and Chaffee (1994) detail their chronology in a range of tables and other forms of graphical illustrations.

held up as the yardstick. However, the project of objectivity is complicated by the entrance of subjectivity and individual experience. The writers of these histories (Schramm, Chaffee, and Rogers) are themselves prominent scholars, and students and friends of the individuals they identify as the founding figures. Parts of the historical accounts are based on their personal recollections, and occasionally, they surface in the stories as actors on the scene of history, as the students of great scholars, participants in meetings, or collaborators on research projects. Indeed, Chaffee and Rogers (1997) explained that their purpose "is to describe, based on our own recollections as well as the work of others, how Wilbur Schramm came to found the field he called communication study" (p. 1). By describing the field of communication through the tales of a small number of great individuals, situated in particular places, the writers of these accounts ultimately center themselves in the hierarchy of communication epistemologies and institutions featured in the narratives.

Rogers and Chaffee (1994) recognized that the unique, emotionally charged, and subjective contributions of the storytellers shape the historical account, yet they embraced the ideal of the impartial scholarly discourse. For example, they explained their method in the following terms:

> Although we have attempted to document, by either primary or secondary sources, our major points, we have also been participant observers in the historical process that we describe here. Because we have relied at points on our own recollections, and those of others we have known well over the years, this monograph is best understood as a personal document both in the sources we have developed and in our interpretation of events. Nonetheless, we offer it as a scholarly product that will help others in the field of communication to appreciate what went into its founding. (p. 1)

The authors' recognition of their presence on the scene of history is used as a means of disciplinary legitimation, but rarely for the purpose of reflection on the claims to disciplinarity. As Peters (1986a) suggested, using the example of Schramm's discussions of the development of communication theory, self-reflection can be used as a "tool of apologetics for the field's existence, [in which case it assumes] a public relations rather than an intellectual function" (p. 543). Such self reflection, in Schramm's hands, became a useful public relations tool for the discipline of mass communication research because it perpetuated "ingenious social research on social problems" (Peters, 1986a, p. 543) without necessarily interrogating the intellectual foundations of such social research. Self-reflection allows the author to speak from a position of undisputed—and rightfully so—epistemic authority, whereas the assumptions that underlie this authority are left untouched. Chaffee and Berger (1987) opened their influential essay, "What Communication Scientists Do," by pointing to the conscious choice of refraining from interrogating the assumptions of their branch of research:

> The concept of a science of human communication rests upon the optimistic assumption that behavior can be both understood and improved through systematic study. Further, it assumes that improvement must be based upon understanding, which is the primary goal of a science. Like all assumptions, these beliefs are not tested within the science itself. Instead they provide a working point of view, which derives its validity in the long run from the value of the knowledge produced. If we did not believe that we could understand human communication, and so perhaps improve upon it, we would not undertake scientific study with these goals in mind. (p. 99)

An important implication of these assumptions is the idea that a normative orientation entailed in the desire for social change and progress can peacefully coexist with a scientific enterprise, and that we should appreciate such goals on the basis of the value of the research, rather than on the basis of an a priori scrutiny that fails to appreciate the usefulness of research. It is a pragmatic understanding of research, but also a conservative one: What turns out to be valuable is compelling research, as judged by already-existing and always-perpetuated standards of excellence. This, in turn, implies that the ultimate judges of quality and truth in mass communication research are the established central figures; the broadly recognized experts. Foremost among these experts are those who brought the field into being and gave it prominence in the academy and the larger world.

Chaffee and Rogers (1997) wrote about finding the manuscript for Schramm's autobiographical history of communication research that there:

> were no footnotes or citations to be found, either in the computer files or elsewhere in the papers that he left. ... No one has ever been better qualified to write on the subject Schramm chose for this book. One of the most remarkable academic innovators ever known, he had been the central figure in the process embodied in this title. (p. ix)

Chaffee and Rogers thus suggested that the founder's personal authority and experience is worth more as a measure of validity than the scientificity inherent in the academic convention of footnotes and citations.

One way in which the tension between scientificity and subjectivity is resolved in the biographical histories is through a deliberate rejection of the project of reflexivity, in favor of crafting a disciplinary ritual that requires a high priest, or a mythical hero, to rally around. Rogers and Chaffee's (1994) monograph opens with the recognition that this:

> "received history" of Schramm's invention of the field was a concise tale, one that we recounted to our students and colleagues over the ensuing years. We are pleased to have become part of this history, and to have known its central figure both personally and professionally. ... As is often the case with one's favorite stories, though, it is not quite true—and certainly it is not the whole story. (pp. 1–3)

By recognizing the constructed nature of their "favorite story," they highlighted its usefulness as a convenient anecdote that legitimates communication studies in a concise, easily digestible form. This recognition is also important in exploring and staking out the limits of their claims. In effect, Rogers and Chaffee did not portend to write a soul-searching reflection on communication study—they did not wish to interrogate our understanding of the past, but share their remembrances of it. They gracefully acknowledged the interests they brought to the writing of the histories and shed some light—if subtly—on their own stakes in writing a disciplinary history. Although they did not delve into the claims they made about disciplinary history, they provided an important and difficult kind of reflexivity in addressing their own role in the construction of history, thereby recognizing that history is a creature of human invention.

The structure of the biographical history: The emphasis on the form of research. One of the greatest challenges of disciplinary history writing lies in integrating the description of historical circumstances with that of the development of theory and methodology. The biographical histories, couched in a social science tradition, tend to focus on the form of the research of the scholars they write about, rather than the ideas underlying their research (for a discussion on Freud's research methods in detail, see Rogers, 1994, pp. 70–77). When discussing particular works, the emphasis is placed on identifying and analyzing methodological innovation. It is clear from the narrative that the important contribution of research projects lies in methodologically advancing the study of communication. When theory is discussed, it is often couched in terms of the research questions of particular traditions. Rogers (1994) wrote of critical scholars that they "focus on emancipation. They ask: Who gains and who loses from social research?" (p. 123). Likewise, Chaffee and Rogers (1997) wrote about Merton's "Rovere" study of influence that "Merton and the bureau wanted the study to answer questions of greater generality: Who in a society has influence, over whom and for what, and how is such influence exerted?" (p. 59). The biographical authors imply, then, that knowledge of theory development is necessary to be able to apply the theory empirically. In other words, our concern with history can also help to train us in methodology (for a similar argument, see Bernstein, 1976, p. 15). This idea is echoed at the narrative level of the biographies. Schramm (as cited in Chaffee & Rogers, 1997) wrote about Hovland that:

> [He] had been running experiments to test theories about conditioned responses and rote learning at Yale. It was not a great stretch conceptually for him to turn his efforts to experimentation with military indoctrination films. ... Hovland's report *Experiments on Mass Communication* was the third of four volumes of a set edited by Stouffer and generally known as *The American Soldier*. Stouffer's own methodological brilliance shone through best in the fourth volume, which introduced the world to such innovative measurement techniques as Guttman scaling. (p. 34)

The passage celebrates the methodological flexibility of social scientific research. It points to the ways in which the method supersedes the underlying theory.

Hovland, as the master of experiments, skipped easily from one theory to the next. Stouffer's "methodological brilliance," manifested in his invention of "innovative measurement techniques" earns him a place in this history. Likewise, Schramm (as cited in Chaffee & Rogers, 1997) wrote about Merton's (Merton, Fiske, & Curtis, 1946) study of the famous 1939 telethon, hosted by Kate Smith, and designed to sell war bonds:

> Using survey data and intensive interviews, Merton went about finding why Smith's performance was so remarkable effective. The explanation was the chemistry of Smith's personality, the appeals that she used, and the situation in which the radio program was heard. The striking aspect of Merton's analysis was the skill with which the individual pieces of data were generalized into broad patterns of interwoven cognitions, values, affects, and behaviors. The book must have opened the eyes of many scholars to the close relationship between social psychological theory and field research. (p. 57)

Here, Merton et al.'s (1946) study is summed up in terms of the methods of "survey data and intensive interviews," of "explanation," "data generalized into broad patterns," and the "close relationship between social psychological theory and field research." The emphasis on method offers us an insight into the specificities of how this study was designed and how it revolutionized the methods of the discipline. In doing so, then, the structure of the biographical history valorizes and perpetuates a methodological preoccupation. It subtly constructs a rationality for the social science of mass communication research, one that is easily defensible as scientific and rigorous.

INTELLECTUAL HISTORIES

The Narrative Level: Contextualizing Communication Study

The other group of histories, here represented by Hardt's (1992) *Critical Communication Studies* and Schiller's (1996) *Theorizing Communication*, seeks to complicate the development of mass communication research by situating its history as an integral, if small part of a larger, dynamic context. Indeed, Schiller's (1996) *Theorizing Communication,* although identified as a history of communication study in the United States, casts its net much wider to form a comprehensive theory that integrates the concepts of communication and labor. Schiller examined the distinctions between manual and intellectual labor as they manifest themselves in the larger society as well as in the interests of mass communication researchers throughout the last 200 years of American history and the last 40 years of British history. In doing so, Schiller charted the continuity between the pragmatist philosophers of early 20th-century Chicago, to the early propaganda research of the interwar period, and finally on to the emergence of British cultural studies in Great Britain during the 1960s. As Peters (1998) noted in his review of *Theorizing Communication,*

> the book does not claim to be a complete history of everything relevant to theorizing communication. Feminism and face-to-face communication, for instance, both receive glancing treatment. Rather, it is a genealogy, focusing on mass communication, that aims to recover lost promises and diagnose wrong turns. The chief wrong turn in the history of communication theory is the loss of an adequate vision of labor. (p. 139)

Schiller (1996) suggested that the thought of communication study is fittingly understood to be a consequence of the inability "to integrate, or even to encompass, 'labor' and 'communication' within a single conceptual totality" (p. xi). In exploring what he saw as a false dualism between the two concepts, he called for the understanding of communication study from a "contextualist" approach to history. He explicitly articulated a desire for a reflexivity that derives from a consideration of the historical conditions under which our knowledge is produced—the intellectual labor of communication theory.[12] Schiller traced how events such as the introduction of the telegraph, the world wars, and the unrest of the 1960s have shaped our understanding of labor and communication and, more broadly, our intellectual history as researchers of communication and culture. In doing so, he centered, on the American side, on the work of such pragmatist thinkers as John Dewey, George Herbert Mead, and Ezra Park. Across the Atlantic, he focused on the cultural studies work of scholars like Stuart Hall and Raymond Williams. Seeking to create a unified tale of communication study, he drew an entirely different trajectory from that of the biographical scholars. It is one that criticizes the impartiality, or, as Hardt (1992) put it, "ahistorical nature" (p. 221) of the social sciences, and instead embraces the normative sensibility that has characterized critical and cultural scholarship.

Hardt's (1992) project was to "argue for the proximity of critical communication studies to social and political reality and its potential to contribute to the welfare of society" (p. xi). Although he pointed out in his introduction that he did not proclaim to write "a comprehensive intellectual history of communication and media studies, but rather an invitation to contemplate the need for such a history," (p. xi) he wove in a comprehensive range of mass communication research over time and through space. Like Schiller, he spanned the early 20th century Pragmatist school, the social science dominance of the World War II and Cold War eras, and the Frankfurt School and contemporary British cultural studies. In doing so, he probed our understanding of the categories of mass society and democracy, so central to a critical conception of mass communication. To understand the problems in-

---

[12]Schiller (1996) wrote that rippling "across the field of vision of communication study from generation to generation, the epic question of 'intellectual' labor has been episodically remodulated and reshaped" (p. 185).

herent in the desire to transplant critical and cultural scholarship to a U.S. context, he explored American communication scholars' appropriation of and response to European schools of thought. Ultimately, Hardt wished to show that the

> dilemma of American communication studies continues to lie in its failure to comprehend and overcome the limitations of its own intellectual history, not only by failing to address the theoretical and methodological problems of an established academic discipline, but also by failing to recognize the potential of radical thought. (p. 237)

Hardt (1992) did this by suggesting that the dominance of a social scientific effects paradigm has impoverished our understanding of communication and culture. It has resulted in a narrow view of human beings as actors on the stage of social life, one that ignores the potential of communication studies for "an informed critique of the contemporary conditions of society" (p. 9).

Schiller (1996) and Hardt's (1992) histories can be read as intentional countermoves to the biographical explanations in their orientation toward theory and context. Indeed, Hardt defined his work in sharp opposition to biographical accounts by pointing out that he "ignored the obsession to identify 'father' figures among communication researchers. [Instead, he suggested that] influences were far more widespread or diverse than can be subsumed under what I consider a directed and self-serving definition of fraternal leadership" (p. xii). Nevertheless, his myth of origins, as outlined in the chapter titled "Discovering Communication," heavily draws on the thought of pragmatist philosophers, such as Dewey and James, to demonstrate that the history of communication theory and research in the United States:

> has been guided by notions of democracy and the impact of technology on the nature of communication. It emerged from philosophical considerations and sociological practices that were enamored with the progress of science, but also embraced humanistic and literary interests in language, symbols and communication. Throughout this development, the idea of the critical, stimulated by the advancement of knowledge and provoked by the social and political consequences of social change, has persisted as an example of intellectual responsibility and moral leadership, beginning with the rise of American Pragmatism. (p. 31)

This tale, then, is specific and narrow in pinpointing the pragmatist origins of our field. It is one that without hesitation identifies a normative and subjective rationality for mass communication research, rather than the scientific legitimacy vouched for in the Rogers–Chaffee–Schramm school of thought. Similarly, Schiller (1996), in his emphasis on labor, challenged readers to recognize that relations "of production within and around communication institutions exist only within an environing social field or formation" (p. 197). Transcending an individualist explanation, Schiller and Hardt (1992) both called for a contextualization that recognizes the place of complex forces pushing and pulling the flow of the ideas that make up communication theory. Whereas historical causation in the biographical histories is often explained in terms of the action of charismatic figures, Hardt and Schiller saw intellectual influences as embroiled in conditions often beyond the control of the individual. Indeed, one has to search long and hard for any indication of individual agency in Schiller's history—here, thought is understood to emerge out of collectivities. Speaking the language of structural Marxism, Schiller saw the social system as constitutive of the individual. Although he discussed the work of individuals, they are seen as products of the groups to which they belong. Biographical information about scholars is useful because it helps to classify them. Individuals are thus representatives or examples of political, cultural, and economic developments; they fit into categories such as intellectual refugees, critics, dissenting researchers, radicals, and alienated individuals, to name just a few. For example, he wrote about Althusser, to describe the work of Hall and other cultural studies scholars:

> Within this larger matrix, the distinctive attempt of the Althusserian Marxism on which Hall drew was to seek a special warrant for the scientific enterprise. Althusser viewed science as a determinate social labor, "distinct from other practices." But the place ascribed by him to science, or theory, within the totality went well beyond this legitimate differentiation. Althusser explicitly sought to ground theory in terms of "intellectual" labor's putative contribution to an evolutionary transformation of society. (p. 146)

Schiller (1996) aptly moved the spotlights from Althusser's person to the concept of "Althusserian Marxism" and on to Althusser's view of scientific knowledge production, rather than the story of his life. He thereby underlined the view of individuals as the purveyors of ideas and concentrated on the analysis of these ideas. The history of the individual is deemed irrelevant. Where the particularities and peculiarities of individuals and institutions make for colorful anecdotes that form the backbone of the biographical histories, personal details are mostly absent from the intellectual histories because they have not shaped the history of ideas. Indeed, the movement of the narrative through time and space seems entirely unproblematic; the physical flow of ideas is so fickle and intangible in the narrative of the intellectual histories—particularly in Schiller's account as to appear invisible. Schiller easily moved back and forth between decades and continents to show a continuity of ideas rather than the process of their journey, which is so thoroughly illuminated in the biographical histories.

The Structural Level: The Emphasis on Content

Schiller's (1996) and Hardt's (1992) narratives borrow from their authors a critical sensibility, coupled with an analysis of the relation between the essence of a theoretical stance and its relation to other ideas and political, economic, or social realities. In other words, just like the biographical histories, the structure of the intellectual histories subtly supports the epistemology advanced at the narrative level; one of a critical and cultural approach to the study of communication. Hardt described the work of Carey in terms of his political ideas and the theoretical concerns of his projects:

> Carey believes that American Cultural Studies can advance without reducing "culture to ideology, social conflict to class conflict, consent to compliance, action to reproduction, or communication to coercion" ... He relies on the work of Raymond Williams, whose emphasis on the question of culture seems to provide more suitable linkages with the American tradition of cultural history. In fact, Carey's writings on culture and cultural history, in particular in connection with his critique of journalism history, coincide with an increasing interest in social history. (p. 201)

Hardt (1992) recognized that Carey's is an opinion; something he "believes." He refrained from phrasing Carey's idea in the social scientific language of finding or proving or concluding, seeing his scholarship as emerging out of a process of critical reasoning. By adopting this interpretive strategy, he implied that although ideas may have a life of their own, they erupt and evolve in the minds of scholars. In summing up Carey's influences, he emphasized the importance of connections and links between people only insofar as such links provide the breeding ground for ideas. Although the intellectual histories mostly sidestep the discussion of how individuals engage in institutionalizing communication study, they suggest that those who originate the ideas, as representatives and products of their location, also change them in the process.

The Subjective Dimension in Intellectual Histories: Critique As Authority

The intellectual histories carried out explicitly political projects: As indicated earlier Schiller's (1996) was one of centering Marxist theory in the study of communication, and Hardt (1992) worked toward justifying a radical agenda as the rallying point for communication studies (cf. Schiller, 1996, p. 237). In this process, the two authors took a critical look at the events of yesteryear, with the hindsight of history. This is particularly true for their writing about social science research in communication. For example, Schiller (1996) wrote about early American mass communication research:

> [That the] purportedly "limited effects" of the mass media were elevated by mainstream research only as the structural underpinnings of institutionalized communication were willed off-limits. ... Delimiting the scientist in his laboratory sharply from

the society that surrounded him, Klapper sought, by keeping social relations at arms length, also to keep them at bay ... the fundamental social purpose and institutional structure of the contemporary mass media could be nimbly skirted. (p. 59)

Schiller (1996) came out strong in his resistance to the dominant paradigm of communication studies by pointing to its lack of awareness of the social and political nature of communication. In this move, he distanced himself from the ideal of objectivity and the detachment of science by showing the ahistorical nature of a social scientific ideology that he saw as suffocating in "methodological fixation" (p. 60). He legitimated his own epistemological choices by showing how the competing paradigm comes out gasping for the conceptual richness and normative rationality that arrives with contextualized research. For example, he indicted the social scientific traditions emerging out of the late 1940s in the following terms:

The social psychological study of communication processes ... developed at a distance from a second, concurrent, conceptual tradition, known as "information theory." But information theory acted only to reinforce the field's newfound detachment from the study of social relations. ... Information theory helped to accredit an academic communication study as a Cold War social science fit for institutional accreditation. (p. 64)

Although Schiller (1996) and Hardt (1992) turned toward reflection by entering political and social contexts into the equation of history, and critiquing discourses that evade such action, they refrained from a thorough reflection on their own stakes, except for cursory acknowledgments in their prefaces. Both scholars, however, are important players in the field of communication research, and openly engaged in the political battles to define communication research. Both are highly influenced by and working within a school of thought that until recently attained only limited recognition in many of the central historical and epistemological discussions of the field, but now has become centrally important—that of critical communication scholarship. They have been the reluctant witnesses to the trajectory of the dominant effects paradigm, and in their act of configuring the historical field, they are changing the very history to reflect the problematic, conflict-ridden, and contested journey of that paradigm. Contextualizing history to change it, however, is not a sufficient criterion for reflexivity: By centering and advancing their definition of the field in their narratives, and criticizing other ones, they also identify a particular narrative of origins that justifies their own work. To write a reflexive account in the service of disciplinary renewal, the writer needs to take a further step by explaining why he or she has engaged in that undertaking.

Hardt (1992) and Schiller (1996) fell short of reflexivity but they blew fresh life into disciplinary debates for other reasons. If the organizing principle of the biographical histories is one of constance and disciplinary maintenance, that of the intellectual histories, grounded as they are in the paradigm of critical theory, is one of struggle and mobilization. Amidst the attempts to fix disciplinary boundaries and justify epistemologies, their work represents a respectable rebellion. It is a rebellion because it departs from notions of "compromise or friendly accommodation in the spirit of common interests [and instead signals] the emergence of real differences and radical changes" (Hardt, 1992, p. 21). It is a rebellion because it is premised on the idea that only "if a series of additional conceptual dislodgments can be affected, will a long-obstructed road once again be thrown open" (Schiller, 1996, p. 193), the road to intellectually rich and responsible inquiry in mass communication research. Like any rebellion, it is counterhegemonic: It chastises the supporters of the status quo—the dominant paradigm—for not "getting it"—in this case, not getting the richness of communication studies, and its potential for leaving its imprint on society instead of ignoring it. To counteract the reconstructive and reaffirming ritual of the biographical histories, their critiques represent both deconstruction and destruction. By challenging the "received wisdom [to reflect on] the struggle for the domination of a field of social research" (Hardt, 1992, p. 22), they offered us the breaking down of barriers that Bourdieu (1991) saw as so necessary for the solidification of epistemic authority. As Jay (1993) argued, historiography "requires … a willingness to intervene destructively as well as constructively, to shatter received wisdom as well as reconfigure the debris in new and arresting ways" (p. 1).

Reflexive Rebellion and Ritual: The Use of Disciplinary Histories

At its most general, I have raised the question of why we should we be interested in writing and reading disciplinary histories and what they could and should be used for. As I argued, histories play a crucial role in the debate about disciplinary legitimation that has become all the more urgent in recent years but has always been around, throughout the life of a young discipline suffering under the weight of an ever-present identity crisis prompted by a skeptical academy eager for cost cutting. Historical accounts may give us direction, identity, and coherence in the intradisciplinary critique of our activity: We discipline ourselves through storytelling, and our stories, in turn, shape what we do today by advancing particular rationalities, sustained and proven by history.

More specifically, I have taken up the question of whether we, as mass communication scholars, are up to "anything but self-reproduction" (Peters, 1986a, p. 551); of whether our endeavors at studying mass communication, and at studying the history of studying mass communication, yield the basis for a reflective appreciation and critique of our position. If we wish to move toward self-understanding and integration, this article demonstrates that there are at least two different ways to go: The biographical and intellectual histories suggest radically different ends that interplay with the overarching project of disciplinary legitimation.

The intellectual histories, matched with Bourdieu's (1990, 1991) good advice, remind us that to understand the origins and development of communication research, we need to ask how the field is tied to historical and cultural circumstances. We need to reexamine the historical record and the canon of communication study with an eye to locating it in a larger and more complex picture, a picture too messy and contestable to constitute a neat fairy tale, but more suited for the kind of self-understanding we require and desire (for a similar suggestion in anthropology, see Marcus & Fischer, 1986). If we ought to, as Bourdieu (1991) suggested, turn inward to be socially responsible practitioners of research, we are best served by taking the Schiller–Hardt route to historiography. Although these histories cannot escape, and do not sufficiently problematize, their role in the legitimation of communication study, they take a stab at contextualizing our research activity. Biographical histories, on the other hand, celebrate and maintain existing definitions of the field by nurturing a body of communication study folklore. They promote the social integration of communication scholars as social scientists and the unity of the field but do not purport or desire to examine the assumptions of such integration. However, they provide an important source of reflexivity in outlining the biases and predispositions of the authors in writing the histories. They offer us an honest acknowledgment of the constructed nature of historical accounts.

All this is not to say that the biographical approach lacks an interest in intellectual history, or to suggest that the intellectual histories do not celebrate mythical heroes of their own. Instead, this article points to the dominant modes of discourse within social scientific and humanistic traditions, to appreciate their claims about historical processes in general and about mass communication research in particular. More than anything, the coexistence of these two modes of historical accounts reveals the range of answers to the question of what is important in history: It reveals the richness of the field in which we work and forms a basis for a future of grounded hindsight.

The central question of this article is whether the production of historical accounts represents a possibility for a reflexive turn in communication studies. The brief answer to this question is a qualified "no": The histories offer us an archaeology of knowledge that digs out only very select layers but also alerts us to the fact that we have a past equally worthy of celebration and critique. They craft a collective memory for mass communication researchers that gives us a way to see ourselves as part of something grander. Whether pointing to Dewey and Carey or to Lewin and Schramm as the central figures and heroes, the histories, if implicitly, show us what is special about American mass communication research: They let us in on how the circumstances of the first half of the 20th century made our activity relevant to the lives of people, and they try to show us ways in which we may, once again, attain such social relevance. Thus, they flex our historical muscles and expand our opportunities for reflection. Nevertheless, it has become apparent that the historiographic approaches of our chroniclers stop short of true reflexivity: Whereas the intellectual histories shy away from discussion of the writers' stake in the production of the account, the biographical histories stay away from the political context that shaped the histories.

In the process of legitimating disciplinary missions, these narratives of origin inevitably fix us in particular understandings of our origins. By defining and organizing our field, they also delimit the parameters of our discovery. This should, perhaps, not come as a surprise: Although disciplinary histories represent a first step toward self-examination, this discussion also shows that the very nature of the genre makes reflexivity almost impossible. The paradox of disciplinary history and, perhaps, of attempts at disciplinary renewal in general, is that we need reflection for renewal and dynamism. At the same time, we also need unified theories and tales for the purpose of creating the coherence a field of inquiry requires. The two, as this discussion shows, are not easily reconcilable, but both are present in the disciplinary histories that we have at our disposal.

A share of the burden, then, must rest on the community of scholars who are the readers of the disciplinary histories: We need to read competing histories; open up a dialogue about their meaning; and understand, appreciate, and critique their claims. We can explore how the production of historical knowledge helps us better understand the present. To borrow Craig's (1999) helpful turn of phrase, a close reading of disciplinary histories may offer us a

> common awareness of certain complementarities and tensions among different types of communication theory, so it is commonly understood that these different types of theory cannot legitimately develop in total isolation from each other but much engage each other in argument. (p. 124)

A reading of intellectual and biographical histories challenges us to consider what institutional demands and personal and political interests drive our research. It challenges us to problematize the bifurcation of the discipline of mass communication research into social scientific and humanistic approaches—one that limits the questions we can ask and challenges our coherence and relevance as a field. We can begin to appreciate that our research does not take place in a vacuum but has real implications in the realms of individual and collective action. Reflexivity, like psychoanalysis, will not always yield pretty insights, but it is a necessary step toward locating ourselves within larger contexts. Reflexivity can empower us and enrich our task by opening our eyes to the fact that academic practices interact with and affect the outside world of economics, politics, and culture.

REFERENCES

Aronowitz, S. (1988). *Science as power: Discourse and ideology in modern society.* Minneapolis: University of Minnesota Press.
Barthes, R. (1995). *Mythologies.* New York: Hill & Wang.
Benson, T. W. (Ed.). (1985). *Speech communication in the 20th century.* Carbondale: Southern Illinois University Press.
Bernstein, R. J. (1976). *The restructuring of social and political theory.* New York: Harcourt Brace Jovanovich.
Bourdieu, P. (1990). *In other words: Essays towards a reflexive sociology.* Stanford, CA: Stanford University Press.
Bourdieu, P. (1991). Epilogue: On the possibility of a field of world sociology. In P. Bourdieu & J. Coleman (Eds.), *Social theory for a changing society* (pp. 373–388). New York: Sage.
Bourdieu, P., & Wacquant, L. J. D. (1992). *An invitation to reflexive sociology.* Chicago: University of Chicago Press.
Carey, J. W. (1992). *Communication as culture: Essays on media and society.* New York: Routledge.
Carey, J. W. (1996). The Chicago school and mass communication research. In E. E. Dennis & E. Wartella (Eds.), *American communication research: The remembered history* (pp. 21–38). Mahwah, NJ: Lawrence Erlbaum Associates, Inc.
Chaffee, S. H., &. Berger, C. R. (1987). What communication scientists do. In C. H. Berger & S. H. Chaffee (Eds.), *Handbook of communication science* (pp. 99–123). Newbury Park, CA: Sage.
Chaffee, S. H., & Hochheimer, J. L. (1985). The beginnings of political communication research in the United States: Origins of the "limited effects" model. In E. M. Rogers & F. Balle (Eds.), *The media revolution in America and Western Europe* (pp. 267–298). Norwood, NJ: Ablex.
Chaffee, S. H., & Rogers, E. M. (Eds.). (1997). *The beginnings of communication study in America: A personal memoir by Wilbur Schramm.* Thousand Oaks, CA: Sage.
Craig, R. (1999). Communication theory as a field. *Communication Theory, 9*(2), 119–161.
Czitrom, D. J. (1982). *Media and the American mind.* Chapel Hill: University of North Carolina Press.
Deetz, S. A. (1994). Future of the discipline: The challenges, the research, and the social contribution. In S. A. Deetz (Ed.), *Communication yearbook 17* (pp. 565–600). Thousand Oaks, CA: Sage.
Delia, J. G. (1987). Communication research: A history. In C. Berger & S. Chaffee (Eds.), *Handbook of communication science* (pp. 20–98). Newbury Park, CA: Sage.
Dervin, B., Grossberg, L., O'Keefe, B. J., & Wartella, E. (Eds.). (1989). *Rethinking communication.* Newbury Park, CA: Sage.
Durkheim, E. (1971). *The elementary forms of the religious life.* London: Allen & Unwin.
Foucault, M. (1972). *The archaeology of knowledge.* New York: Harper & Row.
Foucault, M. (1979). *Discipline and punish: The birth of the prison.* New York: Vintage.
Gerbner, G. (Ed.). (1983). *Ferment in the field.* Philadelphia: Annenberg School Press.
Hardt, H. (1992). *Critical communication studies: Communication, history and theory in America.* London: Routledge.
Jay, M. (1993). *Between intellectual history and cultural critique.* New York: Routledge.

Knuf, J. (1993). "Ritual" in organizational cultural theory. In S. A. Deetz (Ed.), *Communication yearbook 16* (pp. 61–103). Thousand Oaks, CA: Sage.
Kuhn, T. S. (1962). *The structure of scientific revolutions.* Chicago: University of Chicago Press.
Lazarsfeld, P. F. (1941). Remarks on administrative and critical communication research. *Studies in Philosophical and Social Sciences, 9,* 2–16.
Lipari, L. (1999). Polling as ritual. *Journal of Communication, 49*(1), 83–103.
Marcus, G., & Fischer, M. (Eds.). (1986). *Anthropology as cultural critique: An experimental moment in the human sciences.* Chicago: University of Chicago Press.
Merton, R. K., Fiske, M., & Curtis, A. (1946). *Mass persuasion: The social psychology of a war bond drive.* New York: Harper & Row.
Mohanty, S. P. (1997). *Literary theory and the claims of history: Postmodernism, objectivity, multicultural politics.* Ithaca, NY: Cornell University Press.
Nothstine, W. L., Blair, C., & Copeland, G. A. (1994). Professionalization and the eclipse of critical invention. In W. Nothstine, C. Blair, & G. A. Copeland (Eds.), *Critical questions: Invention, creativity, and the criticism of discourse and media* (pp. 15–70). New York: St. Martin's.
Novick, P. (1988). *That noble dream: The "objectivity question" and the American historical profession.* New York: Cambridge University Press.
Peters, J. D. (1986a). Institutional sources of intellectual poverty in communication research. *Communication Research, 13,* 527–559.
Peters, J. D. (1986b). *Reconstructing mass communication theory.* Unpublished doctoral dissertation, Stanford University, Stanford, CA.
Peters, J. D. (1993). Genealogical notes on "the field." *Journal of Communication, 43*(4), 132–139.
Peters, J. D. (1995). Historical tensions in the concept of public opinion. In T. L. Glasser & C. T. Salmon (Eds.), *Public opinion and the communication of consent* (pp. 3–32). New York: Guilford.
Peters, J. D. (1998). Theorizing communication: A history [book review]. *Journal of Communication 48*(1), 138–140.
Peters, J. D. (1999). *Speaking into the air: A history of the idea of communication.* Chicago: University of Chicago Press.
Robinson, G. J. (1988). "Here be dragons": Problems in charting the U.S. history of communication studies. *Communication, 10,* 97–119.
Robinson, G. J. (1996). Constructing a historiography for North American communication studies. In E. Dennis & E. Wartella (Eds.), *American communication research: The remembered history* (pp. 157–168). Mahwah, NJ: Lawrence Erlbaum Associates, Inc.
Rogers, E. (1994). *A history of communication study.* New York: Free Press.
Rogers, E., & Chaffee, S. (1994). Communication and journalism from "Daddy" Bleyer to Wilbur Schramm: A palimpsest. *Journalism Monographs, 148.*
Rorty, R. (1979). *Philosophy and the mirror of nature.* Princeton, NJ: Princeton University Press.
Rosaldo, R. (1993). *Culture and truth: The remaking of social analysis* (2nd ed.). Boston: Beacon.
Ross, D. (1991). *The origins of American social science.* New York: Cambridge University Press.
Said, E. W. (1983). Opponents, audiences, constituencies, and communities. In W. J. T. Mitchell (Ed.), *The politics of interpretation* (pp. 7–32). Chicago: University of Chicago Press.
Schiller, D. (1996). *Theorizing communication.* New York: Oxford University Press.
Sigman, S. J. (Ed.). (1995). *The consequentiality of communication.* Hillsdale, NJ: Lawrence Erlbaum Associates, Inc.
Simpson, C. (1994). *Science of coercion.* New York: Oxford University Press.
Stripas, T. (1998, November). *Facing facts: Why universities love cultural studies (and what to do about it).* Paper presented at the National Communication Association convention, New York.
Wartella, E. (1996). The history reconsidered. In E. Dennis & E. Wartella (Eds.), *American communication research: The remembered history* (pp. 169–180). Mahwah, NJ: Lawrence Erlbaum Associates, Inc.

Wartella, E., & Reeves, B. (1985). Historical trends in research on children and the media: 1900–1960. *Journal of Communication, 35*(2), 118–133.

White, H. (1987). *Metahistory: The historical imagination in nineteenth-century Europe.* Baltimore: Johns Hopkins University Press.

SCHOLARLY MILESTONES ESSAY

The Extensions of Men: The Correspondence of Marshall McLuhan and Edward T. Hall

Everett M. Rogers
Department of Communication and Journalism
University of New Mexico

Marshall McLuhan, the Canadian media guru, and Edward T. Hall (1959), the American anthropologist who wrote The Silent Language *and founded the field of intercultural communication, exchanged over 133 letters during the period between 1962 and 1976. Their correspondence provides insight into the evolution of such important ideas as the conception of the media as extensions of man, media technological determinism, and McLuhan's dictum that the medium is the message. Although these ideas are usually attributed to McLuhan, who wrote about them in two important books,* The Gutenberg Galaxy *(1962) and* Understanding Media: The Extensions of Man *(1965), Hall had considerable influence in their development. Although Harold Innis is widely acknowledged for shaping McLuhan as a communication technological determinist, the exchange between Hall and McLuhan helped develop the latter's theory about the impacts of communication technology on the human senses. Here we see how important intellectual ideas often grow out of communication between scholars, allowing them to test and extend their thinking in a collaborative mode.*

To say that any technology or extension of man creates a new environment is a much better way of saying the medium is the message.
—Marshall McLuhan to Edward T. Hall
(letter dated September 16, 1964, in the Edward T. Hall Papers, University of Arizona Library)

Requests for reprints should be sent to Everett M. Rogers, Department of Communication and Journalism, University of New Mexico, Albuquerque, NM 87131–1171. E-mail: erogers@unm.edu

The purpose of this scholarly milestone essay is to analyze the extensive correspondence between Marshall McLuhan and Edward T. Hall in the 1960s and 1970s, an exchange through which they worked out their thinking about such important ideas as that of the media as the extensions of man, "the medium is the message," and media technological determinism.[1] These conceptual ideas are generally credited to McLuhan, and they boosted his public fame as a media guru. However, this analysis suggests that Hall played a very key role in their development. (McLuhan also influenced Hall's theories, although the evidence for this flow is less clear in their letters and in Hall's publications.) This essay questions the conventional scholarly wisdom that the primary, and sole, intellectual influence on McLuhan's theorizing was Harold Innis's media determinism. I conclude that McLuhan's basic perspective on technological determinism may have come from Innis, but that Hall was at least an equally important influence in how this paradigm was applied to mass communication, especially concerning the media technologies' impacts on the human senses.

MARSHALL MCLUHAN AND EDWARD T. HALL

The year 2000 marks the 20th anniversary of the death of Marshall McLuhan (1911–1980), the Canadian communication theorist and professor of English, who spent much of his career at the University of Toronto, where he headed the Centre for Culture and Technology. He earned his PhD in English Literature at Cambridge University, and his first scholarly work was in literary criticism (in fact, McLuhan was always a literary scholar, as James Carey [personal communication, August 3, 1999] pointed out). A "new McLuhan" emerged in the 1960s who was a marked contrast to the earlier McLuhan as literary critic and cultural observer (Duffy, 1969, p. 9). The new McLuhan developed a theoretical system of communication technological determinism, influenced at least to some degree by fellow Canadian, Harold A. Innis.[2] McLuhan became famous in 1962 with publication of *The Gutenberg*

---

[1]Some 131 of the 133 McLuhan–Hall letters are archived in the Edward T. Hall Papers, Special Collections, University of Arizona Library. Correspondence from 1962 to 1963 is in Box 8, Folder 27; from 1964 to 1967 in Box 8, Folder 28; and from 1968 to 1977 in Box 8, Folder 29. Only two additional letters are included among the 36 McLuhan–Hall letters in the Marshall McLuhan Papers, National Archives of Canada, Ottawa, in Box 25, Folder 64. The 133 letters seem to represent a rather complete set of the McLuhan–Hall correspondence, as can be inferred from the way in which almost every letter refers to the previous letter. Most of this correspondence consists of letters written at approximately monthly intervals, somewhat like a conversation. For purposes of simplicity, the McLuhan–Hall papers are cited in this article as the Hall Papers, or the McLuhan Papers, depending on the archive in which they are stored.

[2]McLuhan widely acknowledged his intellectual debt to Innis, an influence which may have occurred during the 1940s and 1950s, prior to Hall's correspondence with McLuhan, but mainly seems to have occurred after Innis died in 1952 (in fact, McLuhan helped increase Innis's posthumous reputation). Although both Innis and McLuhan were faculty members at the University of Toronto, they were in separate academic units—McLuhan in the Department of English (and the Catholic college, St. Michael's) and Innis in the Department of Political Economy—and they seldom met. One meeting was ar-

Galaxy, and was regarded as a celebrity after his 1964 book *Understanding Media.* In fact, Bissell (1988) stated, "No academic of our generation was more widely known than Marshall McLuhan" (p. 74).

McLuhan was a critic and analyst of the communication media's impacts on individuals and society, which, he argued, occurred by changing individuals' sensory organization and thought (Carey, 1967). McLuhan was considered controversial and evidence for his theoretical formulations, which he drew from novels and other literary texts, was considered impressionistic by many communication scholars who regarded data from surveys, experiments, and content analyses as more valid. The reviewers of McLuhan's books generally regarded many of his claims as preposterous, his methods as questionable, and his writing style as puzzling. Some of their reviews were ravaging. McLuhan's friend, the anthropologist Edmund Carpenter (letter to Hall, July 19, 1966, in the Hall Papers, Box 2, Folder 12), noted that McLuhan, after a particularly critical review, should blow his nose on the *New Yorker.* McLuhan steadfastly refused to answer his critics.

Most of McLuhan's important contributions were made prior to the mid-1960s, when a San Francisco-based public relations company[3] marketed McLuhan as an international guru, and then peddled him as a highly paid business consultant. "Promotional methods previously reserved for products and stars, especially rock stars, were now used on behalf of an academic, all stops out" (Carpenter, 1992, p. 11). "Celebrity stains whatever it touches, and he had more celebrity than any other professor in recent decades" (Fulford, 1991, p. 4). McLuhan became a nonstop lecturer to IBM and other companies' executives, and while his speaking fees escalated, his originality ebbed. Perhaps his peak in public popularity occurred with his 1976 appearance in the movie *Annie Hall.* As Carey (in press) noted, "His fame obeyed the law of celebrity: The rate of ascent is strictly mirrored in the rate of descent." During the 1970s, McLuhan's popularity dropped, and ill health cut short his intellectual activities.

Edward T. Hall (1914–) grew up in New Mexico where he worked with road construction crews of Navajos and Hopis, and earned his PhD in anthropology at Columbia University. From 1950 to 1955, Hall was employed by the U.S. State Department's Foreign Service Institute (FSI) in Washington, DC, where he developed a theory of communication and culture. This perspective was published as Hall's (1959) book *The Silent Language,* which became the founding document for the

---

ranged by Professor Tom Easterbrook of Innis's department, but the two scholars fought about the Spanish Inquisition (which McLuhan, a converted Catholic, defended). Thereafter, the two maintained a distinctly cool relationship (Jeffrey, 1989). Edmund Carpenter (1992), one of McLuhan's closest academic collaborators, concluded that Innis's influence on McLuhan has been overestimated: "I remain unconvinced of his allegiance to Innis. ... Innis was never Marshall's mentor, not really. Marshall followed noone" (p. 8).

[3]The public relations firm, Gossage and Feigen, was officed in a former firehouse in San Francisco and has been called the "pump house gang."

new field of intercultural communication (Rogers & Steinfatt, 1999).[4] Hall's book became a best-seller, and he became a public figure, appearing in *Playboy* and *Psychology Today* interviews. He moved into a circle of leading American intellectuals, including the anthropologist Margaret Mead, the sociologist David Riesman, the futurist (and designer of the geodesic dome) Buckminster Fuller, and others.

The McLuhan–Hall letters began in January 1962,[5] and by their 14th letter (in mid-April 1962), "Dr. McLuhan" and "Dr. Hall" gave way to "Marshall" and "Ned." At first their exchanges centered on the main ideas in their books, Hall's (1959) *The Silent Language* and McLuhan's (1962) *The Gutenberg Galaxy,* especially the idea of technologies as extensions of man. Initially, McLuhan preferred the terms *outerings* or *ablations,* but soon the word *extensions* dominated in their exchanges. McLuhan wrote to Hall (February 6, 1962, Hall Papers), in one of his first letters:

> I use the term "ablation" from Claude Bernard's *Experimental Medicine,* where I first encountered it. But for years I have been studying the various media of communication as extensions of our various senses. Each sense has a *grammar* of its own, well understood by the painters, musicians, etc. I'm very much concerned to establish contact with those who have pursued this approach to human technologies as externalizations or extensions of our senses and our faculties. When I mentioned this matter some time ago to Ted Carpenter, he replied that he knew of only one anthropologist [it was Hall] who had even speculated about this matter.

The 133 letters represented a dialogue about their evolving theories, books they were reading and wished to call to the other's attention, and reactions to each others' publications and career moves.[6]

Hall first met McLuhan in May 1963 (more than a year after their correspondence began) when the latter gave a lecture in Washington, DC, where Hall was then living. Afterward, McLuhan wrote to Hall (letter, May 23, 1963, in Molinaro, McLuhan, & Toye, 1987, p. 383): "My visit with you is resonating most delectably

---

[4]The impact of this important book on Hall himself is indicated in his letter to McLuhan (November 12, 1969, Hall Papers): "By writing it [*The Silent Language*], I changed everything in myself as well as for a few others."

[5]McLuhan's first letter to Hall was mailed to him in care of his New York publisher, Doubleday, but McLuhan soon obtained Hall's address through their mutual friend, Edmund Carpenter. Carpenter was responsible 8 years previously (in 1954) for publication of an article by Hall and George L. Trager in *Explorations,* the interdisciplinary journal edited mainly by Carpenter. Carpenter's initial contact with Hall (and with several of his colleagues from the Foreign Service Institute) had occurred at a conference in Louisville organized by their mutual friend Raymond Birdwhistell (Carpenter, 1992).

[6]Hall and McLuhan, as their archives show, each carried on an extensive correspondence with many other scholars. However, the 133 letters they exchanged with each other outnumbered the letters either of them exchanged with others, with the exception of McLuhan's some 400 letters to his mother, which were personal, rather than professional, in nature.

in the caverns of my memory." Hall responded (letter, June 23, 1963, Hall Papers): "Your visit ... stirred up so much in the far recesses of my mind that I have been waiting for the intellectual dust to settle before replying."

McLuhan was an admirer of Hall's (1959) *The Silent Language,* and began their exchange of letters in 1962 to raise several questions about "the extensions of man" idea. McLuhan remarked, on rereading *The Silent Language* in 1969 (McLuhan said that he had to reread the book because brain surgery to remove a tumor had rubbed out several years of his previous reading), "It is a ball!" (letter, McLuhan to Hall, November 3, 1969, Hall Papers). McLuhan told Hall (letter, March 9, 1966, Hall Papers) that he was "absolutely entranced with *The Hidden Dimension,*" Hall's (1966) book about nonverbal communication. However, the interpersonal relationship between Hall and McLuhan was not always smooth, as when they disagreed about credit for theoretical ideas, such as the extensions of man.

EXTENSIONS OF MAN

One of the most important ideas attributed to Marshall McLuhan is that the mass media are extensions of man, with new communication technologies allowing individuals to be exposed to news events from afar, and to exchange messages with others at long distances. McLuhan was a *technological determinist,* believing that technology is the main cause of social changes in society. More specifically, McLuhan believed that the mass media and other communication technologies shaped society, a viewpoint adapted from his fellow Canadian at the University of Toronto, Harold A. Innis (1950, 1951).[7]

McLuhan (1962) stated, "All media, from the phonetic alphabet to the computer, are extensions of man that cause deep and lasting changes in him and transform his environment" (p. 13). For example, a crane is an extension of the arm, and wheels are extensions of the feet. Communication technologies extend the human mind, allowing it contact with far-off parts of the world.

The idea of extensions of man, however, goes back to Hall (1959), who stated in *The Silent Language,* "Today man has developed extensions for practically everything he used to do with his body" (p. 79). Hall cited the evolution of weapons, clothes, houses, furniture, power tools, television, telephones, books, money, and transportation. McLuhan (1962, p. 4) quoted at length from Hall's *The Silent Language* on the extensions of man, in his book, *The Gutenberg Galaxy,* in which he analyzed print media as extensions of the human senses (and as altering the senses).

---

[7]And also from Lewis Mumford (1934) whose *Technics and Civilization* was more often cited by McLuhan (1951) in his *The Mechanical Bride* than was Innis (personal correspondence with James Carey, August 3, 1999; Carey, 1998–1999). Carey was undoubtedly correct when he pointed out that the notion of media as extensions of man was an idea in the atmosphere at the time, so it is somewhat difficult to pin it down to any single scholar.

Early in their correspondence, McLuhan (letter to Hall, January 27, 1962, in the Hall Papers) stated, "Your page 79 [in *The Silent Language,* Hall's statement about the extensions of man] has become ever more crucial in my work." Evidence of McLuhan's (1964) subsequent focus on extensions of man is evident in his book *Understanding Media: The Extensions of Man.*

Hall, in a letter to McLuhan (dated February 13, 1962, in the Hall Papers) explained to McLuhan that he got the idea of extensions of man from Buckminister Fuller (1940/1962).[8] Hall and McLuhan disagreed about who should get credit for the idea of extensions of man. In a February 27, 1962 letter to his friend and admirer, the Jesuit scholar Walter J. Ong (Molinaro et al., 1987, p. 287), McLuhan asked: "Have you encountered the work of E.T. Hall? He says he got the idea of our technologies as outerings of sense and function from Buckminister. I got it from nobody." Hall (1976), in his book *Beyond Culture,* stated:

> Marshall McLuhan used to talk about innerings and outerings (processes he could see at work in man), and few people knew what he meant until he began speaking in terms of extensions—a term he borrowed from the author—in *The Gutenberg Galaxy* (1962). (Note 4 to chap. 2, p. 216)

Hall sent McLuhan a copy of his 1976 book, *Beyond Culture,* in page proofs. McLuhan responded to Hall in a December 8, 1975 letter (Hall Papers): "Of course I am unhappy about page 135, where you accuse me of unacknowledged borrowing. How happy I would have been to give you full credit had I recognized the source at the time of writing." In his December 19, 1975 reply (Hall Papers) to McLuhan's December 8 letter, Hall said that McLuhan was not to be unhappy about the note, as the matter of acknowledgment had not been mentioned on page 135, and that "We all get things from each other."

Buckminister Fuller (Molinaro et al., 1987, p. 308) said that McLuhan acknowledged (to him) use of his concept and phasing of the "mechanical" and other "extensions of man," which Fuller (1935) had first published in his Preface to *Nine Chains to the Moon.*[9] McLuhan had met Fuller at the 1962 Delos Symposium, held on the yacht of Constantine Doxiadis, a wealthy Greek architect and futurist. Each summer, Doxiadis invited a dozen or so leading intellectuals for a week or two of talk while they drifted through the Aegean Sea. Nevertheless, it was Hall, through correspondence with McLuhan and Fuller, who traced the exact source of Fuller's first use of the idea of extensions of man.

---

[8]The notion of extensions of man, although not referred to as "extensions" can be traced to Sigmund Freud's (1929/1953) *Civilization and Its Discontents:* "Man has become a god by means of artificial limbs, so to speak, quite magnificent when equipped with all his accessory organs; but they do not grow on him and they still give him trouble at times" (p. 778).

[9]A more detailed exposition by Fuller on extensions of man is his *Untitled Epic Poem on the History of Industrialization* (1940/1962).

Despite their dispute about their respective roles in the origin of the idea of extensions of man, Hall and McLuhan thought highly of each other. For example, McLuhan (Molinaro et al., 1987) recommended Hall as a participant in the 1964 Delos Symposium: "He is worth a half-dozen Margaret Meads" (p. 296). Hall and McLuhan were both participants in the 1965 Delos Symposium, along with leading intellectuals in architecture, history, sociology, anthropology, and other fields.

Certainly Hall and McLuhan both sharpened their understanding of the extensions of man model through their exchanges. For instance, Hall wrote to McLuhan (May 24, 1962, Hall Letters):

> I have the feeling that writing in many instances should be consciously designed to do the work of the senses at a distance, that is, writing should be an extension—ablation of all senses. Good writing does this. ... With the invention of writing, man created a time machine. This means that you have sensual writing, spoken writing, and the most difficult of all to talk about: Conceptual writing, which is in effect writing about thinking.

PROXEMICS AND AUDITORY SPACE

During the early 1960s, Hall was conducting research on *proxemics,* the role of space as it affects human communication, a topic which fit with how the media altered human sense ratios. For example, in one of his most noted observations about proxemics, Hall (1955) stated:

> A U.S. male ... stands 18 to 20 inches away when talking face to face to a man he does not know very well; talking to a woman under similar circumstances, he increases the distance about four inches. A distance of only 8 to 13 inches between males is considered ... very aggressive. Yet in many parts of Latin America and the Middle East distances which are almost sexual in connotation are the only ones at which people can talk comfortably. (p. 87)

Hall wrote to McLuhan (August 20, 1962, Hall Letters):

> I would not be at all surprised to discover that people perceive each other's size as a highly variable feature in which the self and others expand and shrink depending upon the relationship and what's going on. ... Space is certainly one of the most communicative of the basic communication systems.

Somewhat thereafter, McLuhan called Hall's attention (November 3, 1962) to the changing conceptions of the human senses:

> Pupil of the eye was called the *apple.* Apple projected images of daily life. Eye as organ of perception rather than projection not accepted until later Seventeenth [Century]. ... If electricity outers the central nervous system, then a collective consciousness is mandatory. The subconscious must be liquidated? Regards, Marshall.

Hall, some months later, responded (February 6, 1963, Hall Letters):

> I was re-reading your November 3 letter and came across the reference to the apple of the eye which projected images rather than receiving them. This checks with your statement elsewhere that the picture was an object, not a representation. I could imagine that the shift from object to representation, and object reception to projection occurred more or less at the same time. Do you have any more documentation on this?

This particular exchange about the apple of the eye illustrates how Hall and McLuhan educated each other about certain topics, thus extending each other's knowledge and understanding of human sensory experiences.

Hall wrote to McLuhan (February 20, 1964, Hall Papers):

> Incidentally, if you are interested in a very fine example of auditory space, get hold of a record called "Fort and I." In it these two comedians imitating two Maine fishermen take off in a dory called the "Bluebird." All of the sound effects are produced by either one or the other of them, including the starting of the motor and its pump-pump-pump as it glides through the Maine fog on the smooth waters of the harbor. ... Burke sets the scene by introducing you to close auditory space first by sniffing the fog. Then they establish far distance with a fog horn coming from a buoy. The "Bangor Packet" comes out of the fog, bears down on the "Bluebird" and smacks it amidships. The whole scene is auditory and yet at the same time incredibly visual.

Auditory space (or acoustic space) became a favorite concept of McLuhan's, with strong encouragement from Hall, as the preceding quotation suggests.[10] McLuhan identified examples of how sounds conveyed a sense of distance and direction.

McLuhan wrote to Hall (June 23, 1967, Hall Papers): "Your work is always in my thoughts. By the way, the word 'stereo' is Greek for 'solid'—i.e., for tactility, or interface. The immediate after-image of touch is interval, not connection, ergo the closure for the interval creates rhythm." Here we see an illustration of how McLuhan extended Hall's interest in *haptics,* the study of how touch affects human intercultural communication (Rogers & Steinfatt, 1999).

Hall and McLuhan continued to advance their thinking about extensions of man and the sensory impacts of the media. McLuhan wrote Hall (March 4, 1964, Hall Papers):

> Just a brief query apropos your remark in your last letter that repetition is a kind of sensory deprivation. Would this afford any light on the matter of technological extension

---

[10]McLuhan's interest in auditory space may have come from multiple sources. Carpenter (1992) stated that McLuhan learned of this concept from D. Carleton Williams, a psychologist at the University of Toronto who participated in McLuhan's Seminars in Communication and Culture (described later in this article), and who published an article, "Acoustic Space," in the journal *Explorations* (Williams, 1955).

and ensuing numbness? If technology is extension or amplification of a faculty or sense, it seems also to involve this factor of repetition in large measure. There is the mystery of non-perception affecting amplification. There is the Greek intuition of extension as narcosis in the legend of Narcissus.[11]

Perhaps the several preceding quotations from the McLuhan and Hall letters provide some sense of the richness of their exchange. When mapped on their scholarly books, being written during this same time period, an observer can understand something of the "kitchen" in which their theories were being developed. They worked out their key ideas through their private correspondence, testing and extending their theories by explaining them to each other, prior to publishing them in their books.

THE MEDIUM IS THE MESSAGE

McLuhan argued that the impacts of the new communication technologies, like television, for instance, occur not just on the conscious level of an individual's knowledge and opinions. A new medium may also affect individuals' sense ratios and patterns of perceptions. Thus McLuhan said that "the medium is the message," implying that the way information is presented is at least as important as the information itself.[12] For example, McLuhan argued that Gutenberg's printing press, invented in 1437, changed how individuals in society acquired information from primarily oral communication to a sequential (linear) mental experience. Thus, Gutenberg was the key inventor of the Renaissance; his communication technology caused the cultural discontinuity that led to the rebirth of European civilization between 1450 and 1600. The phonetic alphabet and the printing press modified the human senses, in that linear thinking was encouraged by reading left-to-right (or, as in several cultures, right-to-left) lines on a page (McLuhan, 1962).

Here McLuhan built directly on the media technological determinism of Harold Innis, as he acknowledged. McLuhan (1962), in *The Gutenberg Galaxy,* stated, "The alphabet is an aggressive and militant absorber and transformer of culture, as Harold Innis was the first to show" (p. 48), in his *Empire and Communications* (Innis, 1950). McLuhan (1962) also said, "In short, Harold Innis was the first person to hit upon the *process* of change as implicit in the *forms* of media technology. The present book [*The Gutenberg Galaxy*] is a footnote of explanation to his work" (p. 50).

Innis was a scholar of political economy who analyzed, each in a separate book, the role of the fur trade, the Canadian Pacific Railroad, and the cod fisheries in the

---

[11]Narcissus in Greek myth was a youth who pined away in love with his own image and was transformed into the flower that bears his name. Narcosis is a drug-induced unconsciousness.

[12]Carpenter (1992) claimed that McLuhan adapted his phrase from a lecture, "The Method Is the Message," by Ashley Montague that they both attended.

development of Canada. This technological determinism then was applied to communication media in Innis's (1950, 1951) final two books, in which he analyzed the role of orality, stone tablets, papyrus, and other forms of communication on the rise and fall of empires. The changing technology of communication acted to reduce the cost and increase the speed and distance of communication, and thus to extend the geographical size of empires. Innis was historical, empirical, interpretive, and critical (Carey, 1967). His approach to a scholarly topic, such as the impacts of communication technologies on empires, was to investigate what had been written about it through history, impose his theoretical framework of technological determinism on it, and then to critique this deterministic relationship.

McLuhan took Innis's paradigm of media technological determinism, applying it not to such consequences as social and political organization, but to sensory organization and thought. This application of media technological determinism to sensory change pervaded the McLuhan–Hall papers during the 1960s. For example, McLuhan (letter to Hall, February 21, 1962) said, "Any environmental factor which favors the intensification of a single sense (for example, the ear, by means of the drum) fosters new closure of the other senses and faculties, and new ablations." In an April 5, 1962 (Hall Papers) letter to Hall, McLuhan stated:

> What I became aware of in studying media was that a high definition medium like radio had a visual closure, whereas a low definition auditory image, such as the telephone, does not result in visual closure. The same reversal of characteristics is true of all media, depending whether they are of high or low intensity.

Here one can detect the hot media–cold media distinction that McLuhan (1965) was to popularize 2 years later, when his *Understanding Media* was published.

After reading the proofs of *The Gutenberg Galaxy,* Hall (letter, May 4, 1962) told McLuhan of one of his observations about cultural differences in the human senses:

> Arabs do not judge distance from other people usually the way we do, but kinesthetically and olfactorily [such as by smelling garlic on a conversation partner's breath]. They use their eyes as true distance receptors for taking in a view. As a consequence they suffer horribly from claustrophobia.

McLuhan responded (letter, May 14, 1962, Hall Papers), "What you say about the unique sense-mix in the Arab perception of space must equally apply to the sense-mix of any given language." As illustrated here, McLuhan and Hall in their correspondence typically reacted to each others' theoretical probes in a questioning or an extending manner, bringing in illustrations from their insights, experiences, and reading. Hall and (especially) McLuhan were not exchanging empirical data but rather understandings gained from their observations and conceptualizations.

The notion of the medium as the message fits with media technological determinism, but implies that it is a kind of subconscious effect of the media. Hall

(1959), influenced by Freudian psychoanalytic theory, in *The Silent Language,* argued that much of nonverbal communication was out-of-awareness (Rogers & Hart, 1998; Rogers & Steinfatt, 1999, p. 65). McLuhan (1965, p. viii), in *Understanding Media,* commended Hall for explaining, in *The Silent Language,* that individuals are not aware of the ground rules of their environmental systems or cultures. Hall (letter, August 20, 1962, Hall Papers) wrote to McLuhan,

> I think that some people have been trained, or possibly for some other reasons, have a greater capacity than others to pick up the subliminal effects of media. We call them variously prophets and insane, depending upon the time and the circumstances.

McLuhan (letter, January 10, 1964, Hall Papers) wrote to Hall:

> One curious aspect of the approach to sensory typology as a field of study is that it appears plausible and acceptable at once to scientists and layman alike. This baffles me, accustomed as I am to reactions of incredulity and hostility. It even arouses some doubts in my mind about the validity of the whole thing.

Thus it seems that McLuhan was surprised at the popularity of his ideas about the sensory impacts of the media.

HOT AND COOL MEDIA

McLuhan (1965) distinguished between "hot" and "cool" media in his book *Understanding Media.* The basic distinction is that a hot medium (like radio) has much detail supplied by the source, so that little needs to be added by the audience individual. Not much information is left to be filled in by the receiver. In contrast, a cool medium (like television) provides meager information and low definition, as the pixels must be connected instantaneously by the audience individual to give meaning to the otherwise hazy message (McLuhan, 1965, p. 22).[13]

Hot and cool media differ in audience *involvement,* defined as the degree to which an individual actively participates in decoding a media message. Unlike many of McLuhan's other ideas, the notion of hot and cool media could be tested empirically by communication researchers. McLuhan (letter to Hall, January 21, 1971, Hall Papers) approved of Herbert Krugman's (1966, 1971) experiments test-

---

[13]It is possible that McLuhan's hot–cool classification of media may have influenced Hall (1976) to categorize cultures as high-context versus low-context, on the basis of the amount of information that is implied versus stated directly in a communication message. A *high-context culture* is one in which the meanings of a communication message are found in the situation and in the relationships of the communicators or are internalized in the communicators' beliefs, values, and norms. A *low-context culture* is one in which the meanings of a communication message are stated clearly and explicitly, without depending on the context of the communication situation. For example, European American cultures are generally low-context and individualistic. The more collectivistic Asian cultures tend to be high-context.

ing audience individuals' involvement in the media.[14] Krugman measured involvement as the degree to which respondents connected magazine versus television advertisements with their own life experiences. The operation of involvement was the number of bridging experiences mentioned by each respondent per minute. For example, responses to a travel ad included: "It made me think of traveling there myself," and "My husband flies all the time. ... I think wouldn't it be great to go."

In general, communication scholars ignored McLuhan's hot–cool conceptualization in their research, although it was often taught in introductory communication courses at the time.[15] However, the concept of involvement played an important role in mass communication research, such as in formulations of stages in the process of media effects on individuals (Ray, 1973), investigations of parasocial interaction (Rubin & McHugh, 1987), and studies of the effects of entertainment-education in stimulating interpersonal communication among peers about an educational issue (Singhal & Rogers, 1999). However, McLuhan is seldom credited today for attracting research attention to the concept of audience involvement.

THE GLOBAL VILLAGE

A further concept popularized by McLuhan, and reflected somewhat indirectly in the McLuhan–Hall letters, is the *global village,* defined as a world that is increasingly interconnected by communication technologies and tending toward a global culture. Large cities across the world today resemble each other in the consumer products sold, movies, air conditioning, traffic, airports, and fast food (Rogers & Steinfatt, 1999, p. 263). The gradual trend toward a more universal culture, at least at a superficial level, was noted by McLuhan (1962): "Certainly the electro-magnetic discoveries have recreated the simultaneous 'field' in all human affairs so that the human family now exists under conditions of a 'global village.' We live in a single constricted space resonant with tribal drums" (p. 31).

The popularity of the term *global village* was furthered by McLuhan's book, with Quentin Fiore, *War and Peace in the Global Village* (McLuhan & Fiore, 1968). They foresaw the end of the Cold War, and the coming of a new era in which

---

[14] However, Krugman's (1966) research may not have been directly stimulated by McLuhan's theory of hot and cool media; at least Krugman did not cite McLuhan. Later, Krugman (1971) noted that his research findings fit with McLuhan's hot–cold involvement theory (Marchand, 1989/1998). In general, McLuhan was hostile to attempts by communication researchers to test his theories.

[15] Both McLuhan and Hall were invited to be keynote speakers at the International Communication Association in 1977 in Berlin. Hall (letter, June 24, 1977, Hall Papers) wrote to McLuhan after his return (McLuhan was unable to go), "I had not realized the degree to which this group [ICA] that dedicates itself to communication has managed to define it almost entirely in terms of words and numbers, even the intercultural and 'non-verbal' parts of it." This participant observation was noted by Hall in the final letter in the McLuhan–Hall exchange.

computer-related technologies of communication would stimulate a greater degree of diversity and division in society, as culturally unalike people were interconnected. McLuhan's book of predictions about the 21st century, co-authored with Bruce Powers (McLuhan & Powers, 1989) and published nine years after his death, was called *The Global Village*. Today, much more so than almost three decades ago when McLuhan first coined the term, we indeed live in a global village, one interconnected by the Internet. So McLuhan was prophetic about the global village, although he did not anticipate the communication medium (the Internet) through which it would occur.

Hall's influence on McLuhan regarding the global village was much less than in the case of the extensions of man or the sensory impacts of newer media. The McLuhan–Hall letters, however, suggest the tendency for Hall, an anthropologist who had traveled and studied in various cultures, to encourage McLuhan to consider the applicability (or limitations) of his theories to cultures outside of North America. Hall would question McLuhan from time to time as to whether one of his statements about the sensory impacts of new media would hold up in a non-Western culture. Perhaps Hall's commentary about the spatial sense of Arabs, cited earlier, is illustrative. McLuhan was fascinated with tribal and other non-Western cultures, and seemed to need relatively little urging from Hall to think globally and cross-culturally. Hall supplied many examples of intercultural similarities and differences in media determinism and in the sensory impacts of communication media in their ongoing dialogue.

MCLUHAN'S RELATIONSHIP TO THE FIELD OF COMMUNICATION STUDY

One of the most important roles played by McLuhan was to promote the emerging interdiscipline of communication study, as noted by Jeffrey (1989), who described him as "a catalyst offering inspiration, a fertile and provocative if unsystematic thinker who made an indelible contribution to the commencement of communication as an interdisciplinary research enterprise" (p. 4). While his contemporary founding figure in the United States, Wilbur Schramm, sought to institutionalize communication study by integrating it into already existing university departments of journalism and speech, McLuhan's strategy was to promote the scholarly study of communication as an interdiscipline.[16]

What was the process through which McLuhan promoted his perspective of communication study as an interdiscipline? With Edmund Carpenter, McLuhan re-

---

[16]The interdisciplinary scope of McLuhan's interest in human communication is amply illustrated in his correspondence with Hall, which ranges across poetry, literature, criticism, social science, and brain physiology, in addition to other fields.

ceived a grant of $44,000 from the Ford Foundation to establish the Seminars in Communication and Culture at the University of Toronto in 1953.[17] These seminars involved five faculty from the social sciences and humanities (McLuhan, Department of English; Carpenter, Department of Anthropology; Thomas Easterbrook, Department of Political Economy; Carleton Williams, Department of Psychology; and Jacqueline Tyrwhitt, School of Architecture and Town Planning), and offered fellowships to 10 graduate students in the five departments to participate in the weekly seminars about human communication (other students could enroll in the seminars for credit). The seminars were characterized by considerable conflict, as the participants sought to develop common understandings in their discussions of human communication, despite their differences in disciplinary background.[18] McLuhan complained that the other seminar participants failed to understand him; he ended the three years of the seminars with the paranoid statement that "All ignorance is motivated" (Fulford, 1991, p. 3).

Some of the Ford Foundation funding was used by McLuhan to launch an interdisciplinary journal, *Explorations,* in 1953, the objective of which was to bridge the social sciences and humanities (Jeffrey, 1989). This journal was published from 1953 to 1959, and served as an important outlet for McLuhan's ideas. Marchand (1989/1998) stated that all of McLuhan's main theoretical contributions are traceable to the first eight issues of *Explorations.* Certainly this journal helped launch McLuhan's reputation among scholars.

The University of Toronto established the Centre for Culture and Technology in 1963, which grew out of the seminars, and which was created to keep McLuhan in Canada in the face of attractive offers from U.S. universities (Jeffrey, 1989).[19] This interdisciplinary center was not allowed to grant independent degrees, nor can it today: It continues as a small research institute centering on a handful of scholars devoted to teaching and research on McLuhan's theories, and to extending them to

---

[17]The seminars evidently grew out of an informal gathering every weekday at 4 p.m. around a table in the coffee shop of a museum on the University of Toronto campus. McLuhan, Carpenter, Tyrwhitt, and others talked until the place closed (Carpenter, 1992). McLuhan's general style was to advance his ideas by talking about them with others.

[18]An example of how the seminar participants talked past each other is provided by Carpenter (1992): "Carl [Williams] provided the first breakthrough, He used the phrase 'auditory space.' ... Marshall changed it to 'acoustic space' and quoted Symbolist poetry. Jackie [Tyrwhitt] mentioned the Indian city of Fatehpur Sikri. Tom [Easterbrook] saw parallels in Medieval Europe. I talked about Eskimos" (p. 5).

[19]McLuhan wrote to Claude Bissell, President of the University of Toronto (in a March 23, 1971 letter, McLuhan Papers, Box 39, Folder 27):

> My motive in returning to Canada [from Fordham University in New York, where he had been teaching for a year on leave from the University of Toronto] was ... my fear of acceptance. I knew there was no danger of this in Canada. It is very salubrious to have a daily charade of human malice and stupidity, mingled with warmth and insight. In the U.S., surrounded by an atmosphere of success and acceptance, I could have lost my bearings very quickly. I am invited every week to accept academic appointments to the U.S.A.

contemporary problems of the new media. For instance, one course, Understanding Media, is presently co-taught by Eric McLuhan, Marshall McLuhan's son, and by Frank Zingrone, a friend and scholar of Marshall McLuhan.

The Centre, since its establishment in 1963, has been housed in the Coach House, a modest and venerable building on the University of Toronto campus, surrounded by more modern university buildings that tower over it. In McLuhan's day, the Centre consisted mainly of his office and his secretary's, plus a small seminar room where McLuhan held the Seminars in Communication and Culture for his interdisciplinary following of graduate students. This seminar was the workshop in which McLuhan created and explained many of his theories, which were then published, first in the journal *Explorations,* and then in his books, *The Gutenberg Galaxy* (1962) and *Understanding Media* (1965). The Coach House and the Centre were essentially a one-man show that accommodated McLuhan's interdisciplinary approach to communication study.

McLuhan was well aware of the PhD programs in communication underway at U.S. universities, but he generally disdained them as "almost entirely slanted toward hardware expertise" (letter to Claude Bissell, President of the University of Toronto, dated May 10, 1973, Box 19, Folder 27).[20] McLuhan did not feel that most U.S. communication scholarship was interdisciplinary enough; perhaps his attitude reflected his lifelong sense of himself as a "superior outsider" (Jeffrey, 1989), something akin to Simmel's stranger (Rogers, 1999; Rogers & Steinfatt, 1999). McLuhan considered himself a "pattern-watcher" (Jeffrey, 1989, p. 5), as he explained in a lengthy *Playboy* interview (McLuhan, 1969).

In short, the paradigm of human communication represented by Marshall McLuhan differed from the paradigm established by Wilbur Schramm, which grew out of the earlier work of the political scientist Harold Lasswell, the sociologist Paul F. Lazarsfeld, and the social psychologist Carl Hovland (Rogers, 1994).[21] McLuhan stressed the differences between his paradigm and the dominant paradigm of mass communication study in the United States. McLuhan wrote to Hall (August 26, 1975):

---

[20]This remark seems to imply that communication study in the U.S. was too professional or vocational, in McLuhan's opinion. While certain skills in using broadcasting technology were taught in U.S. universities, at least to undergraduates, McLuhan's jibe was an extreme overstatement, and suggests his lack of understanding of U.S. universities' departments of communication in the early 1970s. Nevertheless, McLuhan had visited the University of Illinois, a leading communication school, in the summer of 1960 (Carey, 1998/1999).

[21]McLuhan (1965), in his book *Understanding Media,* criticized both Schramm for his studies of television effects on children (pp. 19–20) and Lazarsfeld for his studies of radio effects (pp. 297–298), as Jeffrey (1989) noted. Such criticism of the dominant paradigm by the founder of an opposing paradigm is typical of most scientific revolutions (Kuhn, 1960/1972). McLuhan's criticism of Schramm's and Lazarsfeld's communication research might be interpreted as based on McLuhan's preference for a different epistemology.

What I call a "theory of communication" is a study of the *effects* of work on a particular public. The Shannon–Weaver model of information theory (encoder, channel, and decoder) simply ignores the laws of the situation, i.e., the Shannon–Weaver model is identical with the bias of Western man, which excludes the possibility of environmental influence. In fact, the environment presupposed by the activity of communication is categorized as "noise" in the Shannon–Weaver paradigm.[22]

McLuhan's paradigm for communication study was lastingly interdisciplinary, historical, and focused on the technology of communication. Given McLuhan's emphasis on the sensory impacts of communication technologies, it is strange that his theories do not receive more attention from contemporary communication scholars, as the study of the new media gained increasing attention in recent years.[23] Perhaps McLuhan's paradigm for communication study was not more fully appreciated by U.S. communication scholars because he operated out of a scholarly tradition of literary criticism, rather than social science. Yet the cultural studies paradigm, which stems from the British literary critic Raymond Williams, has been accepted by many U.S. communication scholars (Jeffrey, 1989).

A contrast in acceptance of intellectual influences is provided by Hall's considerable influence on the field of communication study, leading to the specialty of intercultural communication (Rogers & Hart, 1998; Rogers & Steinfatt, 1999). Intercultural communication as a field of study and research grew out of the intellectual roots of Freudian psychoanalytic theory, anthropology, and linguistic determinism (especially the theory of Benjamin Lee Whorf and Edward Sapir). These strains came together at the hand of Hall in the FSI, a U.S. Department of State training center, from 1950 to 1955.

Hall and his colleagues at FSI recognized the out-of-conscious dimensions of human communication, such as nonverbal communication, which were particularly important to the Foreign Service diplomats that the FSI trained. Hall's (1959) book, *The Silent Language,* which distilled the perspectives on intercultural communication developed at the FSI, was well-accepted by communication scholars. Hall is celebrated today as one of the most important founders of intercultural communication and of nonverbal communication, and courses on these topics (Hall gave both their names) are taught in most communication departments. In contrast, Marshall McLuhan and his theories of communication media determinism are seldom mentioned by contemporary American communication scholars, despite the growing impacts of the new media on society.

---

[22]McLuhan's critique might be more true of Weaver's interpretation of the Shannon (1949) model than of Shannon's model itself, a mistake made by many readers of the Shannon and Weaver essays bound in a book of which they are listed as co-authors (Rogers, 1994).

[23]The comprehensive study of the impacts of the printing press by Elizabeth Eisenstein (1979), however, was stimulated by McLuhan's provocative but gargantuan hypothesis, as she acknowledged.

One indicator of the scholarly attention given to McLuhan and to Hall is provided by their number of citations in the Social Science Citation Index through 1997. McLuhan is cited 1,438 times, compared to Hall's 2,580 citations, with most of these citations occurring prior to the 1990s (which is understandable, given that their most important books were published prior to 1980).

CONCLUSIONS

I argued in this essay, on the basis of their extensive correspondence, that Edward T. Hall was a strong intellectual influence, heretofore unrecognized, on the conceptualizations of Marshall McLuhan, while McLuhan seems to have been of lesser importance in influencing Hall's published work. The media determinism of Harold Innis on McLuhan has been acknowledged (and probably overstated) by McLuhan and by most analysts of McLuhanism, for example, Duffy (1969), Carey (1967), Marchand (1989/1998), and Gordon (1997). The strong influence of Hall on McLuhan, although McLuhan referenced Hall and quoted directly from Hall's (1959) *The Silent Language,* has not been widely appreciated by scholars. Thus the McLuhan–Hall letters speak to us of a powerful, previously unrecognized influence on McLuhan's theories.

Hall, through the idea of extensions of man, influenced McLuhan in his media technological determinism, and helped focus this explanation of social change on sensory impacts of different media, leading to McLuhan's idea of the medium as the message. Hall's influence on McLuhan's classification of hot–cool media and the concept of the global village is less specifically evident in the McLuhan–Hall letters, although the progress of McLuhan's thinking on these issues was facilitated by Hall.

More generally, perhaps the McLuhan–Hall letters suggest that many important ideas in any scholarly field come about not through the introspective process of a single individual, but via a process of communication and social construction involving two or more individuals.[24] When the two scholars come from rather different backgrounds, but share a common interest in the same intellectual issue, their exchange can be particularly rich for both participants.

This essay is based on an analysis of the extensive correspondence between Marshall McLuhan and Edward T. Hall. Such personal letters are one type of essential materials for analysis by historians of science, who bemoan the present day use

---

[24]Which can be construed as a critique of McLuhan's contributions; Carpenter (1992) stated, "Writers commonly speak of Marshall's original ideas. He had none. Be grateful. They would have been right off the wall. His genius lay in perceiving, not creating" (p. 7). McLuhan was a synthesizer of other scholars' ideas through a process of reading and discussion with others. The degree to which McLuhan's theoretical contributions built on the work of others (except for Innis) has not been fully appreciated, nor was it acknowledged by McLuhan.

of e-mail, which does not leave a lasting written trail. This communication technology, the Internet, widely utilized by today's scholars to replace letters, also provides excellent illustrations of the concepts of the extensions of man, media determinism, hot–cool media (e-mail is presumably cool because such messages do not convey the nonverbal context which must be filled in), and the global village.

Finally, as Steven Chaffee has suggested in personal correspondence (June 28, 1999), the McLuhan–Hall letters of study here are extensions of these two brilliant scholars into our own time and place. As they debated the role of the media as extensions of humans, McLuhan and Hall were extending their own thought processes to each other, and now, to us.

ACKNOWLEDGMENTS

I thank William Hart for helping me discover the McLuhan–Hall Papers and to appreciate their importance in understanding the history of mass communication study. I also thank Steven Chaffee for his thorough critique of a previous draft of this article, Donald F. Theall for his reactions to a previous draft, James W. Carey for his helpful comments, and Edward T. Hall for his reactions to this article. I also thank three archival sources: The Edward T. Hall Papers, University of Arizona Library, Special Collections, Tucson, AZ; the McLuhan Centre for Culture and Technology, University of Toronto, Canada; and the Marshall McLuhan Papers, National Archives of Canada, Ottawa.

REFERENCES

Bissell, C. T. (1988). Herbert Marshall McLuhan. *The Antigonish Review, 74–75*, 11–14.
Carey, J. W. (1967). Harold Adams Innis and Marshall McLuhan. *The Antioch Review, 27*, 5–39.
Carey, J. W. (1998–1999). McLuhan, genealogie et descendance d'un paradigme [McLuhan, geneology and descendants of a paradigm]. *Quaderni, 37*, 111–131.
Carey, J. W. (in press). Review of Glenn Willmott's *McLuhan, or modernism in reverse. Critical Studies in Mass Communication*.
Carpenter, E. (1992). Remembering *Explorations. Canadian Notes & Queries, 46*, 3–14.
Duffy, D. (1969). *Marshall McLuhan.* Toronto, Canada: McClelland & Stewart.
Eisenstein, E. (1979). *The printing press as an agent of change.* New York: Cambridge University Press.
Freud, S. (1953). *Civilization and its discontents* (J. Riviere, Trans.). Chicago: University of Chicago Press. (Original work published 1929)
Fulford, R. (1991). All ignorance is motivated: Re-examining the seedbed of McLuhanism. *Canadian Notes & Queries, 45*, 3–8.
Fuller, R. B. (1935). *Nine chains to the moon.* New York: Lippincott.
Fuller, R. B. (1962). *Untitled epic poem on the history of industrialization.* New York: Simon & Schuster. (Original work published 1940)
Gordon, W. T. (1997). *Marshall McLuhan: Escape into understanding: A biography.* New York: Basic.
Hall, E. T. (1955). The anthropology of manners. *Scientific American, 192*, 85–89.

Hall, E. T. (1966). *The hidden dimension.* Garden City, NY: Doubleday.
Hall, E. T. (1959). *The silent language.* Garden City, NY: Doubleday.
Hall, E. T. (1976). *Beyond culture.* Garden City, NY: Doubleday.
Hall, E. T., & Trager, G. L. (1954). Culture and communication: A model and an analysis. *Explorations, 1,* 137–149.
Innis, H. A. (1950). *Empire and communications.* New York: Oxford University Press.
Innis, H. A. (1951). *The bias of communication.* Toronto, Canada: University of Toronto Press.
Jeffrey, L. (1989). The heat and the light: Towards a reassessment of the contribution of H. Marshall McLuhan. *Canadian Journal of Communication, 13*(4–5), 1–29.
Krugman, H. (1966). The measurement of advertising involvement. *Public Opinion Quarterly, 30,* 583–596.
Krugman, H. (1971). Brain wave measures of media involvement. *Journal of Advertising Research, 11,* 3–9.
Kuhn, T. S. (1972). *The structure of scientific revolutions.* Chicago: University of Chicago Press. (Original work published 1960)
Marchand, P. (1998). *Marshall McLuhan: The medium and the messenger.* Toronto: Random House of Canada. (Original work published 1989)
McLuhan, M. (1951). *The mechanical bride: Folklore of industrial man.* Boston: Beacon.
McLuhan, M. (1962). *The Gutenberg galaxy: The making of typographic man.* Toronto, Canada: University of Toronto Press.
McLuhan, M. (1965). *Understanding media: The extensions of man.* New York: McGraw-Hill.
McLuhan, M. (1969, March). *Playboy* interview: Marshall McLuhan. *Playboy,* pp. 53–74, 159.
McLuhan, M., & Fiore, Q. (1968). *War and peace in the global village.* New York: Bantam.
McLuhan, M., & Powers, B. C. (1989). *The global village: Transformations in world life and media in the 21st century.* New York: Oxford University Press.
Molinaro, M., McLuhan, C., & Toye, W. (Eds.). (1987). *Letters of Marshall McLuhan.* New York: Oxford University Press.
Mumford, L. (1934). *Technics and civilization.* New York: Harper.
Ray, M. L. (1973). Marketing communication and the hierarchy of effects. In P. Clarke (Ed.), *New models for mass communication research* (pp. 147–176). Newbury Park, CA: Sage.
Rogers, E. M. (1994). *A history of communication study: A biographical approach.* New York: Free Press.
Rogers, E. M. (1999). Georg Simmel and intercultural communication. *Communication Theory, 9,* 58–74.
Rogers, E. M., & Hart, W. (1998, November). *Edward T. Hall and the field of intercultural communication.* Paper presented at the annual meeting of the National Communication Association, New York.
Rogers, E. M., & Steinfatt, T. M. (1999). *Intercultural communication.* Prospect Heights, IL: Waveland.
Rubin, R. C., & McHugh, M. P. (1987). Development of parasocial interaction relationships. *Journal of Broadcasting and Electronic Media, 31,* 279–292.
Shannon, C. E. (1949). The mathematical theory of communication. In C. E. Shannon & W. Weaver (Eds.), *The mathematical theory of communication* (pp. 29–125). Urbana: University of Illinois Press.
Singhal, A., & Rogers, E. M. (1999). *Entertainment-education: A communication strategy for social change.* Mahwah, NJ: Lawrence Erlbaum Associates, Inc.
Williams, D. C. (1955). Acoustic space. *Explorations, 4.*

BOOK REVIEWS

John Corner. *Critical Ideas in Television Studies,* New York: Oxford University Press, 1999, 139 pp., ISBN No. 0–19–874221–5 (cloth), ISBN No. 0–19–874220–7 (paper).

Reviewed by Matthew C. Ehrlich
Department of Journalism
University of Illinois at Urbana–Champaign

The Oxford Television Studies series is designed to "reflect on particular problems of history, theory, and criticism which are specific to television and which are central to its critical understanding" (p. ix). This short book is a part of that series. The author, John Corner, is a professor in the School of Politics and Communication Studies at the University of Liverpool and is an editor of the journal *Media, Culture and Society.* He has written and edited several other articles and books on television studies.

As Corner describes it, his research "has involved working with both the social science and the humanities' approaches to television, [and in this book he] attempts to make connections with both, giving particular emphasis to work which bridges the two" (p. 1). He does so by reviewing scholarly research over the past 50 years on aspects of television that cut across genre and nationality and by highlighting some of the central ideas about the medium. His goal is not so much to develop an overarching theory but to help frame critical discussion, or as he says, "to give support to the more genuinely argumentative ways of thinking and writing about television" (p. 11) as we enter the new millennium.

After a brief introduction, Corner devotes one chapter to television as an institution and then one chapter each to aesthetic concerns, including image, talk, narrative, and flow. He proceeds with separate chapters on production, reception, pleasure, and knowledge before concluding with a glimpse at "Television 2000." Each chapter covers a lot of ground quickly. For example, the one on flow (the concept

---

Requests for reprints should be sent to Matthew C. Ehrlich, Department of Journalism, University of Illinois at Urbana–Champaign, 119 Gregory Hall, 810 South Wright Street, Urbana, IL 61801.

that television can be understood not in terms of discrete programming elements but as a continuous stream of image and sound) reviews the history of the concept dating from Raymond Williams before concluding that it is now largely passé. The chapter on reception touches on a 1950s' Dallas Smythe article, research on uses and gratifications, Stuart Hall's encoding–decoding model, Ien Ang's examination of the show *Dallas,* and feminist-based studies of the "domestic contexts of reception"—all within 12 pages.

In this regard the book's breadth is impressive, but it does not come close to providing a comprehensive overview of each of the aspects of television Corner discusses here; indeed, it could not do so if it were 10 times longer than it actually is. Corner candidly acknowledges this limitation. Although he aims to cut across national boundaries, he predominantly focuses on the British television system and those working within British television studies. There is certainly nothing wrong with that, but in so doing he downplays or omits work that has been of particular interest to American scholars. For example, Corner does not cite the research of George Gerbner and his colleagues on the *scary world syndrome,* the notion that heavy viewers of television violence see the world as a more threatening place than others do. The point is not that Corner or others are obligated to tip their hats to Gerbner. It is that U.S. researchers have focused heavily on violence in television and other media, reacting partly to intense public debate following incidents like the 1999 Colorado high school shootings. Hence, an American undertaking a task similar to that Corner sets for himself—to highlight critical ideas about television that have emerged from the scholarly literature—would be far more likely to cite Gerbner and the many others who have studied television violence and give that issue far more prominence than Corner does. As it is, he restricts his discussion of violence to his chapter on pleasure; that is, the pleasure individual viewers may derive from different kinds of violent depictions. Other issues like children's television and political advertising that U.S. scholars have examined closely receive little attention here. Consequently, it is possible that some of those scholars will find this book of limited interest.

Nevertheless, the perspective Corner offers holds significant value. Compared with the United States, Britain has had a far stronger tradition of public service broadcasting and, at least until recently, a system far less dependent on commercial support. One suspects that is a major reason why the school of British television studies that Corner represents has tended to view television in less monolithic and apocalyptic terms than some American observers have. The British school has paid more attention to aesthetic elements like image and narration, giving more credence to the idea of an active, discerning audience that is not merely amusing itself to death. For scholars not well versed in this work, this book is a useful primer that raises provocative questions. Although it does not completely bridge the gap between the social science and the humanities approaches to television, it does suggest the value of taking a broader approach that borrows liberally from both bodies of research and interrogates the assumptions that each has made. Finally, Corner's closing call for research on television that is better grounded in history and that makes better comparisons across genres and nations is one that all scholars may heed.

Norma Odom Pecora. *The Business of Children's Entertainment,* New York: Guilford Press, 1998, 190 pp., ISBN No. 1–57230–280–1 (cloth).

Reviewed by Sharon R. Mazzarella
*Department of Television–Radio
Roy H. Park School of Communications
Ithaca College*

The academic literature on children's entertainment traditionally has fallen into one of two categories: (a) analyses of content (Seiter's [1993] wonderful *Sold Separately* comes to mind) and (b) studies of how children are affected by such content (see, e.g., MacBeth's [1996] *Tuning in to Young Viewers*). Norma Odom Pecora's *The Business of Children's Entertainment,* on the other hand, offers something that has been sorely lacking in studies of children's entertainment—a detailed, painstakingly researched examination of the economics behind the programs, toys, and movies that make up such a large part of children's culture. Although the economics of these industries are often touched on in other studies of children's entertainment, none offer as extensive an analysis as this.

Divided into eight chapters, Pecora's book begins with a historical examination of how children have come to be defined as consumers and as audiences. Her point is that, although not new, such definitions of children have become, in recent years, more accepted and more likely to be the basis for decisions made regarding what content and products to produce for children. For example, she points out that although product licensing is not a new phenomenon—remember Davy Crockett hats and Shirley Temple dolls?—recent years have seen the "acceleration of the process and the takeover of all aspects of children's play and imagination" (p. 153).

Focusing primarily on television, as most analyses of children's entertainment do, Pecora also offers glimpses into other facets of the children's entertainment industry. For example, her extended discussion of the economics of the toy industry in chapter 3 is particularly enlightening as it shows how market consolidation, year-round marketing, extended shelf life, and the proliferation of product licensing have changed the nature of the toy industry. Furthermore, she devotes an entire chapter (chap. 6) to briefly outlining the economics of a variety of other industries

---

Requests for reprints should be sent to Sharon R. Mazzarella, Department of Television–Radio, Roy H. Park School of Communications, Ithaca College, Ithaca, NY 14850–7253.

providing children's entertainment—books, recorded music, movies, and so on. Ideally, I would like to have seen coverage of several of these industries expanded more, and I find the lack of coverage of the Internet, World Wide Web, and CD–ROM industry glaring. Of course when this book was written, these three media outlets were not the powerful forces in children's entertainment that they are now.

Overall, there are two main strengths to this book, the first of which is the wealth of industry statistics and other data, much of which are incorporated into informative figures and tables. As a result of meticulously combing a variety of industry sources, Pecora offers highly useful data on all facets of children's entertainment industries including lists of children's films in production, comparative lists of network children's programming airing during given years, revenue sources, money generated from sales of licensed products, and so on. Unfortunately, given the realities of publishing time lines (i.e., the fact that statistical sources are often 2 or more years behind to begin with, not to mention the time it takes to get a book such as this in print) several of the statistics are older than I would have liked. With some data coming from the mid-1980s and early 1990s, at times, I found myself wishing for more current data. For example, in chapter 2 Pecora includes a figure highlighting the increases and decreases in the number of network children's programs aired from 1948 through 1992. Given the ramifications of the Children's Television Act of 1990, it would be interesting to see data from more recent years.

The second main strength of this book is chapter 4, which consists of case studies of three product-based programs, the *Smurfs, He-Man,* and *Thundercats.* Beginning with the point that "Mutually beneficial arrangements bring about a culture of play driven by characters available at Toys 'R' Us" (p. 60), Pecora offers an in-depth economic analysis of the players and "arrangements" behind the creation of each of these three programs and their product lines. Although often lumped together, Pecora shows that not all product-based programs are created in the same manner, and that more recent product-based programs are characterized by an "increasing linkage between the toy and program production lines" (p. 73).

Also compelling is chapter 5, ironically titled "Alternatives," which examines the economics of Nickelodeon (originally aired without commercials), the Disney Channel (which contains no formal commercials, but is, in reality, one continuous commercial for Disney), and the Public Broadcasting System. The interesting point of this chapter is that these alternatives are not—at least in terms of their economics—and that cable and public television for children, originally intended to provide alternatives to more commercially produced fare, actually fit the corporate model used in other forms of children's television and entertainment.

Overall, this book should appeal to a wide range of readers, as it provides an easy-to-read, well-documented description of the economics of the children's entertainment industry. For the novice, it also provides an introduction to the history of television, of children's television, and of the toy industry, as well as a clear explanation of how product licensing and program syndication work. For the more advanced scholar, its impressive array of industry data can function as a reference tool. For those of us teaching graduate or undergraduate classes in children's entertainment, *The Business of Children's Entertainment* makes an excellent companion to traditionally assigned readings that analyze content and examine effects. I just wish Guilford would publish a paperback edition to make it easier to assign this book for class.

REFERENCES

MacBeth, T. M. (Ed.). (1996). *Tuning in to young viewers: Social science perspectives on television.* Thousand Oaks, CA: Sage.

Seiter, E. (1993). *Sold separately: Parents and children in consumer culture.* New Brunswick, NJ: Rutgers University Press.

Barry Dornfeld, *Producing Public Television, Producing Public Culture*, Princeton, NJ: Princeton University Press, 1998, 240 pp., ISBN 0–691–04468–6 (cloth), ISBN No. 0–691–04467–8 (paper).

Reviewed by Kevin M. Carragee
Department of Communication and Journalism
Suffolk University

In recent years, demands for a more contextual approach to media texts and media audiences have become commonplace. Few studies, however, have realized the ambitious goals of these demands. Barry Dornfeld's *Producing Public Television, Producing Public Culture* provides a telling demonstration of the insights derived from a study that locates the production of media texts within broader political, economic, and organizational contexts.

Dornfeld provides a rich ethnographic examination of the production processes that shaped the content of *Childhood,* a seven-part educational documentary series on the Public Broadcasting System (PBS); the series was first broadcast in 1991. His approach seeks to understand "media texts in relation to specific agents, practices and social contexts" (p. 11).

This contextual approach allows Dornfeld to explore a variety of significant and challenging issues. For example, he examines the organizational and social contexts that influenced the decision-making process of *Childhood*'s executive producers. By providing a nuanced analysis of this process, Dornfeld explores the complex question of authorship in a television documentary series. Given the documentary's cross-cultural focus on childhood development, the study also centers on the ways in which the program represented other cultures. In examining these and other issues, Dornfeld devotes attention to how structure and agency shaped the development and content of *Childhood*.

Dornfeld carefully charts the ways in which the origin and development of the series was rooted in the specific cultural and political setting of PBS in the early 1990s. *Childhood*'s origin was linked to multiple strategic needs of PBS: the broadening of its audience, the avoidance of programming that would offend its already vociferous conservative critics, and the production of programming with a multicultural focus. These structural considerations shaped the program in multiple ways, including the producers' decision to exclude an approach that would empha-

Requests for reprints should be sent to Kevin M. Carragee, 41 Temple Street, Boston, MA 02114.

size the ways in which poverty has shaped children's lives internationally and historically.

Dornfeld's analysis of the collaborative authorship of *Childhood* traces the multiple decisions, negotiations, and conflicts that shaped the content of the documentary. The treatment of the multiple tensions evident in how the producers developed and shaped the documentary's content is particularly illuminating. The study focuses on the tensions between education and entertainment, between pedagogical significance and audience pleasure, and between the desire for both cultural specificity and universal characteristics in the portrayal of the families depicted in the series. These tensions are frequently evident in the conflicts between the executive producers and the researchers who served as both advisors and on-camera hosts for the program. For example, the researchers objected to some sequences because of their banality or because of overgeneralizations contained in them; in response, the producers often justified material because of "its cinematic, dramatic, or otherwise rhetorical qualities" (p. 139). Dornfeld's discussion captures the challenges confronting the producers in transforming scientific and intellectual concepts into what they hoped would be compelling images and sounds.

This book takes on added significance because it examines a number of areas that have been neglected in recent cultural studies and mass communication scholarship. Dornfeld correctly notes that the recent emphasis on the ways in which audience members interpret media texts has "left in its wake a shallow pool of research on production processes" (p. 13). Too often media texts have been treated as autonomous signifying systems, cut off from their origin in media organizations. In contrast to researchers who privilege audience activity, Dornfeld repeatedly emphasizes the ways in which the production and reception of media texts are intertwined. For example, he points out that *Childhood*'s content was shaped by the experiences of its executive producers as both creators and viewers of long-form documentaries.

Dornfeld's study also fills another gap in the research literature by examining a public television documentary series, a genre often ignored because of the recurring research focus on television's entertainment programming.

Producing Public Television, Producing Public Culture provides an exemplary illustration of the opportunities and challenges of ethnographic research at a time when far too many studies use the term *ethnography* in a far too casual and unsystematic manner. Dornfeld's approach to ethnography is reflective; he discusses the specific challenges of conducting an ethnographic examination of individuals and institutions that have a degree of power and social prestige. His role as a participant-observer on *Childhood* (he acted as a researcher on the series) and his background as an independent filmmaker enrich the analysis of the formal properties of the program.

Although Dornfeld makes an impressive contribution to our understanding of the production processes shaping a television documentary, some limitations are evident in this work. Dornfeld notes that the executive producers of *Childhood* had the right to review and comment on his manuscript; these comments, in turn, produced editorial changes, but these revisions are not defined. The lack of detail in this discussion stands in sharp contrast with the reflective approach to ethnography that characterizes much of the book.

Other limitations stem from a somewhat problematic extension of concepts derived from cultural studies. In his discussion of the internal debates on the content of the documentary, Dornfeld classifies the interpretations of the executive producers as dominant readings and evaluations, whereas the views of others, including the academic advisors, are categorized as oppositional interpretations. This extension of Hall's work on decoding positions ignores the broader ideological meanings originally associated with the concepts of dominant and oppositional readings; that is, these readings were defined by their relation to hegemonic meanings and values.

Dornfeld also applies another concept derived from cultural studies scholarship when he contends that the shared authorship of the documentary produced a text characterized by polysemy. Unfortunately, the textual polysemy of *Childhood* is more assumed than demonstrated, especially in regard to major ideological inconsistencies and contradictions within the text. His discussion of polysemy also would benefit from an examination of the considerable research debate that has focused on this concept.

A discussion of these limitations should not mask the many ways this book enriches our understanding of the production of a television documentary. Dornfeld has made a significant contribution to restoring "the agents of production to a more central place in media theory" (p. 188).

Richard H. Reeb, Jr. *Taking Journalism Seriously: Objectivity As a Partisan Cause,* Lanham, MD: University Press of America, 1999, 326 pp., ISBN No. 0-7618-1276-8 (paperback).

Reviewed by Mead Loop
*Department of Television–Radio
Roy H. Park School of Communications
Ithaca College*

When I was in graduate school, a former journalism professor assigned this essay question: Would you as a newspaper editor knowingly hire a socialist? Alone in my class, I wrote that I would not hire someone whose ideas were fundamentally at odds with our constitutional protection of a free press.

Author Richard Reeb would likely agree in *Taking Journalism Seriously: Objectivity As a Partisan Cause.* Reeb bases his advocacy of objectivity in journalism on the political principles of America's founding fathers. Rather than defending objectivity on the contemporary favorites of historical or scientific determinism or rejecting it outright, Reeb calls for an understanding of the original intent of America's founders to create a better government. By doing so, Reeb puts objectivity in a more philosophically sound and practically useful context.

Reeb begins his expanded version of his doctoral thesis by looking at two of journalism's biggest stories during the Vietnam War—the CBS documentary "The Selling of the Pentagon" and *The New York Times* publication of the Pentagon Papers. He finds CBS guilty of manipulation and distortion in its documentary and finds the *Times* wanting in its ability to act as a thoughtful critic in analyzing the Pentagon Papers.

The editing of comments out of context in the case of CBS was clearly nonobjective, but Reeb also believes CBS's advocacy of journalism's mantra of the public's right to know at all costs blinded it to objective truth seeking. Although the watchdog function of the press is important, framing every issue as a right-to-know one hinders reporters' ability to address the more fundamental issue of better government. CBS lacked the will and the philosophy to explore a perspective other than the right-to-know one.

Requests for reprints should be sent to Mead Loop, Department of Television–Radio, Roy H. Park School of Communications, Ithaca College, Ithaca, NY 14850.

Reeb restricts his critique of the *Times* to the quality and justification of what was published, not the narrower ruling on the constitutionality. He faults the *Times* for being unable to be selective regarding what to publish. The author believes neither the *Times*'s good intentions nor a string of facts without meaning are enough to satisfy the requirements of objectivity if publication fails to support the end of promoting good government.

The *Times* was not able to analyze U.S. policy with much substance because of the journalists' creed of strict neutrality. By rooting out any set of political values or philosophy (which only reveals a wrong set of values and bad philosophy), news media lack the frame for substantive discussion because criticism ceases to be an "objective" reportorial function.

Where are the roots of contemporary value-free reporting? Reeb cites the influence of Walter Lippmann and James Reston. Reeb shows Lippmann's "objectivity" was actually subjectivism because of its grounding in historicism—men are wholly products of their age—and scientism—where men's whims are more important than principles of political right. The author also faults Reston for abandoning the guide of "principled foundations of republican government" in his reporting and instead adopting the adversarial role most journalists have regarding those spending taxpayer money. Reeb wants journalists to foster statesmanship in the media and to examine how helpful or harmful they have been to the health of our republic.

Reeb's prescription is similar to the one Robert Bork made explicit before his confirmation to the Supreme Court was defeated: adherence to the principles of America's founders. The prerequisite is understanding natural rights theory, in which journalists acknowledge there is a knowable objective reality. From the metaphysical realm to the political realm of philosophy, then, come the Declaration of Independence with its "self-evident truths" and the U.S. Constitution.

Reeb writes, "There is nothing inconsistent, therefore, about striving for objectivity in the press while expressing a partisanship for the republican regime which makes freedom of the press responsible" (p. 240). That which furthers republican government can be considered objective; values at fundamental odds with our system of government, then, block true objectivity, which he broadly defines as "openness to the truth, whether universal or particular, theoretical or practical" (p. 241).

Objectivity is not neutral or value-free. It needs the application of political principles as a guide for reporting in context, and a journalist can be a partisan for public enlightenment. Reeb writes, "The great value of news reporting is a truthful account of political events so that the people may make a sound judgment about men and measures. The press may well be objective, but only if its political judgment is sound" (p. 117).

Reeb finds the writings of Jefferson, Madison, and Hamilton sound. Where he could have been more clear is describing the crucial link between objectivity and all realms of life. The self-evident truths of life, liberty, and the pursuit of happiness are a political concept derived from the metaphysical axiom that existence exists. Once the law of identity—"A" is "A"—is understood, then an objective philosophy does not permit splitting the value of promoting a proper role for government from the purpose of a journalist covering it.

Ultimately, Reeb presses for an objectivity based on judgment. Although he does not mention the ideas or philosophy of Objectivism and founder Ayn Rand, he understands her credo, "judge and be prepared to be judged," and fittingly applies it to journalists.

ANNOUNCEMENT

CALL FOR PAPERS

SPECIAL ISSUE:
INTERNATIONAL COMMUNICATION HISTORY

Guest Editors: Hazel Dicken-Garcia, University of Minnesota
K. Viswanath, The Ohio State University

Mass Communication & Society—the official journal of the Mass Communication & Society Division of the Association for Education in Journalism and Mass Communication—invites scholars of all theoretical and research perspectives to submit papers for publication in a special issue of the journal, "International Communication History." Hazel Dicken-Garcia, professor of journalism and mass communication at the University of Minnesota, and K. Viswanath, associate professor of journalism and communication at The Ohio State University, are the guest editors.

As an area of research, International Communication History transcends intercultural communication, histories of individual nations' journalism, journalists, media institutions and press systems. The interest is not, per se, in biographies of individual journalists of given countries, or in individual countries' journalism developments. Rather, the focus is on the intellectual history of international communication. Such evolution calls for a treatment of topics that are global, historical and comparative.

Among the types of questions being asked in international communication history are: What has been the history of the idea of development of international communication? How have conceptualizations of, and questions about, international communication changed over time? What theories have organized the way international communications has been studied and written about over time? What has been the history of news flows across national and international boundaries? How have communication technologies affected international relations among (and/or between specific) nations over time? What has been the history of defining communication as a human right?

(continued)

Manuscripts should be no longer than 30 pages total, follow APA style, and must be received no later than September 1, 2000. Five copies of the manuscript should be sent to:

Dr. Hazel Dicken-Garcia 612–625–4381
School of Journalism & Mass Communication E-mail: dicke003@maroon.tc.umn.edu
111 Murphy Hall, 206 Church Street S.E.
University of Minnesota
Minneapolis, MN 55455

ANNOUNCEMENT

CALL FOR PAPERS

SPECIAL ISSUE: RACE AND REPRESENTATION IN MASS MEDIA

Guest Editor: Debra Merskin, University of Idaho

Representation of racial and ethnic minorities in the mass media is an important area of research that impacts society, individuals, and media industries. How non-White members of society are represented or not represented in media content may have a significant impact on how people internalize meaning about themselves and others. Traditionally, message producers have often relied upon stereotypes to communicate beliefs about individual group members.

This special issue will explore, from a critical perspective, the portrayal of racial and ethnic minorities in mass media content. Articles may examine a number of areas, including: (a) representation in advertising, print or broadcast media, (b) representation and critical/cultural theories, (c) representation and audiences or producers, (d) global representations, (e) the effect of representations on children, and (f) social change and changes in representation. Papers are encouraged that advance thinking of critical race issues within a theoretical context. Submissions may be interdisciplinary in approach.

Manuscripts should be no longer than 25 pages total, follow APA style, and must be received no later than June 1, 2000. Five copies of the manuscript should be sent to:

Debra Merskin
School of Journalism
and Communication
University of Oregon
Eugene, OR 97403–1275

541–346–4189
E-mail: dmerskin@darkwing.uoregon.edu

COMMUNICATING UNCERTAINTY
Media Coverage of New and Controversial Science

Edited by
Sharon M. Friedman
Lehigh University
Sharon Dunwoody
University of Wisconsin-Madison
Carol L. Rogers
University of Maryland

A VOLUME IN LEA's COMMUNICATION SERIES

Exploring the interactions that swirl around scientific uncertainty and its coverage by the mass media, this volume breaks new ground by looking at these issues from three different perspectives: those of communication scholars who have studied uncertainty in a number of ways; those of science journalists who have covered these issues; and those of scientists who have been actively involved in researching uncertain science and talking to reporters about it. In particular, it examines how well the mass media convey to the public the complexities, ambiguities, and controversies that are part of scientific uncertainty.

In addition to its new approach to scientific uncertainty and mass media interactions, this book distinguishes itself in the quality of work it assembles by some of the best known science communication scholars in the world. This volume continues the exploration of interactions between scientists and journalists that the three coeditors first documented in their highly successful volume, *Scientists and Journalists: Reporting Science as News*, which was used for many years as a text in science journalism courses around the world.

Contents: Preface. Introduction. **Part I:** *Interpreting Uncertainty.* **S.C. Zehr,** Scientists' Representations of Uncertainty. **S.H. Stocking,** How Journalists Deal With Scientific Uncertainty. **E. Einsiedel, B. Thorne,** Public Responses to Uncertainty. **S. Dunwoody,** Scientists, Journalists, and the Meaning of Uncertainty. **P.M. Boffey, J.E. Rodgers, S.H. Schneider,** Interpreting Uncertainty: A Panel Discussion. **Part II:** *Science in the Public Arena.* **S.H. Priest,** Popular Beliefs, Media, and Biotechnology. **S.M. Friedman,** The Never-Ending Story of Dioxin. **D.E. Chubin,** An Uncertain Social Contract: The Case of Human Resources for Science. **D. Blum,** Reporting on the Changing Science of Human Behavior. **D. Dumanoski, W.H. Farland, S. Krimsky,** Science in the Public Arena: A Panel Discussion. **Part III:** *Beyond the Basics.* **C.L. Rogers,** The Importance of Understanding Audiences. **K.E. Rowan,** Effective Explanation of Uncertain and Complex Science. **R.J. Griffin,** Using Systematic Thinking to Choose and Evaluate Evidence. **R.R. Colwell, P. Girshman, C.B. Marrett, P. Raeburn, F.S. Rowland, T. Siegfried,** Beyond the Basics: A Roundtable Discussion.
0-8058-2727-7 [cloth] / 1999 / 288pp. / $79.95
0-8058-2728-5 [paper] / 1999 / 288pp. / $32.50

Lawrence Erlbaum Associates, Inc.
10 Industrial Avenue, Mahwah, NJ 07430
201/236–9500   FAX 201/760–3735

Prices subject to
change without notice.

Call toll-free to order: 1-800-9-BOOKS-9...9am to 5pm EST only.
e-mail to: orders@erlbaum.com
visit LEA's web site at http://www.erlbaum.com

Subscription Order Form

Please ❏ enter ❏ renew my subscription to

MASS COMMUNICATION AND SOCIETY
Volume 3, 2000, Quarterly

Subscription prices per volume:

Individual: ❏ $35.00 (US/Canada) ❏ $65.00 (All Other Countries)
Institution: ❏ $185.00 (US/Canada) ❏ $215.00 (All Other Countries)

Subscriptions are entered on a calendar-year basis only and must be prepaid in US currency -- check, money order, or credit card. **Offer expires 12/31/2000. NOTE: Institutions must pay institutional rates.** Individual subscription orders paid by institutional checks will be returned.

❏ Payment Enclosed

  Total Amount Enclosed $_____

❏ Charge My Credit Card

  ❏ VISA ❏ MasterCard ❏ AMEX ❏ Discover

  Exp. Date_____

  Card Number _____

  Signature _____
      (Credit card orders cannot be processed without your signature.)

Please print clearly to ensure proper delivery.

Name_____

Addres_____

_____

City _____ State _____ Zip+4 _____
      Prices are subject to change without notice.

Lawrence Erlbaum Associates, Inc.
Journal Subscription Department
10 Industrial Avenue, Mahwah, NJ 07430
(201) 236-9500   FAX (201) 236-0072

ADVERTISING AND THE WORLD WIDE WEB
Edited by
David W. Schumann
University of Tennessee, Knoxville
Esther Thorson
University of Missouri, Columbia
A VOLUME IN THE ADVERTISING AND CONSUMER PSYCHOLOGY SERIES

The chapters provide a wide-ranging view of issues addressing how advertisers can proceed on the Internet and World Wide Web. An initial chapter traces the development of Web advertising from its very beginnings as it was represented and discussed in the pages of *Advertising Age*. Although there is a noticeable trend to define Web advertising by comparing it to traditional media, it is clear that Web advertising just won't fit the old mold. Keith Reinhard of DDB Needham actually articulates this linkage between the old and new in his invited chapter.

What the reader will encounter in *Advertising and the World Wide Web* is a solid conception of how Web Advertising is different from anything that has come before. There are numerous discussions on consumer and advertiser interactivity, the role of Web advertising within larger campaigns, audience segmentation, and alternative Web-based promotion formats. The five sections cover definition and theory, structure, specific applications, legal issues, and the voice of the practitioner. Although there remain a few nay-sayers concerning the future of Web advertising, the reader will be able to see just how incredibly high-impact this new medium has become and the vast potential that it holds for future promotional endeavors.

Contents: Preface. **E. Thorson, D.W. Schumann,** Introduction. **Part I:** *Definition, History, and Theoretical Foundations.* **E. Thorson, W.D. Wells, S. Rogers,** Web Advertising's Birth and Early Childhood as Viewed in the Pages of Advertising Age. **H.A. Roehm, C.P. Haugtvedt,** Understanding Interactivity of Cyberspace Advertising. **A.E. Schlosser, A. Kanfer,** Current Advertising on the Internet: The Benefits and Usage of Mixed-Media Advertising Strategies. **D.R. Fortin,** "New and Improved!" Advertising and Cyberspace: Using Specific Conduits to Access Browsers and Seekers. **Part II:** *Structure, Function, and Effectiveness.* **L.L. Henke,** Children, Advertising, and the Internet: An Exploratory Study. **J.F. Davis,** Effectiveness of Internet Advertising by Leading National Advertisers. **G.J. Nowak, S. Shamp, B. Hollander, G.T. Cameron,** Interactive Media: A Means for More Meaningful Advertising? **C. Frazer, S. McMillan,** Sophistication on the World Wide Web: Evaluating Structure, Function, and Commercial Goals of Web Sites. **J. Hoerner,** Scaling the Web: A Parasocial Interaction Scale for World Wide Web Sites. **M. McDonald,** CyberHate: Extending Persuasive Techniques of Low Credibility Sources to the World Wide Web. **A.M. Brill,** Online Newspaper Advertising: A Study of Format and Integration With News Content. **J.K. Meyer,** The Adoption of the World Wide Web for Online Catalogs: A Diffusion Analysis. **E. Coupey,** Advertising in an Interactive Environment: A Research Agenda. **Part III:** *Public Policy Issues.* **S. Davidson,** Cyber-Cookies: How Much Should the Public Swallow? **S. Davidson,** From Spam to Stern: Advertising Law and the Internet. **Part IV:** *Applications.* **K. Reinhard,** Old-Fashioned Salesmanship in a Newfangled Medium. **L.R. Kahle, R. Madrigal, N.P. Melone, K. Szymanski,** An Audience Survey From the First Gridiron Cybercast. **D.W. Schumann,** Conversations With Practitioners. **M.G. Samet,** Fifty Million Data Points--Consumer Behavior on the Web. **C. Walters, T. Denova,** Loopy: Keeping You in the Loop. **B. Goerlick,** Interactive Media: An Agency Perspective. **D. King,** Relevance, Originality, and Impact: A New Marketing Communications Model. **D.W. Schumann, E. Thorson,** Thoughts Regarding the Present and Future of Web Advertising.
0-8058-3148-7 [cloth] / 1999 / 328pp. / $59.95
Special Prepaid Offer! $29.95
No further discounts apply.

Prices subject to change without notice.

Lawrence Erlbaum Associates, Inc.
10 Industrial Avenue, Mahwah, NJ 07430
201/236–9500   FAX 201/760–3735

Call toll-free to order: 1-800-9-BOOKS-9...9am to 5pm EST only.
e-mail to: orders@erlbaum.com
visit LEA's web site at http://www.erlbaum.com